Ancient Civilizations

THE NEAR EAST AND MESOAMERICA

C. C. Lamberg-Karlovsky
Harvard University

Jeremy A. Sabloff
University of New Mexico

WAVELAND
PRESS, INC.
Prospect Heights, Illinois

Illustrations on pages 1, 43, and 119 are reproduced from *Handbuch der Vorgeschichte,* C. H. Beck Verlag; courtesy of H. Muller-Karpe.

For information about this book, write or call:
Waveland Press, Inc.
P.O. Box 400
Prospect Heights, Illinois 60070
(312) 634-0081

to
GORDON RANDOLPH WILLEY
colleague
mentor
friend

A community which cannot or will not realize how insignificant a part of the universe it occupies is not truly civilized.

Brian Aldis, *Non-stop*

Foreword

Was King Kong big? Yes, compared to a compact car; no, compared to the World Trade Center in New York City. In order to be understood, phenomena must be captured and reported in scale and perspective.

The comparative method does just that. It describes phenomena on the basis of both their shared similarities and their differences from one another. This process incorporates a generalist approach looking for universal patterns and a particularist approach seeking what makes each individual case unique.

This is the method that C. C. Lamberg-Karlovsky and J. A. Sabloff have chosen to tell the story of the archaeology of early civilizations. They use it to open up to the novice the fascinating details of the ancient civilizations of the Near East, India, and Mesoamerica. At the same time they use it to illustrate the intriguing scientific search for what these civilizations held in common.

This process of describing early civilizations also places our own society in a new perspective by marking the first appearances of many of the most familiar elements of our everyday lives. These early civilizations were composed of large populations, many crowded into urban centers, bound together by economic, legal, political, and religious institutions and their ever-expanding bureaucracies. These early civilizations also began to remake the natural landscape into an artificial environment of public works, large buildings, and the thousands of material items which filled everyday existence. These new forms of human behavior and their material products began to change the face of the world and today we are a living part of trends begun millennia ago.

The story of the comparative study of early civilizations is important and other authors have told it. Lamberg-Karlovsky and Sabloff, however, have succeeded in telling it in a way uniquely their own. The ingredients of their achievement are diverse. C. C. Lamberg-Karlovsky has led several expeditions to the Near East, the largest to Tepe Yahya in Iran. Jerry Sabloff is a veteran of several digs in Mexico and Guatemala, including his latest excavations on the island of Cozumel. The two authors have independently won recognition in their chosen research areas and in the field of archaeology in general for producing exciting data and ideas.

At Harvard they taught an introductory archaeology course. It was a good one. It could have been based on their familiarity with the latest information from the field; it could have been based on their even-handed coverage of the civilizations presented—their rise, internal structure, external relations, and fall. It could have been based on their civilization reader (*The Rise and Fall of Civilizations: Modern Archaeological Approaches to Ancient Cultures—Selected Readings*, Benjamin/Cummings Publishing Company), which allowed students to read first-hand the archaeologists who have made major contributions to our knowledge of the past. But I suspect it was based most on the mix of their personalities and the heated debates that warmed their classroom. It is this enthusiastic interaction that brings archaeology to life and that Lamberg-Karlovsky and Sabloff have injected into this book. It is a unique accomplishment, one that undergraduates especially will appreciate.

My initial reference to King Kong was not too far-fetched. When the first civilizations appeared, they were something totally new on the face of the earth. The authors of this book have now captured what we know of these civilizations and put them and those of us who study them on display. This show is worth the price of admission.

W. L. Rathje
University of Arizona

Preface

For centuries people have been aware of and amazed by the monumental remains of ancient cultures, yet the concept of civilization and the attempts to isolate and define the evolutionary process which led to the development from simple hunting and gathering groups to complex societies are relatively new concerns. For example, as late as the end of the eighteenth century, when James Boswell urged Samuel Johnson to include the very word "civilization" in his *Dictionary of the English Language,* the latter resisted its inclusion, preferring the more accepted word "civility" (from the Greek *civilities,* the city).

If the word "civilization" itself is of relatively recent popularity, then the concepts determining the study of its nature, its rise and fall, are more recent yet. It has taken about a millennium to develop an evolutionary consciousness—that is, a concern with unraveling the processes which enabled certain cultures to evolve more complex systems than others. Philosophers have long speculated over the nature and duration of the human past, but the empirical evidence derived from archaeological excavations is less than two centuries old. Through the development of archaeological methods and the archaeological recovery of past civilizations, historical speculations and philosophical conceptions were transformed into a more empirical discipline. In Chapter 1 of this book, we turn to a selective review of some of those writings which laid the foundation for the formation of the science of archaeology and the rigorous study of ancient civilizations.

Traditionally, archaeologists have attempted to define a civilization by trying to answer the question of what attributes and institutional configurations, such as writing, a class system, cities, great art styles, or standing armies, allow a particular society to "qualify" as being a civilization. Archaeologists searched for answers to this question by trying to reconstruct ancient societies at given points of time. For example, they sought to understand how Classic Maya civilization functioned around A.D. 700 or how Sumerian civilization appeared in the third millennium B.C. Recently, however, archaeologists have turned away from making attribute lists to the study of culture change. The reason for this is that descriptive definitions of the past provide no explanation as to how and why peoples reached a complex stage of social and cultural development. Thus archaeological interest has now turned to the *processes* of how simple societies develop into complex ones. To modern archaeologists, civilization represents a developmental process which leads to the growth of societies with complex social, political, economic, and ideological institutions. But if the evolutionary processes, the diachronic dimension, are an aspect necessary for understanding, so are the synchronic dimensions of interaction between distinctive institutions within a civilization. Thus, in order to understand and define the civilization process, we need to study not only the developmental processes which led toward bureaucracies, long distance organized trade, military conquest, political institutions, etc., but also the structure and nature of the interrelations of these different institutions. In this way the understanding of the rise of a civilization then becomes an understanding of the developmental processes of cultures' complex structure. The civilization itself, such as the Maya or the Sumerian, can best be defined when its institutions are treated as if they were adaptively integrated, i.e., in a state of homeostatic equilibrium in their institutional interactions. This is very different from the old attribute list approach, as we shall see below.

The fall of a civilization can be seen in the processes which lead toward the disequilibrium of institutional integrations and stresses to which the civilization fails to adapt. The study of the integrative and developmental processes along this continuum—the rise of, nature of, and fall of a given civilization—provide definition for an understanding of the civilizational process. It is to the study of this civilizational continuum among several cultures of the New and Old World that our attention will be turned.

Purpose and Scope of the Book

This book is meant to serve as an introduction to the archaeological studies of the Near East, Indus, and Mesoamerica for general readers and undergraduate students. Unlike Brian Fagan's work, *Peoples of the Earth,* which courageously attempts to synthesize all of the prehistoric world, or John Pfeiffer's *The Emergence of Society,* which focuses on a variety of important problem areas in the study of complex societies, we have emphasized the geographical areas of our own expertise in Chapters 2 through 4 in order to illustrate some of the trends in the development of ancient civilizations. Chapters 3 and 4 offer extensive discussions on the growth of civilization in the Near East and Mesoamerica, respectively. A separate chapter (2) has been devoted to the rise of agriculture and settled village life in the Near East due to the wealth of relevant archaeological materials. In contrast, our discussion of the rise of agriculture and settled villages in Mesoamerica is included as an introductory section of Chapter 4 because of the *relative* paucity of data on these important developments.

Traditionally, introductory archaeology courses often attempt to give students an overview of prehistoric developments from the origins of the human species to the beginnings of Western civilization. Students are offered a plethora of names and places in order to give them an appreciation of the variety of ancient cultural developments through time and space. An alternate way to approach the introductory course is to offer students a more limited repertoire of ancient cultures while at the same time giving them a more in-depth feeling for some of the questions and issues with which archaeologists are concerned.

This book serves the latter kind of course. We have consciously limited our focus to the Near East/Indus and Mesoamerica in order to give students a better grasp of the culture history of these areas than they might receive in books with wider scopes. While materials from the civilizations of the Andes in South America, of China, of Southeast Asia, or of other areas certainly would be relevant to the concerns of this book, we have not included them so that we could avoid the superficiality which characterizes books that attempt large-scale world prehistories.

Even though the principal focus of the book is culture historical, we have tried to give students a feeling for the kinds of ideas which excite archaeologists currently working in Mesoamerica and the Near East. In many cases, alternate interpretations are noted so teachers can further explore the issues raised. The tentative status of many hypotheses also is emphasized in order to avoid giving students the false impression of certainty which pervades some introductory works. Finally, Chapter 5 offers some of the leads which archaeologists have begun to explore in their attempts to grapple with the fascinating, yet exceedingly complicated, questions of cross-cultural regularities in the development of complex societies.

The intent of the book is to summarize both older and more recent considerations of ancient civilizations and to give the reader a glimpse of the kinds of questions anthropological archaeologists currently are asking in their studies of civilizations of the past. For students who wish to follow up some of the ideas presented here, this book should provide them with the necessary background to read such theoretical works as Robert McC. Adams, *The Evolution of Urban Society,* or W. T. Sanders and B. Price, *Mesoamerica: The Evolution of a Civilization.* In addition, interested readers are referred to the selected references at the end of the book for readings which will enable them to pursue questions they might have.

In order to simplify the text for the beginning student and to avoid recurrent citations, we have, on the whole, footnoted only direct quotes. The books and articles on which we relied in writing the five chapters which make up this book are listed in the notes section at the end of each chapter and full citation information is given in the selected references. These listings are not meant to be exhaustive bibliographies on the subjects but simply offer the principal works to which we have had reference.

Acknowledgments

We are indebted to many for assistance given over the past two years. For a number of years both of us taught a General Education class at Harvard entitled the Rise and Fall of

Civilizations. This course inspired us to collaborate on a reader published by Benjamin/Cummings under that same title and to consider doing a book which dealt with aspects of the development of complex societies in the New and Old Worlds. The feedback from our students and the comments from our graduate teaching fellows were of great aid to us as we began to think about the topics included in this book.

Initially James Wilmeth of Benjamin/Cummings helped us to define our scope and offered us consistent encouragement even when our own enthusiasm waned. Following Mr. Wilmeth's departure from Benjamin/Cummings to pursue his advanced education in anthropology, Larry Wilson assumed the principal role of guiding the volume to completion. To him we owe a deep debt of gratitude not only for his professional competence which has greatly enhanced the book, but for his interest and personal concern with the project. Jean Stein, as developmental editor, tightened up our manuscript, cast out repetitions, and struck out inconsistencies, greatly enhancing the final product in the process. Margaret Moore, as production editor, guided us smoothly through the laborious task of dealing with photographs, figures, maps, etc., while gently forcing us to adhere to the rigid schedule of reviewing her superbly edited galleys. Daniel Jones, photographic archivist at the Peabody Museum, assisted us in securing necessary photographs. Additionally, to those colleagues who provided us with photographs we gratefully acknowledge this assistance by crediting their names to the photos.

We sincerely hope that we have acknowledged all those who assisted us in providing photographs as well as maps, figures, etc. If we have erred or overlooked a credit, it was most certainly not intentional and our red-faced apologies are forthcoming.

Several of Lamberg-Karlovsky's portions of the book were read by a number of his students, particularly Dr. Thomas Beale and Daniel Potts. I am most grateful for their assistance. Finally, over the years one person above all has been directly engaged in aspects of my research, whether in the field or at home. Public recognition cannot repay the debt owed my wife.

Sabloff also wishes to acknowledge the useful comments of Professor Dennis Heskel as well as several anonymous readers of early drafts of the text. The constructive criticisms of my wife, Dr. Paula L. W. Sabloff, have led to major improvements of this work, and I am deeply grateful to her for this aid and for her constant encouragement.

In addition, we wish to thank Larry Daniel and Margaret Gutierrez for typing the final draft of the manuscript.

Lastly, it is with great pleasure that we dedicate this book to Gordon Randolph Willey, who has done so much to further the growth of archaeological knowledge of ancient civilizations and to stimulate our own thinking on this subject.

C. C. Lamberg-Karlovsky
Harvard University

Jeremy A. Sabloff
University of New Mexico, Albuquerque

Contents

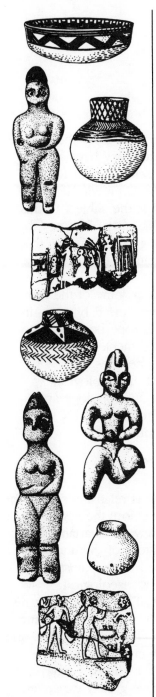

1. The History of History

The archaeological data and interpretation that form the bulk of this book clearly do not exist in a vacuum. They have an intellectual background that provides a useful context for the student who wishes to understand the development of ancient civilizations. That intellectual background is the subject of this chapter. Here we hope to provide a brief "history of history" by looking at the various stages of developing consciousness that have taken place in people's conceptualizations of past cultures and civilizations.

In the first half of this chapter, we look at some of the most important trends in past ways people have viewed history—in Mesopotamia, in ancient Greece, and in Europe both in Medieval times and in the Age of Enlightenment. We will, moreover, be examining more recent perspectives. The remainder of the chapter looks broadly at archaeological discoveries and the modern discipline of anthropology and, more specifically, at the ways these two influences have transformed our view of ancient civilizations.

A Résumé of Historical Views

Our knowledge of the cultures of antiquity is relatively recent, for historical records had been long lost even before the beginning of the European Middle Ages. Beyond a few antiquarian and Biblical references, the prehistory and history of the ancient Near East and other early centers have had to be painstakingly reconstructed almost exclusively through archaeological fieldwork. Within the past century and a half, intensive programs of archaeological exploration and excavation have led to many rediscoveries—among them the Sumerian civilization in 1899 and the Minoan, Harappan, Shang, and Olmec civilizations of the Aegean, India, China, and Mexico within only the past fifty years. These rediscoveries of past civilizations have greatly expanded our appreciation of human diversity through the ages. Recognition of this diversity is part of our present-day outlook; it was not a perspective of antiquity.

ANCIENT VIEWS OF THE PAST

The best place to begin an examination of past views of history is in the ancient Near East, an area bordered by the Caucasus on the north, Egypt on the south, the Aegean Sea on the west, and the highlands of eastern Iran on the east. Within this area was the "Mesopotamia" referred to by Greek writers, and it was here, by the sixth millennium B.C. if not earlier, that the first urban cultures took form. The cultures which inhabited Mesopotamia, the lands between the Tigris and Euphrates rivers of present-day Iraq, are called Sumerian, the earliest literate civilization of Mesopotamia, which was chronologically followed by the Akkadian, Babylonian, and Assyrian. Of the Sumerians we will have more to say in Chapter 3.

Some of our most valuable information about the historical outlook of these ancient civilizations comes from deciphered writings from Egypt and Mesopotamia. Although only a small proportion of texts has yet been translated, those documents have allowed us a glimpse of ancient attitudes, myths, legends, and everyday life that would be impossible without the thousands of tablets that archaeologists have recovered.

In dealing with texts from the remote past, the modern reader meets with conceptual barriers which become a constant source of misunderstanding and misinterpretation. Just as the physical plan, the social structure, the economic foundations—and almost every other aspect of a civilization—have varied from one culture to another over time, so has the way people think.

This is especially true of perceptions of history. The historical consciousness as we know it is a recent development. Only in the past few hundred years have the study and placement of historical processes in their "proper" sequence and perspective been a concern of history and science. Even now our understanding of the historical process continues to change from one generation to the next. Each period of time appears to have derived its own valid "truth" in reference to its own social framework.

That is why modern historians, as they try to outline the ancient Mesopotamian's attitude toward the past, are tempted to use concepts, attitudes, and categories that would have been alien to the Mesopotamian. In the thousands of written inscriptions relating to economic, political, legal, literary, and daily affairs discovered in the archaeological remains of third-millennium Sumer, for instance, the word for *history* is wholly absent. This absence does not indicate a lack of interest in the past, for numerous inscribed clay tablets suggest the contrary to be true. Instead it signifies a completely different world view—including a different approach to history.

A basic principle of both Mesopotamian and Egyptian thought was the virtually total lack of distinction between heaven and earth. To the Mesopotamian and the Egyptian, every mundane matter depended on divine action—from appointments of kings and victories at war to the birth of infants. The questions of why or how past events occurred seemingly never troubled the Mesopotamian or the Egyptian, because everything—including cultural change—was controlled by celestial powers! This conception explains one aspect of the ancient Near Eastern idea of history—the complete absence of reference to causes of the kind we require today in understanding historical processes. The search for a cause could hardly go beyond that of divine causation.

Related to divine causation is the belief in *divination,* the ability to predict the future. Divinations became a highly developed practice in the ancient Near East (and in early Mesoamerican civilizations as well); indeed, they are responsible for most of the historical records we now have.

In Egypt and Mesopotamia, scribes recorded both events and the omens that attended these events. Records of omens appearing before major events were carefully compiled for future reference in predicting the will of the gods. In this way, the compilation of events and omens served a real and practical purpose to the ancient "historian."

Because of the function they served, these very ancient records are just that—descriptions of events. The personal beliefs and theological or philosophical insights of the scribes who kept the records are conspicuously absent in cuneiform literature. In this respect, the "historical" perception of the ancient Near East is vastly different from that of the Classical world of the Greeks and from later Judeo-Christian traditions. The newer outlooks, and the "truths" which they inspired, are as different from Mesopotamian or Egyptian traditions as the social institutions which fostered them.

CLASSICAL HISTORICAL VIEWS

According to Hecataeus of Miletus (ca. 550 B.C.), the first Greek historian of whom we have any knowledge, the ideal in Greek historical writing was the eyewitness account. The historian's function was to act as a judge, making careful notes from eyewitnesses and evaluating testimony. Impartial reconstruction of past events was recorded as the history of the immediate past.

While Greek historical writing is like that of ancient Mesopotamia in that both provide accurate descriptions, there are some very basic differences. For one, the Greek historian was concerned with historiography—the methods and principles that govern the writing of history.* A concern for historical methodology was part of the classical tradition but was unknown to ancient oriental civilizations. Of course, the limitations of classical historiography are all too apparent to us now. The time constraints of dealing only with events within the memory of living witnesses may seem unduly restrictive to modern historians accustomed to relying on archaeological or archival data and excavations. But these sources of evidence were not to become a concern for another two thousand years, and the point remains that the classical historians were the first to derive a methodology for studying the past.

The Greek historians were also the first to concern themselves with a theoretical framework for understanding the past. They no longer perceived history as wholly directed by divine ordination. Rather, they looked for other causes and effects. The classical historians were concerned with questions of historical directionality and cause, the cumulative effects of the growth of civilizations, the purposive growth of civilizations, and the irreversible aspects of history.

---

*A formal description of this historical method is first provided by Polybius. His treatment of the Roman conquests became the model for classical historiography.

Plate 1.1   Aristotle.

An overriding theme among classical historians was the belief in the *cyclicality of history:* the view that history repeats itself in a series of events that recur regularly and usually lead back to the starting point. It might be noted in passing that some ancient Mesopotamian peoples also had a cyclical view of the past, but this view regarded divine direction as the only moving force. To Aristotle and Plato, the cyclical course of history provided a model of change as well as development in both immediate and remote times.

The Greek historians' view of the cyclical nature of cultural growth continues to have a remarkable impact even today. Take the twentieth-century comment of Oswald Spengler that each civilization "passes through the age phases of the individual man. It has a childhood, youth, manhood, and old age."[1] In this remark we can find a direct analogy in the writings of Heraclitus, Aristotle, Plato, Polybius, Lucretius, and Seneca.

One important element of the tradition of cyclicality was the classical world's concern for a developmental perspective which

Plate 1.2 Plato.

emphasized origins. Thus Aristotle, when investigating the nature of the state in his *Politics,* noted that: "He who considers things in their first growth and origin, whether the state or anything else, will obtain the clearest view."[2]

The concern for origins led to inquiries into the nature of knowledge in many other disciplines, including science, ethics, politics, and art, and the answers helped to provide the Greeks with a framework for viewing history. Attempts to answer the question "What sort of being must being be when being becomes?" led Plato to outline social evolution from prestate conditions and primitive states to the rise of civilization in both *The Laws* and *The Republic.*

The Greek historian's concern with cyclical development formed the basis for another element of the classical perspective: the idea that future events could be predicted through an understanding of the past. This notion can be seen in the historical treatises of Thucydides (471–400 B.C.), who shares

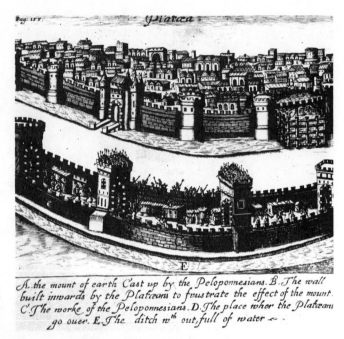

Plate 1.3 Frontispiece from a London 1629 edition of Thucydides, *History of the Peloponnesian Wars.* (Courtesy of Houghton Library, Harvard University.)

the mantle, "Father of History," with Herodotus (490 – 409 B.C.). Thucydides found a repeating pattern in history: a rise of civilizations that was inevitably followed by a fall—the result of increasing pride and arrogance. Power led to wealth; wealth led to indulgence and pride; and these in turn led the civilization to believe itself exempt from the laws of human behavior. The result was the civilization's downfall. A clear illustration of this pattern was the rise and fall of the Persian Empire, described in Thucydides' *History of the Peloponnesian War.* By the same process, Thucydides predicted, Athens was doomed to a similar fate.

In their recording and interpretation of past events, the classical historians laid some foundations for Western social thought that are still very much with us today. Evidence for this can be seen throughout classical writing in an overriding concern for understanding the origin of things; a belief that developmental processes followed definite patterns and a concern for isolating the causes that underlie those patterns; a belief that all things within nature are set to specific purposes; and an emphasis placed on methodology to provide guidelines for scientific inquiry.

While much of our own historical tradition has roots in early classical views, the dominant Western perspectives have undergone many changes in the interim. The first major shift accompanied the rise of the Judeo-Christian tradition.

SAINT AUGUSTINE'S LINEAR DESIGN OF HISTORY

While the Greeks perceived the pattern of history as cyclical, there existed another, quite distinct, contemporaneous view. The biblical tradition of the Old Testament saw history as linear, the work of divine providence guiding events toward the fulfillment of a final purpose. The fusion of these two contrasting views added an important new perspective to Western historiography. This fusion is best illustrated in the writings of St. Augustine (A.D. 354–430), whose historical perspective has influenced Western civilization for well over fifteen hundred years.

In the fifth century, non-Christians blamed the fall and sack of Rome in 410 on the turning away from their pagan gods. In his monumental study, *The City of God* (written between A.D. 413 and 426), St. Augustine set out in ten volumes to show that there was a different cause. The fall of Rome was part of the purposive design of history leading to the establishment of a new Christian civilization.

In his book, St. Augustine introduced two basic ideas. The first was that history follows a linear path. Unlike the cyclical conception of classical historians, Augustine's linear view of history was universal, encompassing all civilizations and moving in a definite direction and by a definite design, all imposed by God's will. "He made in time not from a new and sudden resolution, but by His unchangeable and eternal design."[3] Within Augustinian tradition, history was "going somewhere": it was an irreversible process moving along a predetermined course. (The revelation of this divine plan was to become a primary concern of scholars through the age of the Renaissance.)

A second important element of St. Augustine's conception was that progress over earlier times was inevitable. The notion of

Plate 1.4 St. Augustine, Bishop of Hippo, author of *City of God*.

progress—that is, that each civilization represents a higher order of development than its predecessor—was to influence later views of history again and again. Modern conceptions of historical progress, whether Marxian or empirically deductive, have their origin in this Judeo-Christian view of a purposive history.

The synthesis of Judeo-Christian and classical traditions presented by St. Augustine was to become the most influential single book on the nature of the historical process in early Western civilization. Augustine's book has continued to have an impact on Western thought well past Renaissance times: perhaps its best-known lineal descendant in recent times is Toynbee's *A Study of History,* discussed later in this chapter.

St. Augustine presented five new perspectives, and elements of each of these still influence historical thinking to a greater or

Plate 1.5 Giambattista
Vico (1668–1744).

lesser extent. First is the notion of a universal history: all of
history incorporates all humankind; and all of the past is seen as
related to God's purpose. Second is the view that history is not
to be written in terms of years, centuries, events, or even
civilizations. Instead, the basic reference point of history is the
unfolding of a directed, purposeful plan dictated by divine will,
and events in history are seen as points along this predetermined course. A third element of Augustinian tradition is
the rejection of classical cyclicality. Historical processes are
linear: they follow a single path from beginning to end. Fourth,
history is seen as dynamic, not static. It deals with action—that is,
the movement of events and history toward specific goals—and
not with immutable patterns such as cyclicality. And, finally, both
reason and rationale underlie history, and these reasons and
rationales are subject to study. These perspectives dominated
both Medieval and Renaissance historical writing; not until the
eighteenth century were they seriously challenged.

Plate 1.6 René
Descartes (1596–1650).

THE RISE OF SCIENTIFIC VIEWS

Vico's Spiral Theory

The first major historian and historiographer to formulate
principles outside the Augustinian tradition was Vico of Naples
(1668–1744). Modern conceptions of history can be said to begin
with Vico, who created a science of history that paralleled the
principles of scientific method devised by Francis Bacon.

Vico's mission was to vindicate (and at the same time recast)
history, which at that point was experiencing what we would call
a "credibility gap." Descartes (1596–1650), whose views were
representative of many thinkers of that time, had held history in
contempt, believing it to be a less worthy study than the more
precise disciplines of mathematics, physics, and astronomy. Vico
strongly disagreed. He set out to show, *verum factum,* that the
truth is the truth, whether it is revealed through the scientific
method of physics or through the study of history. In his book
Scienza Nuova (1725) (the frontispiece of the first edition is
shown in Plate 1.7), Vico proposed a general plan for a whole new
mode of thought: the examination of elements to determine

Plate 1.7 Allegorical frontispiece of *Scienza Nuova,* by Giambattista Vico.

patterns. This, he insisted, was the purpose of historical studies, and he set down a number of guiding principles to trace the development of cultural traits like class consciousness, myths, and technology. According to Vico, these patterns characterized all cultures. For this reason, his book stands as a landmark in the development of history as a comparative science.

Vico combined an interest in investigating origins with his greatest innovation: the emphasis on formulating laws of historical development. Vico believed that there existed laws of history that could be recognized and stated systematically.

Vico's law of history combined elements of both the classical conception and the Augustinian tradition. From the Greeks, Vico borrowed the notion of universal stages in the cycles of civilizations—the idea that each civilization passes through the same phases of development: from "Stone Age" to "Bronze Age" to "Iron Age" (a theory first formulated by Hesiod in the seventh century B.C.). Vico's theory also incorporated the linear concept of progress accepted by St. Augustine and his successors—with a significant modification: he recognized that the Europe of A.D. 1000 was not at the same level of progress as Homeric Greece. Vico's was neither a cyclical nor a linear view of historical progress, but one which combined both in a theory of spiraling development.

This "spiral theory" provides one of the earliest universal models for the rise and decline of civilizations. Vico's belief that there are laws which govern history just as they govern any other science marks the beginning of a new way of looking at history. Alan Donagan has written:

> Vico's principle that what men have made, man can hope to know, is the foundation of modern scientific historiography. First it defines what historians study: namely, whatever survives from past human actions. Secondly, it implicitly specifies their aim: to recover the human thinking, however different from our own it may have been, by which what survives from the past is made.[4]

Vico's Successors

Though Vico's theory was later to influence such diverse thinkers as Kant, Herder, Condorcet, Hegel, and Spencer, his ideas lay dormant for almost a century. Neither the rationalism nor the romanticism of the seventeenth and eighteenth centuries produced a comparable figure. Voltaire (1694–1778), the rationalist, was obsessed almost to the point of blindness in his insistence that the single goal of historical research was to combat superstition; Rousseau (1712–1778), the romantic, never overcame his prejudice against civilization itself as the corruption of all the natural good in humanity. Herder (1744–1803) came closer to the historiographic approach of Vico. He believed that a universal pattern existed in the development of civilizations. But Herder's view was much narrower than Vico's: he could only explain that development through an understanding of "national character."

Vico first used the *positivist approach* in the early eighteenth century; not until the mid-nineteenth century was this approach

Plate 1.8 Jean-Jacques
Rousseau (1712– 1778).
(By permission of the
Houghton Library,
Harvard University.)

finally indelibly present in historical analysis. A positivist
approach, whether in history or in physics, aligns itself in the
belief that all knowledge is based on an understanding of natural
phenomena and that the properties and relations of these
phenomena, whether historical events or molecular structures,
can be fully understood and verified. A positivist would argue that
causes for the rise and fall of civilizations are entirely
determinable and subject to rigorous analysis.

In 1848, Que'telet (1796– 1874), the Belgian founder of
formal statistical approaches, attempted to define the laws of
history. In his *Social Systems and Its Laws,* he calculated the
average duration of five ancient empires to be 1461 years—a time
span which he said equaled the Gothic year of the Egyptian
calendar (and also the life span of the Phoenix!). He then
calculated the standard deviation of his result and seriously
informed his readers that it amounted to 185 years. All of this may
seem quite meaningless to us now—but the idea that
quantification alone can provide explanations is disturbingly

Plate 1.9 G. W. F.
Hegel (1770–1831).

reminiscent of our own modern prejudice that in numbers there
is science. Even though his hypotheses may have been premature
and extreme, Que'telet's methodology was positivist, empirical,
and exploratory.

Hegel's approach was far broader in scope. According to
Hegel (1770–1831), there was a necessary emergence of stages in
civilizational growth by which the process of historical
development could be understood according to defined laws.
History was a rational process; the historian's purpose was to
examine and identify the stages in order to understand the process
of historical development. The elegance and enormous
erudition of Hegel have continued to influence us into the
twentieth century.

One later thinker who was profoundly influenced by Hegel was
Karl Marx (1818–1883)—one of the first to provide an
all-embracing explanation of historical development in his
concept of *historical materialism*. Marx propounded an
elaborate philosophy of history, and he implemented it by an
elaborate economic theory. In Marx's historical materialism,
economic developments are regarded as the prime mover of
social evolution. Transformations in a society's institutional

Plate 1.10 Karl Marx (1818– 1883), pupil of Hegel.

structures are inevitably the result of alterations in the basic economic foundations.

Marx's overall view was not an entirely new one. His conception of cultural evolution as following a set pattern of stages was an idea borrowed directly from Lewis Henry Morgan, a New York lawyer. In his *Ancient Society* (1877), Morgan outlined seven stages of cultural evolution and characterized each by a specific technological invention: fire, the bow and arrow, animal domestication, and so forth. Marx used this same idea, but he built upon it. To him, the rise of these inventions was brought about by economic factors. Changes in material production (and also in the control of the means of production) were the forces determining the social, political, and legal aspects of a society. And so, transformations from one stage to another were the direct result of economic factors.

Nineteenth-Century Views of Progress

In many respects, the eighteenth-century idea of "progress" has been the cornerstone of intellectual modernism. Long before Marx believed that the "cause of anything is also the end toward which movement aims,"[5] a concept of progress had been

legitimized as a valued good toward which civilization moves.
Social change was recognized as a linear development leading
through ever more complex stages toward progress.

Following this lead, nearly all nineteenth-century historians
believed progress to be "not an accident but a beneficent
necessity."[6] Indeed, the laws of progress became a pre-
occupation of nineteenth-century thought. Influenced by the
Darwinian theory of evolution (a population and statistical
model based on randomness and variation), they devised a model
of social evolution which directed cultural change toward a
progressively more complex form of social order: from savagery
through barbarism to civilization. Some versions of this model
were quite complex. Morgan, a firm advocate of progress in his
Ancient Society, even ventured to differentiate among relative
rates of progress within different stages of cultural evolution:

> While progress was slowest in times in the first period, and most rapid
> in the last when the achievements of either period are considered in
> relations to their sums, it may be suggested not improbable of ultimate
> recognition, that the progress of mankind in the period of savagery, in
> its relation to the sum of human progress, was greater in degree than
> it was afterwards in the three sub-periods of barbarism, and that the
> [progress in] barbarism was, in like manner, greater in degree than it
> has been since the entire period of civilization.[7]

There were four central elements of nineteenth-century social
evolutionary theory: belief in the naturalness of change in each
social institution or system; the directional or trendlike character
of change; the necessity of change in each social system (a
necessity which symbolized progress); and, finally, the belief that
change was brought about by uniform, persisting forces. These
concepts, outlined and forged in the nineteenth century, still form
part of our intellectual tradition today. Although they have been
modified, added to, and further abstracted, they remain
fundamental to contemporary studies of social change.

The eighteenth and nineteenth centuries saw another
important movement besides social evolution. The *comparative
method* attained immense popularity as a means of supporting
the idea of progress. The intent of this method was to prove the
validity of cultural evolution from the simple to the complex by
comparing different cultures in both the same and different
periods of time. Thus Auguste Comte (1798–1857) could write
that all the different stages of evolution could be observed
simultaneously throughout the world: "From the wretched

Plate 1.11 Auguste Comte (1798–1857).

inhabitants of Tierra del Fuego to the most advanced nations of Western Europe, there is no social grade which is not extant in some points of the globe, and usually in localities which are clearly apart."[8]

This quote is taken from *The Positive Philosophy,* the work that established Comte as perhaps the nineteenth century's foremost positivist. Comte put forward methodological approaches toward the study of what he called "social physics." His inquiry into history was guided by methods adapted from empirical sciences such as biology, chemistry, and mathematics; its sole purpose was to discover the laws governing the processes of historical change. Comte's view that human society is a subject for objective scientific investigation leading to discoverable laws has exerted, to this day, a powerful influence on social theorists and historians.

To the social evolutionists, the comparative method served as the explanation for cultural evolution, much as natural selection explained evolution in Darwin's biological theory. Sir John Lubbock, one of the pioneers in archaeological inquiry and excavation, echoed a common belief of his day in *The Social and Religious Condition of the Lower Races of Man* (1869): "From the study of modern savages, we can gain a correct idea of man as he existed in ancient times, and of the stages through which our civilization has evolved."[9]

Implicit in Lubbock's statement are the double implications of the comparative method. While this method is "modern" in that it has served as an invaluable tool in gaining much of our twentieth-century knowledge of ancient cultures, it is also inextricably tied with an eighteenth-century assumption. As is all too apparent, the value (and indeed, validity) of the comparative method is wholly dependent on the acceptance of an a priori belief in the idea of progressive development.

While twentieth-century historians have built upon the theoretical and methodological foundations of social evolution and comparative studies, recent perspectives represent more than just a continuation of trends. Our increased knowledge of the past, derived from archaeological excavations in the past fifty years together with the development of the behavioral sciences, has introduced sharp changes in traditional historical outlooks.

TWENTIETH-CENTURY OUTLOOKS

Within the twentieth century, civilizational studies have been transformed by two principal factors. The first is the great expansion of archaeological research that has recovered, within this century, over a dozen buried civilizations which, prior to their excavation, had been erased from human memory. The recovery of these past civilizations has intensified the quest for understanding their development and decline. The second factor transforming the study of past civilizations has been the advances of the behavioral sciences. Social scientists today are not content merely to describe historical events. One must attempt to answer the "how" and "why" of historical change. Social scientists today have a far keener appreciation than their forebears of the influences of ecology, population pressures, and technology, for example, on the process of historical change. At the same time, they are able to apply new methods of analysis through such recently developed tools as computers.

Before discussing the specific contributions of anthropologically oriented archaeologists in the twentieth century, it is worthwhile to review three of this century's foremost exponents of civilizational studies: Spengler, Kroeber, and Toynbee. While Spengler wrote in the 1920s, his intellectual approach is more of the nineteenth century. We are reminded in his work that historical research is itself an intellectual continuum. His method and works are deeply rooted in the traditions of earlier scholarhip. Kroeber, an anthropologist, and Toynbee, a historian, both represent new directions in their search for understanding the processes by which civilizations develop and are transformed.

Spengler's Intuitive Approach

In many respects, Oswald Spengler (1880–1936) could hardly be called a twentieth-century historian. He did not organize his data in terms of cause and effect, or even in an ordered historical sequence. In fact, he was opposed to the use of any method leading to a historical understanding, and he directly opposed positivists like Auguste Comte who wanted to provide laws and methods within historical analysis.

Spengler believed history to be an innate undertaking, a creative ability, an art (an attitude shared by the famous contemporary historian Sir Isaiah Berlin). To Spengler, "culture is a unit of artistic style in all the life manifestations of a people."[10] To the question "Is there a science of history?", Spengler is unrelentingly direct: "There is no science of history, but a quality of divining what actually took place. To the historical vision the actual data are always symbols."[11]

According to Spengler, what actually did take place was a linear process of development within each civilization. To describe this process, Spengler used a biological, or *morphological,* metaphor: each civilization went through stages similar to those in the human life cycle—from birth, to childhood, to youth, to maturity, to old age, to death. He looked at eight major civilizations (Egyptian, Chinese, Semitic, Indian, Hebrew-Arab, Greek-Roman, Western, and Mexican) and concluded that the average life cycle was about a thousand years. Spengler's views are perhaps best portrayed in his most famous work, *The Decline of the West* (1926), in which he viewed the inevitability of the dissolution of Western civilization.

Crucial to Spengler's analysis of Western culture is his view that events of different ages and cultures are analytically contemporaneous. Thus Napoleon was morphologically similar to Alexander the Great. Spengler deemed this morphological comparability not only as an indispensable guide to the past but also as helpful in predicting the future: the West, he said, was awaiting its Julius Caesar.

Spengler was highly critical of many other historians of his time. He contrasted what he called the *Ptolemaic* system of historical analysis with the *Copernican* approach. Ptolemaic systems were ethnocentric, interpreting history from the standpoint of Western civilization and viewing Western culture as a center around which other cultures orbited. In contrast, Spengler's own approach was Copernican. He admitted no privileged position of classical or Western cultures over other cultures.

Spengler's approach was comparative in the broadest sense. He looked at the totality of each civilization and sought to define in each a single *gestalt*—the total form and style of that culture. It is in the methods Spengler used to evoke the gestalt of the civilization that the reader of his works is most puzzled. For in the final analysis, Spengler lacked any method; he believed historical understanding was an "innate" and "creative" act. Such an approach is in direct opposition to the positivist ideas which, since Comte, had had a major impact on historical theory. Thus:

> I see in place of the empty figment of *one* linear history, which can only be kept up by shutting one's eyes to the overwhelming multitude of the facts, the drama of a *number* of mighty Cultures, each springing with primitive strength from the soil of a mother region to which it remains firmly bound throughout its whole life-cycle; each stamping its material, its mankind, in its *own* image; each having *its own* ideas, *its own* passions, *its own* life, will and failing, *its own* death.[12]

This stirring vision of depicting for each civilization its own gestalt was never fully realized by Spengler.

While Spengler's intuitive philosophy of history lacked method, it was rich in relativism, pessimism, and determinism. The outlooks of some other major twentieth-century historians are more representative of an often diametrically opposed tide of historical thinking.

Kroeber's "Pure Systems"

Like Spengler, the American cultural anthropologist Alfred Kroeber (1876–1960) was drawn to the analysis of civilizations. To him, "common sense demands that we accept civilizations as units naturally given in history."[13] Common sense was not, however, an adequate method of analysis in Kroeber's view. Toward the end

Plate 1.12 Alfred L. Kroeber (1876–1960).

of using a more precise analytical approach to understanding civilizations, Kroeber wrote *Configurations of Culture Growth* (1944).

In contrast to Spengler, Kroeber was less interested in the gestalt of a whole civilization than its individual parts. To Kroeber, all cultures are composed of the same parts, which he called "pure systems." These systems include language, fine arts, religion, science, ethics, and so forth. While the pure systems were comparable from one culture to the next, they were wholly interdependent within each civilization: individual civilizations could only be understood as integrated systems.

Kroeber was interested in determining patterns of cultural growth, and his pure systems breakdown provided the method for this analysis. His approach was to quantify the accomplishments of various pure systems within different civilizations. His findings showed that certain elements of cultural growth followed cyclical patterns and that these patterns could be used to determine the rate, peak, duration, and level of cultural growth.

In the end, Kroeber believed that "any explanation is hardly more than the descriptive realization of culture patterns."[14] His search for patterns of cultural growth took him from the mundane analysis of changing styles of wardrobes to the development of modern science and literature. His dislike of intuitive a priorism, his insistence on undertaking empirical, quantitative analysis to determine patterns, his belief that civilizations could only be viewed as single systems of interdependent parts—all set him apart from the approach of Spengler. Indeed, these beliefs set him apart from most of the inductivists of his period, who reasoned from the particular to the general or from the individual instance to the universal. More than most of his anthropological contemporaries he was a positivist thinker, a descendant of Auguste Comte, who used quantification to search for laws of cultural development.

Kroeber's and Spengler's interest in the study of civilization was hardly representative of a universal trend. In sharp contrast were the views of a number of anthropologists in the early part of the twentieth century. Most prominent were Pitirim Sorokin (1889–1968), Franz Boas (1858–1942), and Robert Lowie (1883–1957).

To Sorokin, civilizations are not historic, analytic entities, but vast museumlike congeries—storehouses of material culture on display without a framework. Lowie echoed the same view, calling civilization "that planless hodge-podge, that thing of sherds and patches."[15] And Boas, perhaps the most influential anthropologist in the first part of this century, categorically denied any scheme of cultural evolution, taking a consistently negative view of anthropologists' attempts to structure a universal history of cultures.

Sorokin, Lowie, and Boas all represented a strong reaction against the social evolutionism of the late nineteenth century, denying both the unity of a civilization and the possibility for its empirical analysis. Indeed, their view of civilization as "sort of a dumping ground" where billions of diverse cultural phenomena are thrown together precluded the development of schemes for analyzing cultural change.

Whether or not civilization is an entity ready-made for scholarly analysis, as Kroeber claimed, is still a matter of debate. In either case, the causes of the rise and fall of civilizations have been the subject of a great deal of study in this century. Perhaps the greatest civilizational study of all is that of Arnold Toynbee.

Toynbee's Environmental Determinism

Arnold Toynbee (1881–1976) produced the most ambitious study on civilizations undertaken in this century: *A Study of History.* His work has been the most important and widely discussed study in the philosophy of history since Hegel and Marx.

Toynbee acknowledges two formative influences in writing his tour de force. At the time of World War I, he became aware of what he considered remarkable similarities between his own time and that of classical Greece and Rome. This discovery directed him toward his lifelong search for parallels in historical time and space. A second influence was Spengler's *Decline of the West,* which he became familiar with at the end of the war. Toynbee considered Spengler far too limited, for several reasons: he looked at only eight civilizations; he was too pessimistic; he was inattentive to detail and fact; and he failed to provide adequate explanation of what brings about the rise and fall of civilizations. Yet Toynbee's study bore many resemblances to Spengler's. For Toynbee, the proper units of historical study were whole societies, the entirety of a civilization. Throughout the twelve volumes of his study he showed great concern for identifying unifying concepts—concepts which lead to an understanding of individual civilizations while providing a means for analyzing several civilizations.

Toynbee's notion of "challenge and response" is one instance of his use of a unifying concept in the study of civilizations. Each civilization necessarily addresses itself to particular challenges: environment, population pressures, warfare, and so forth. The manner in which a civilization responds to these challenges can be perceived as a measure of its ability to adjust and survive.

Toynbee isolated twenty-one distinctive civilizations which he believed comprise the history of humankind. In his first six volumes, he set out to discover the factors that led to their rise and fall. He undertook his comparative analysis of civilizations by studying different political, economic, and religious institutions, and he concluded that in all civilizations these institutions developed in a similar manner. Toynbee stated again and again throughout his volumes that "civilizations are wholes whose parts all cohere with one another and affect one another reciprocally."[16]

Plate 1.13 Arnold
Toynbee (1881–1976).
Courtesy of the Harvard
University Photo
Archives.)

Toynbee's study is characterized throughout by an interest in
what he considered the basic unit of history—civilization—and
its various stages of development and dissolution. His approach
was not positivist but effectively intuitive. For Toynbee,
historical "facts" do not and cannot speak for themselves: they are
of necessity "impure" because they are inevitably conditioned by
their perceiver's interests, theories, and interpretations. Toynbee
would have had little difficulty accepting Marx's dictum that
"History is contemporary thought about the past."

Toynbee was not averse, however, to suggesting the why and
how of a civilization's genesis or demise. His answer to why
civilizations arise is again seen in his thesis of "challenge and
response" (fully discussed in his *Study of History,* particularly
volumes 4 to 6 published in 1939), which provides a statement of
environmental determinism: the first civilizations arose out of a
primitive existence by responding to challenges posed by their
physical environment.

Environmental determinism has for centuries been a standing thesis of "principal cause" for the development of civilizations. In dealing with the ancient civilizations of the Old and New Worlds, it is impossible to ignore the conditions which the physical environment imposes on a society. Ellsworth Huntington in his widely read *Mainsprings of Civilization* (1945) supports Toynbee's thesis by showing how climate and geography not only control the character of past nations and civilizations but determine the dominant positions of nations even today.

For Toynbee, civilization develops in response to external causes. The ancient Egyptian civilization, for instance, was a response to the environmental challenge of increasing aridity. The Egyptians drained marshes, irrigated the lands of the Lower Nile, and so created one of the great civilizations of world history. Though civilizations rise in response to external causes, it is internal factors which cause their dissolution. A civilization breaks down when it has not enough creative leadership to respond to new challenges. The dissolution of a civilization is always rooted in inherent defects in the structure of its society.

Kroeber's and Toynbee's attempts to deal with the genesis, nature, and decline of civilizations are readily separated from earlier approaches by two principal factors. Kroeber's effort to introduce a quantitative approach toward an understanding of the nature of cultural growth, and Toynbee's learning and erudition, which make previous attempts at presenting a systematic picture of human history look thin and shabby, have both been of great importance in advancing civilizational studies. The tracing of unsuspected patterns, the inventing of fresh frameworks of classification and interpretation, the importance of quantitative data, and the refusal merely to narrate events characterize this century's studies of civilization. Prior to this century, such figures as Vico were men ahead of their time. Most historians contemporary with Vico were content merely to describe historical events in chronological sequence without discussing the causes of historical change. If there is any simple factor which separates the study of civilizations today from studies of the past, it is in the concern for methods which go beyond history as description and require considerations of causal factors which lead to the "how and why" in the development and transformation of civilizations.

The
Archaeological
Evidence

Around the middle of the nineteenth century, a new influence entered historical perspectives: archaeological evidence. At that time, archaeologists began in earnest the task of recovering past civilizations through excavation. But only since the early part of this century have their findings been incorporated into studies of past civilizations and their theories been introduced into mainstream historical conceptions.

RECENT ARCHAEOLOGICAL CONTRIBUTIONS

In the early nineteenth century, Professor Rasmar Nyerup of Denmark summed up the condition and knowledge of man's past:

> Everything which has come down to us from heathendom is wrapped up in a thick fog: It belongs to a space of time we cannot measure. We know it is older than Christiandom, but whether by a couple of years or even by more than a millennium we can do no more than guess.[17]

Antiquarian interest in the past existed for centuries before the great discoveries of the mid-nineteenth century. As early as 1679, the French Academie des Inscriptions et Belles-lettres was encouraging archaeological research. But these early archaeological excavations could probably best be described as mining operations to retrieve antiquities. Emmanual de Lorraine's 1709 excavations of Herculaneum, for instance, and Charles III of Bourbon's excavations of Pompeii in 1738 were motivated not by a desire to understand past civilizations but by an antiquarian's interest in collecting curios.

The discovery which effectively dates the beginning of the purposeful recovery of ancient civilizations is probably also the most sensational. That is Heinrich Schliemann's excavation of Homeric Troy in 1870. Schliemann's were the first excavations to test literary traditions by archaeological facts. In his day, it was believed that Greek history began with the first Olympiad in 776 B.C.: Schliemann's excavation added half a millennium to that date.

Our own knowledge of past civilizations is relatively recent, since archaeological investigations to recover past civilizations are less than two centuries old. The short list of discoveries provided in Table 1.1 underscores the relative modernity of the discipline of archaeology.

TABLE 1.1   *A Time-Line of Archaeological Discovery*

Egypt

1798–1801   Napoleon's expedition to Egypt is accompanied by several archaeologists who record the ancient monuments there.

1821   Champollion deciphers Egyptian hieroglyphics through study of the Rosetta stone.

1883   The Egyptian Exploration Fund under Sir Flinders Petrie begins archaeological excavation at Tunis.

Mesopotamia

1843   Paul Botta, French consul at Mosul, starts excavating Nineveh, the great Assyrian capital.

1845   Sir Henry Layard starts work at Nineveh.

1852   W. K. Loftus excavates at Eridu and Nippur and in 1854 at Uruk, the Erech of *Genesis*.

1857   Sir Henry Rawlinson "cracks" the cuneiform language of Mesopotamia.

1887   The first American expedition to Mesopotamia. The University of Pennsylvania starts excavations at Nippur.

1891   The Sumerian civilization is discovered through the excavations of Telloh.

1899   Robert Koldewey begins excavations at Babylon.

1899–1906   The French excavation at Susa recovers the Elamite civilization.

1906   Following Georges Perrot's early work, Hugo Winckler establishes the fact that Boghoz-Keui is the capital of the Hittite empire.

Mesoamerica

1841–1843   Stephens and Catherwood publish the accounts of their travels to numerous sites in the Maya area.

1880s–1900s   Important explorations and descriptive accounts by Maudslay, Charnay, Maler, Holmes, Tozzer, E. H. Thompson, and others.

1890s   Peabody Museum of Harvard University begins excavations at the great Maya site of Copan.

1911   Gamio undertakes stratigraphic excavations at Azcapotzalco.

Europe

1847–1864   Excavations at Hallstadt, Austria, evidence the transition from Bronze Age to Iron Age.

1876   The La Tene Iron Age dwellings of Switzerland are discovered and excavated.

1881–1898   General Pitt-Rivers excavates at Cranbourne Chase, England, and establishes excavating techniques which remain the backbone of present-day methodology.

1894   Sir Arthur Evans arrives on Crete and discovers the Minoan civilization through excavation at Knossos.

India–Pakistan

1921   Sir John Marshall starts excavations at Mohenjo-Daro and discovers the great Indus or Harappan civilization.

China

1929–1937   The excavations at Anyang recover the neolithic and Shang civilization of China.

Source: G. Daniel, *A Hundred and Fifty Years of Archaeology* (Cambridge, Mass.: Harvard University Press, 1976).

It should be noted that important data on Mesoamerican civilizations can be found in documents dating from the Spanish Conquest in the early sixteenth century. The writings of Sahagun on the Aztec and Landa on the Maya are particularly notable. But only in the past several decades have we had much evidence to supplement those data. The Olmec civilization, for instance, has only recently been discovered by scholars such as Stirling and recognized to be Mesoamerica's earliest civilization. Again, not until the 1940s did Jimenez Moreno identify Tula as the capital of the Toltecs, while the true size and greatness of the huge urban center of Teotihuacan was only clarified by Millon and his associates within the past decade.* Archaeology is still very much in the process of adding to our fund of historical knowledge.

Recoveries of ancient civilizations undertaken toward the end of the nineteenth century were to have an effect on current theories. The discoveries were instrumental in providing fuel for the role which "progress" was seen to have played in cultural evolution. More than that, they provided the empirical evidence for the existence of past civilizations, many of which had "disappeared" from human history for millennia. With this evidence, the need for understanding not only their nature but also the reasons for their rise and fall was more sharply felt. Archaeological evidence for past civilizations began to demand more than an intuitive, philosophically oriented understanding of cultural evolution. Ideas could no longer exist in a vacuum but required substantive data for their support or negation.

CHILDE'S CONTRIBUTION TO THEORY

The rapid increase in the recovery of ancient civilizations led to the first modern attempts to synthesize these data. In the first half of this century, the outstanding figure in these attempts was Vere Gordon Childe (1892–1957). His voluminous writings date from 1915 and extend to the 1950s. His works continue to influence the generation of archaeologists working today, and

---

*For a more detailed consideration of early research in Mesoamerica and the Americas in general, the reader is referred to a book which one of us coauthored: Gordon R. Willey and Jeremy A. Sabloff's *A History of American Archaeology* (especially Chapters 2, 3, and 4).

he remains the consummate synthesizer of Old World archaeology.

Childe was highly critical of earlier intuitive approaches to examining and explaining history. He was particularly opposed to the "Great Man" approach, racial determinism, and psychic unity, all of which he regarded as of no value in historical analysis. He indicated his feelings on the cyclical nature of history in his comments about Spengler's work: "It is perfectly obvious (especially in the realms of science and technology) that history does not describe a circle but is a cumulative process."[18] Childe also rejected the comparative method, utilizing *ethnographic analogy* (that is, the comparison of living tribal peoples and their material culture and behavior with materials derived from archaeological excavations) in only the rarest instances to illuminate the archaeological record.

In his early writings, Childe built on the theories of Ellsworth Huntington and developed an environmentally deterministic model. This model replaced the nineteenth-century cultural-evolutionary explanation by introducing changing environment as the cause of the rise of civilizations. Later, Childe turned away from environmental determinism as the primary causal explanation. He added another factor more important than geographical environment: the forces of production that are potentially available to a society. Geography and environment were seen as parts of the conditioning background, but for Childe, Marx's materialistic conception offered the most viable explanation of historical processes. He believed that technological development exhibited the greatest potential for ordering the historical process. The material forces of production, he argued, most directly affected the legal, political, and religious superstructure of a society.

Childe incorporated Marx's materialistic explanation in his reexamination of Morgan's theory of social evolution. The result was a masterpiece of archaeological synthesis for Europe and the Near East. Instead of using the traditional ages or stages explanation, Childe viewed the development of cultures as *homotaxial:* cultures that occupied similar levels of development at different times in European and Near Eastern prehistory manifested similar economic, political, and social institutions. This approach led Childe to define stages of civilization according to social and economic patterns. The stage

Plate 1.14 V. G. Childe (1892– 1957). (Courtesy of the Prehistoric Society.)

of "barbarism," for instance, was characterized by the ***neolithic revolution***—beginning food production with the initial appearance of plant and animal domestication. The stage he called "civilization" began with the ***urban revolution***—the first literate communities living in dense settlements (cities) with complex bureaucracies indicative of a state political organization.

Childe called such milestones "revolutions" because they represented dramatic and influential transformations in the development of society. According to Childe, the neolithic revolution was the most important—an idea that has been voiced by other thinkers for centuries. The transformation from living in a "state of nature" as hunters and gatherers to producing food through domestication has long been the subject of speculation for poets, philosophers, and moralists. Remarkable though it may seem, only since World War II has it become a topic for empirical research.

It is evident in Childe's writings that archaeological cultures are to be analyzed on two planes which are separated only for the sake of explanatory convenience. On one level are the principles that govern the integration of institutions, their formation, and functioning; on another level are the principles that caused and directed their evolution and transformation.

Childe's theories have met with some criticism, mostly on the grounds of failing to unite both levels of analysis in one master scheme that both describes past transformations and explains why they took place. Nevertheless, while his contemporaries were constructing trait lists of material remains and writing histories of individual archaeological sites, Childe was incorporating the ideas of Marx, Durkheim, and Malinowski (to mention but a few) in an attempt to explain processes of prehistoric culture within an anthropological framework.

In the final analysis, Childe was the ultimate consumer of theory, not its producer. His synthesizing efforts provided models for determining social organization and economic patterns of prehistoric societies. And his general synthesis of European and Near Eastern archaeology has been the foundation of many changes in archaeological theory, transforming our understanding of ancient civilizations.

Recent Anthropological Perspectives

There have been radical changes in archaeological method and theory in the past two decades in the United States. Previous archaeological theorizing had most often been within the context of culture history. Since World War II, however, the new advances in the discipline have usually been generated within the context of anthropology, the science of human cultural and biological development. As a result, archaeology has recently been concerned more with culture process or change.*

This development marks a major difference in heritage between Old World and New World archaeology. While Old World archaeology developed as a separate discipline with links to other fields such as history and geology, archaeology in the New World has grown as part of the general field of anthropology. (Today, archaeology in both areas is properly seen as the subdivision of anthropology concerned with past cultures.)

In our discussion in this chapter, we can discern two waves of changes that had an impact on civilizational studies. First, we have

*These recent developments have been fully discussed in other texts (see Willey and Sabloff 1974; Hole and Heizer 1977; Binford 1972).

seen that during the early part of this century, anthropology grew to be antievolutionary and antimaterialistic; at the same time, archaeology had become descriptive in its approach, by and large content to classify ancient sites and artifacts as to time and place. While cultural anthropology, that branch of the field concerned with contemporary societies, maintained active theoretical interests, archaeology, at least on an explicit level, became increasingly atheoretical so that many scholars came to view it as intellectually sterile.

While Childe's writings had a major impact on Old World archaeologists, his influence was relatively small in the Americas. But in the 1930s and 1940s, a second wave did take place as evolutionary and materialistic thinking reemerged in American cultural anthropology and filtered into archaeological thought. The field of archaeology began to discard its descriptive emphasis, and the theoretical vitality which characterizes it today began to emerge. In recent years, this theoretical and methodological revival has not only transformed the study of ancient civilizations by archaeologists trained in the New World, but it has influenced those trained in the Old World as well.

If one needed to pinpoint a single year as a turning point in anthropological archaeology's consideration of civilizational development, a strong argument could be made for 1949. In that year, two significant publications appeared. The first was Julian H. Steward's (1902–1972) article, "Cultural Causality and Law: A Trial Formulation of the Development of Early Civilization"; the second was Leslie White's (1900–1975) book, *The Science of Culture*. While both Steward and White were cultural anthropologists, not archaeologists, their publications have had as great an impact on the growth of anthropological archaeology as on cultural anthropology.

The significance of Steward's and White's work lies in their strong support of evolutionary and materialist modes of thought about ancient civilizations. The introduction—or better, reintroduction—of these ideas helped breathe life into an archaeology which had long concentrated on sterile typologies and neglected dynamic models of civilizational development. The new modes of analysis were to provide the intellectual foundation in anthropological archaeology for the restructuring of civilizational studies in the past two decades.

Plate 1.15 Julian Haynes Steward (1902–1972).

STEWARD'S ENVIRONMENTAL EXPLANATION

Steward integrated aspects of evolutionary theory and environmental determinism into his theory. His goal was clear: "The discovery of cultural laws is an ultimate goal of anthropology."[19] He continued:

> Comparative cultural studies should interest themselves in recurrent phenomena as well as in unique phenomena, and ... anthropology [should] explicitly recognize that a legitimate and ultimate objective is to see through the differences of cultures to the similarities to ascertain processes that are duplicated independently in cultural sequences, and to recognize cause and effect in both temporal and functional relationships. ... Any formulations of cultural data are valid provided the procedure is empirical, hypotheses arising from interpretations of fact being revised as new facts become available.[20]

Multilinear evolution was Steward's term for the methodology of empirically searching for limited parallels among different cultural sequences.

Steward's work was a reaction to the then dominant antievolutionary school of anthropology. According to Steward, the antievolutionists' total rejection of all evolutionary formulations because of the excesses of a few earlier evolutionists like L. H. Morgan was like throwing out the baby with the bathwater. He notes: "If the 19th century formulations were wrong, it was not because their purpose was inadmissible or their objective impossible, but because the data were inadequate and insufficient, the methodology weak, and the application of the schemes too broad."[21] In effect, Steward argued that similar cultural ecological adaptations took place in various areas from Mesopotamia to Mexico. While the places and dates were different, the historical sequence was fundamentally the same.

Steward's argument elaborated upon Karl Wittfogel's irrigation hypothesis. His own theory was centered in arid or semiarid areas where maximum agricultural production necessitated irrigation. The tremendous effort of constructing the irrigation works and distributing the water required the growth of a sociopolitical bureaucracy, and this in turn led to the rise of a ruling class. Once completed, irrigation systems also allowed new leisure time as well as population increases. Resulting population pressures led to intrastate and interstate competition and a trend toward empire-building. After a period of cultural collapse and "dark ages," a new militaristic phase led to the formation of new and stronger states. This cycle seemed to hold, Steward argued, in ancient Egypt, Mesopotamia, China, Mesoamerica, and the Central Andes. After reviewing the data, Steward concluded: "Despite many particulars in which these areas differed, the basic cultural patterns or forms, the functional interrelationships between cultural features, and the developmental processes were very much the same."[22]

As we have seen, V. Gordon Childe was also a champion of evolutionary and materialist modes of thought. However, as Marvin Harris has pointed out in his study of the development of anthropological theory, Childe never integrated theory into his cultural-historical writings. Steward, on the other hand, did attempt to test his ideas by using specific cross-cultural data on ancient civilizations. And unlike most earlier writers, he not only used the relatively well known civilizations of the Old World, but also turned to New World data. As Harris has noted: "Steward's ... comparison ... marked the beginning of the use of the New World archaeological evidence to support a cultural-materialist interpretation of the origin of civilization."[23]

Steward's theoretical writings, especially his later collection of essays entitled *Theory of Culture Change* (1955), had a major impact on colleagues and students in the Americas. Three aspects of Steward's ideas have particularly stimulated new directions in archaeological research strategies. The first was the concept and methodology of multilinear evolution. This methodology has led to attempts to formulate civilizational sequences, as described above, and a willingness to compare these sequences to find regularities in development. Steward's second contribution, the renaissance of cultural ecology, has influenced anthropologists to redesign research strategies so that the environment is viewed as an active rather than a passive force. The place of land aridity and irrigation has received special attention as an influence on the development of urban states. A third contribution was Steward's interest in settlement patterns as a major clue in tracing the development of ancient civilizations. The on-site study of settlement patterns has grown as a method for testing ecologically oriented hypotheses about the growth of civilizations.

WHITE'S VIEW: CULTURE AS A SYSTEM

Leslie White's influence on archaeological theory has been neither as immediate nor as direct as Steward's. Nevertheless, his writings have had considerable impact on the growth of archaeology in past decades. Of particular relevance to us are two ideas basic to White's conception. First, cultural change is a regular process; and second, cultures are systems.

In viewing cultural change as a regular process, White broke away from some earlier theorists (most notably Spengler) who had championed the Great Man theory that individuals could singlehandedly change the course of history. White used the example of Akhnaton, the first great Egyptian ruler to advocate monotheism. For this deed, Akhnaton is often cited as one of the significant figures who, alone, altered the course of history. In the words of the great Egyptologist James Breasted: "Until Ikhnaton the history of the world had been but the irresistible drift of tradition. All men had been but drops of water in the great current."[24]

White took the opposite view: "We must conclude that history is still the irresistible flow of the stream of culture and that all men are but chips floating on that stream. . . . [But] the *general trend* of events would have been the same had Ikhnaton been but a sack of sawdust."[25]

In White's view, history is a process which consists of regularized interactions between human cultures and natural environments. The task of anthropologists (archaeologists included) is to direct their energies toward explaining general, repeatable cultural processes through time—not to take a particularistic view that singles out one individual at one point in time. In the Egyptian example just noted, White offers a plausible alternative to the Great Man hypothesis. He argues that Akhnaton's championship of the god Aton as the only god was a ploy in the long-term battle for power between the kingship and the priestly nobility—a ploy that succeeded in fact in stripping the nobility of their power. The trend toward consolidating power would have existed anyway; although he acted as a catalyst to hasten the conclusion, history would have taken the same course even without Akhnaton.

No matter which side of the argument the reader might favor, White's position has been on the upswing in recent archaeological thinking, and it has been helpful in stimulating new interest in searching for regularities in ancient civilizational development.

White's second contribution has had an even more profound influence. That is his explicit consideration of culture as a *system*—a dynamic series of relationships. Although systems thinking has had a long and involved history in other disciplines, White's conception has led to the recent use of systems models in archaeology, in both research strategies and interpretation of process. As White has said: "To understand cultural systems in particular, we must know something about systems in general."[26]

A simple, often-quoted definition of systems says: "The system is conceived as a set of interrelated variables, such that there are repercussions upon some or all of its member variables each time one of them is subjected to certain kinds of change."[27] Many systemic relationships are self-regulated, the classic example being a thermostatically controlled system where a rise in temperature causes the thermostat to shut off the heat and a lowered temperature signals the heat to start again. This kind of system is called a closed system: beyond the cyclical pattern of temperature change and mechanical response, no external factors interfere.

If archaeologists had only closed systems to deal with, their work might be easy. Unfortunately for the archaeologist, human culture is part of an open system that is "dynamic and tends toward growth and differentiation."[28] Human cultures are constantly changing, and their patterns of development can be extraordinarily complex. Specific changes in cultural systems or subsystems can be very difficult, if not impossible, to predict even when all the variables are known. For anthropologists studying modern cultures, all this means that their subject is an elusive one. For archaeologists, the situation is much worse: they often are unable to control, quantify, or even identify a majority of the variables in an extinct cultural system.

Nevertheless, the systems approach seems to have much potential for the archaeologist, and it promises to help provide rewarding new insights into the development of civilizations. While the approach is not an explanatory substitute in and of itself—its chief value has been said to be to shift our focus from things to relationships[29]—it can offer an illuminating framework which archaeologists can use to order their explanations. As we will see in Chapter 4, for example, the use of a systems model recently has helped clear away the so-called mystery of the collapse and disappearance of Classic Maya civilization. Archaeologists have been able to show that the complex interplay of a number of factors over a period of years led to the demise of this apparently thriving civilization in the ninth century A.D.

A LOOK AHEAD

In the last decade, the new trends which had been set in motion by scholars such as Steward and White have been creatively synthesized by the American archaeologist Lewis R. Binford. In a series of forceful publications in the 1960s, Binford argued that archaeologists, instead of just describing and attempting to reconstruct the past, should also direct their energies toward building and testing theories which would explain cultural processes. That is to say, Binford's goal was to *explain* how and why cultures changed through time. He further outlined a methodology which could be used to achieve these ends. The implications of Binford's arguments for the study of civilizations are clear, and their ramifications have been felt throughout the discipline as archaeologists have moved to direct research efforts along lines similar to those proposed by Binford.

As the reader will see in Chapters 2, 3, 4, and 5 of this book, these new research directions are reflected in the emphasis on "how" and "why" questions which are continually raised page after page. How did the Indus civilization develop? Why did the Classic Maya civilization collapse? How did the Aztec empire expand and why did it fall such easy prey to Cortes and the Spanish? What was the role of trade in the growth of Sumerian civilization? Like these questions, the models proposed in response to them echo recent views: that culture is a dynamic system and that cultural change is a regular evolutionary process sharply influenced by such factors as environmental conditions.

This book shows how archaeologists are trying to answer such questions today. In the following pages we will discuss the various models used to organize the vast array of new archaeological data on the ancient civilizations of the Near East and Mesoamerica. We will explore, moreover, the variety of hypotheses which have been proposed to explain different facets of civilizational development. Where considerable disagreements among archaeologists still exist, we will say so, and, if possible, state which views appear to have the most support at the moment. We have provided general descriptions of the major civilizations of the Near East and Mesoamerica, as well as an overview of their historical development, in order for the reader to gain both an appreciation of the achievements of these civilizations and an understanding of the kinds of data archaeologists uncover and utilize in their efforts to give meaning to the past.

The reader may notice that, plentiful though the questions be and sophisticated though their answers may be, generally acceptable explanations are rare indeed. At the present state of affairs, we are just beginning to recognize some regularities in civilizational development that seem to hold across time and space—but even these patterns have not been universally accepted. Nevertheless, there is great optimism among archaeologists that the discipline is on the verge of new breakthroughs. We can only hope that we have transmitted some of this new excitement in the following discussions of the ancient civilizations of the Near East, the Indus, and Mesoamerica.

Notes

1. Spengler (1926:vol. 1, pp. 104ff.).
2. Aristotle's *Politics* (bk. 1:passim).
3. St. Augustine's *City of God* (bk. 7:14).
4. Donagan (1962:vol. 8, pp. 173ff.).
5. Marx (1973:173).
6. Bury (1932:19).
7. Morgan (1877:76–77).
8. Comte (1896:250).
9. Lubbock (1871:325ff.).
10. Spengler (1926:vol. 1, p. 124).
11. Spengler quoted in Gardiner (1959:190).
12. Spengler (1926:194).
13. Kroeber (1944:820).
14. Kroeber (1944:19).
15. Lowie (1920:441).
16. Toynbee (1934–1954:vol. 3, p. 380).
17. Quoted in Daniel (1976:38).
18. Childe (1947:4ff., 43–48).
19. Steward (1949:2).
20. Steward (1949:2–3).
21. Steward (1949:2).
22. Steward (1949:7).
23. Harris (1968:680–681).
24. Breasted (1926:126).
25. White (1949:278).
26. White (1975:15).
27. Wagner (1960:6).
28. Hole and Heizer (1973:440).
29. Hole and Heizer (1977:361).

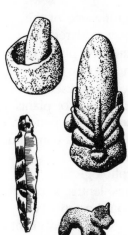

2. Agricultural Communities: The Near Eastern Evidence

43

The transition from hunter-gatherer to food producer is one of the most important in the development of human society; our understanding of it has also been one of the major contributions of archaeological research. Indeed, probably the only subject of equal significance is the emergence of tool-making hominids several million years ago. These changes, perhaps more than any other, have transformed cultural conditions and altered our environment, human biology, and, to a degree, our planet.

The Neolithic Revolution

While archaeologists are agreed on the significance of the Neolithic Revolution, it has not been so easy to determine exactly when food production began. In the first place, the definition of food production is dependent on our understanding of domestication, an ambiguous concept itself. *Domestication* can be defined as the manipulation of plants and animals by humans in such a way as to cause some genetic, or morphological, change; more broadly, it is seen as a continuum of relationships between people, plants, and animals.

On one end of the continuum are morphologically domesticated plants—like wheat, barley, peas, lentils, and bitter vetch. In these plants, changes brought about by artificially induced selective processes can be recognized by paleobotanists studying the remains of seeds. Some morphologically domesticated plants, including maize, dates, banana, and breadfruit, have been so altered that they are forever tied to people, for they have lost their independent power of seed dispersal and germination.

On the other end of the same continuum are plants that have been "domesticated" solely in terms of the growing space people provide for them. These plants, referred to as *cultivated* plants, are difficult if not impossible to distinguish from wild plants, for their domestication is a matter of ecological rather than morphological change.

In the middle range of the continuum lie all degrees of domestication and cultivation. As a result, determining whether or not a past culture has domesticated plants often involves a fair amount of detective work. For instance, the presence of seeds at Nahal Oren in Israel (ca. 18,000 B.C.) of precisely the same cereal plants later domesticated indicates that certain plants may have been selected and cultivated at a very early date.

Determining the extent of animal domestication also involves some inference and guesswork. As with plants, some animals (in the Near East, dogs, sheep, goats, cattle, and pigs) became genetically changed in time. But morphological changes did not take place for many generations, and in some instances they never took place at all. In these cases, paleozoologists must rely on other clues. The high percentage of gazelle bones in some early Neolithic sites, for instance—three times more than any other species—probably indicates their "domestication" or at the very least their selective exploitation. In recent times the red deer, eland, and musk-ox have, for all practical purposes, been domesticated perhaps in the same manner that the gazelle was in the early Neolithic.

As with plants, some animal species are more easily domesticated than others. Studies on the herding behavior of animals suggest that certain species may be preadapted for domestication.[1] The transition from extensive dependence on gazelle to the domestication of sheep and goats may have resulted from the fact that sheep and goats utilize a wider range of foods, are more dependent on water supplies, and are better integrated into a sedentary community.

Because it is difficult to determine the extent of domestication in past cultural systems, assigning agricultural status to a community is often a somewhat arbitrary decision that involves some ambiguity. In short, there are degrees of food production. Anthropologists and archaeologists can, however, agree on a working definition of food production. This definition posits two minimum requirements: first, there must be a reasonably efficient level of food procurement (food acquired through direct production must amount to over half the community's dietary needs for part of the year); and second, both plant and animal domesticates are no longer bound to their natural habitat (that is, plants and animals can survive, with human assistance, in environments to which they are not naturally adapted).

CAUSES OF THE NEOLITHIC REVOLUTION

After hundreds of millennia of predatory food-gathering (hunting and collecting), how did people begin controlling their own food supply and what were the sociocultural consequences of this new development in human history?

Old and New World Contrasts

The answers to the preceding questions are somewhat different for the Old World than for the New World. While most writers have emphasized similarities in the evolving urban societies of the two hemispheres, the processes of development in the two areas were based upon distinctive subsistence economies and cultural patterns. Old World and New World civilizations evolved essentially independently; thus they provide a contrastive opportunity for the study of the rise of civilizations.

The economic foundations on which Near Eastern civilizations were built depended upon wheat, barley, certain legumes (especially peas and lentils), sheep, goats, pigs, cattle, and dogs; later horses and camels were domesticated. These subsistence resources are remarkably different in kind from those which established the economic foundation for the New World. There the principal domesticated plants were maize, beans, and squash. A far more limited group of animals was available to be domesticated than in the Old World. Chief among these were the llama in Peru and the guinea pig in Mesoamerica.

The differences in the subsistence patterns between the two areas at least partially explains their fundamentally distinctive cultural patterns. From earliest times, the Near Eastern subsistence economy supported two distinctive cultural patterns: the sedentary farmers and the nomadic herdsmen. The relationship between these two provides one of the leitmotifs of Near Eastern civilization. This relationship featured some built-in animosity and suspicion, as the two groups contended over grazing rights and property ownership. But it was also symbiotic in many senses, as settled and nomadic groups provided important services and information exchange channels.

Without an understanding of the tensions and interrelations between these two cultural systems, the civilizational process in the Near East can be only partially comprehended. But in the

New World, the foundations for civilization lacked this sedentary farmer – nomadic herdsman relationship. As a result, it provides an essentially different system for the rise of civilization. In this chapter and the next, we will look at the factors that led to the development of civilization in the Near East; Chapter 4 examines Mesoamerican neolithic foundations and the development of civilization.

Theories of Food Production

Until around 1925, when V. G. Childe began to stress the importance of the food-producing or "Neolithic" Revolution, this matter had received little attention as a factor in the development of civilizations. As Chapter 1 showed, the eighteenth- and nineteenth-century scholars posited cultural-evolutionary schemes of universal history, and these idealized explanations were generally accepted. The stages were nicely outlined, each with its consequent impact on the social order. Humanity progressed from "savagery" (hunting and gathering) to "barbarism" (agriculture and pastoralism) to "civilization." It was as simple as that. If it all seemed very neat and logical it was because it was based on no empirical evidence. All was mere speculation: hypotheses were formulated; details were even argued; but the ideas were never tested by actual archaeological fieldwork.

These untested cultural-evolutionary models received their most concise formulation in the writings of Childe.[2] He was interested in the impact a newly introduced food-producing way of life had upon the "savage" hunters and food collectors of Europe following the end of the last ice age. He turned his attention to the Near East as the probable center of origin from which food production was diffused to Europe, thousands of years before conventional ancient history began.

Childe's explanation was a classic of environmental determinism. According to his "oasis theory," the food-producing revolution took place during a time of major climatic changes. With the retreat of the ice sheets from continental Europe in about 10,000 B.C., he argued, the summer rains that watered North Africa and Arabia shifted northward to Europe, resulting in the desiccation of much of the Near East. This desiccation, Childe said, provided the stimulus for adopting a food-producing economy. The drier land yielded less food for hunters and gatherers; thus populations clustered in oases where the natural propinquity of plants, animals, and humans led to a symbiotic relationship binding all three.

Childe's theory provided a masterful explanation. But it is no longer favored for a number of reasons—not the least of which is the absence of evidence for large-scale environmental desiccation at the end of the Pleistocene. More recent explanations have firmer foundations in archaeological data, but still they do not represent a unified view.

Archaeologists feel increasingly uneasy in using the traditional sequence of Paleolithic, Mesolithic, and Neolithic. Recent research has expanded, modified, and confounded this system by introducing such "stages" as Protoneolithic, Aceramic, Prepottery Neolithic, and Preurban or Protourban—all with various subdivisions. This proliferation of stages has resulted in a baffling terminology. We believe it most helpful, and theoretically most illuminating, to approach the data through an understanding of the successive economic patterns which led to food production. In this manner, the development of food production is seen as a successive and increasingly dependent adaptive manipulation of environmental resources.

Within this framework, theories on the origins for domestication tend to be of two types: those that involve the conscious manipulation of animal and plant by humans on economic, religious, or subsistence resources; and those that stress environmental pressures, such as desiccation or glacial advances and retreats which brought about ideal conditions for domestication. Zeuner, a pioneer in paleozoological studies, believed that "social relationships" between people and certain exploited wild animals led inevitably to a symbiotic relationship that resulted in domestication.[3] This focus differs from that of ecologically oriented archaeologists in the Near East. Their approach does not deal with social relationships but with environmental pressures and adaptations of specific ecosystems as forming the primary causes leading to domestication.

An important representative of the second group of theorists is Robert J. Braidwood of the Oriental Institute, University of Chicago. Braidwood was the first to challenge Childe's theories through archaeological excavation, and his excavations at Jarmo (discussed later in this chapter) led him to reject notions of catastrophic climatic change. Braidwood believed that the shift to a food-producing economy resulted from an "ever increasing cultural differentiation and specialization of human communities."[4]

In his study of the neolithic revolution, Braidwood discerned several different levels in the evolution of food production.[5] One level was an "era of incipient cultivation and animal domestication," where individuals first began manipulating plants and animals by herding wild animals, selectively hunting species by age or sex, or removing plant species from their natural habitat and replanting them around their settlements. Such manipulation of the animal and plant world, in order to control one's food resource, is believed to have occurred by 10,000 B.C. in the Near East. Another level was an "era of primary village farming," in which specific plants and animals were fully domesticated and provided the dependent food resources of the community.

Braidwood's levels of socioeconomic evolution did not develop contemporaneously, nor did they inevitably succeed each other. Though it is difficult to support from archaeological evidence, one may assume that the mosaic of interdependence between village agriculturist and nomadic herder was an early development, with the principal actors often changing their respective roles.

Beginning with Carl Sauer's essay in 1952, an ecological approach to the origins of food production has been of paramount importance. Sauer explains the origins of food production in Southeast Asia as a change in adaptation: a change in the manner of interaction between culture and environment.[6] Over ten years later, Lewis Binford added an important dimension to this ecological approach when he suggested that at the end of the Pleistocene, population increases in the Near East forced settlements inland from coastal areas. These population movements led in turn to demographic pressures in areas where potentially domesticable plants and animals could be found. Binford regards the development of agricultural techniques as adaptively advantageous to the populations of these regions. This hypothesis entails a series of causes, but it has a number of weaknesses. For instance, we still await evidence to support the contention that populations moved inland and that demographic pressures existed. Moreover, one wonders why the same process had never been set in motion during earlier interglacials.

Perhaps the most widely accepted theory today has been proposed by Kent Flannery. Flannery advances a hypothesis based on systems models to explain not the cause but the mechanisms for the transition to food production.[7] His hypothesis contains three important assumptions: first, that hunting and gathering populations increased prior to food production; second, that food production began in marginal areas of the mountain zones of Iran, Iraq, and Turkey and the woodland zones of Palestine; and, third, that there were many centers of food production even from the very beginning.

Flannery suggests that preagricultural peoples adapted not to specific environments but to certain plants and animals that inhabited several environments. To exploit these resources successfully, populations had to be in specific areas at specific times. In other words, the procuring of food required a *scheduling* of seasonal movement. The seasonal productivity of different environments is typical of both the Near East and Mesoamerica, where populations were obliged to schedule exploitation of plants and animals in different seasons. For instance, several ecological zones existed in the Near East. Along the Euphrates River terraces were wild goats, joint fir trees, and milk vetch; around the nearby salt rivers and saline plains were wild boar, deer, cats, poplar, and tamarisk trees; and in the low mountain valleys about the Euphrates were oaks, pistachios, almonds, goats, deer, and partridge. The variety of environmental zones with their different seasonal resources required their exploitation at the time of year when each specific resource could be harvested. This differentially scheduled exploitation of varying environments would have characterized incipient cultivation and domestication in both the Old and New Worlds. And within both areas, increasing populations would have had the same effect: that of new groups splitting off to exploit more marginal areas where they would be forced to cultivate the plants brought with them.

THE NEOLITHIC "REVOLUTION": AN OVERVIEW

From the combined theories and research of people like Flannery, Binford, and Braidwood, a sort of composite picture emerges of the beginnings of food production in the Near East.

The geographical area in which this process took place extends from the Anatolian plateau in Turkey to the deserts of Central Asia, and from the uplands of Palestine to the Caucasian range in Russia. The time was during the millennia that followed the stabilization of our modern climate after the last ice age—by 9000 to 8000 B.C. in the highland zones of the Near East.

The process of this "revolution" was neither sweeping nor sudden. Cultural developments are never uniform over large geographical expanses, nor are innovators restricted to a single area. The archaeological record suggests a slow, often faltering adaptation toward food production: a process which in retrospect has sometimes been erroneously perceived as directed toward a final goal of food production. But cultural evolution, like biological evolution, is entirely random. It is not directed toward final goals but only establishes boundaries for that which is possible.

What seems to have happened is that hunting and gathering populations, well adapted to particular environments, remained stable and below the point of resource exhaustion until that equilibrium was disturbed. Disequilibrium may be brought about by either of two factors: environmental change or demographic stress. The absence of clear evidence for the first—the hypothesis originally suggested by Childe—has resulted in more recent models that concentrate on demography as the prime mover in bringing about the domestication of plants and animals.

Flannery took Binford's model of demographic stress and applied it to the Near East. His systems model begins with population growth as the determining factor. This caused some people to move to marginal areas where producers tried to grow plants artificially around the outskirts of optimum zones. Gradually, this necessitated that population's adaptation to a food-producing economy in order to maintain its settlement within the marginal areas.

In this model, food production is both a cause and an effect of demographic change. Indeed, so fundamental a transition as the beginning of food production has obvious social consequences. When people sow crops, food supplies and populations remain in one place. The practice of agriculture tends toward the establishment of permanent settlements, and this in turn leads to the establishment of storage activities, enabling food produced at any time of the year to be consumed at other times. (Animal husbandry has a similar effect in "banking" food supplies: meat can be kept on the hoof until needed.) In this sense, food production is a factor in the establishment of settled communities.

But while food production often leads to permanent settlements, this sequence is not inevitable. There are a number of archaeological sites which indicate the existence of permanent settlements without evidence of domestication. In these ancient communities, a good case can be made for the argument that permanent settlements sometimes necessitate domestication, instead of the reverse.[8] Increasing sedentism (permanence of habitation in one settlement) among forager-fisher populations exploiting reliable food supplies in coastal areas along the Mediterranean or riverine areas (as along the Tigris and Euphrates) may have resulted in population pressures that led to more effective manipulation of food resources. Another effect of these pressures was the "budding-off" of excess population groups searching for new food resources—the same process Flannery describes in his model.[9] This second effect may have provided a selective advantage to groups who were able to develop practices of domestication.

Which came first, the Neolithic Revolution or the development of sedentism? It is obvious that no clear-cut answer exists, and certainly no universal explanation that provides the key in every geographical area. A growing body of archaeological evidence does exist, however, and it is to this that we now turn.

The Era of Incipient Cultivation

From about 12,000 B.C. onward, there are indications that people were beginning to attach increased importance to manipulating plants for food. Saddle querns (stone platforms for grinding cereals) and mortars for grinding cereals, sickle blades for their harvest, and dry lined storage pits appear for the first time on archaeological sites. The earliest appearance of these artifacts does not imply domestication. It does suggest *incipient cultivation:* people were beginning to devise a technology for their manipulation and exploitation of plants for food.

For the time period in which incipient cultivation played a major role, we have scanty archaeological evidence but an abundance of conjecture. Such evidence as does exist comes to

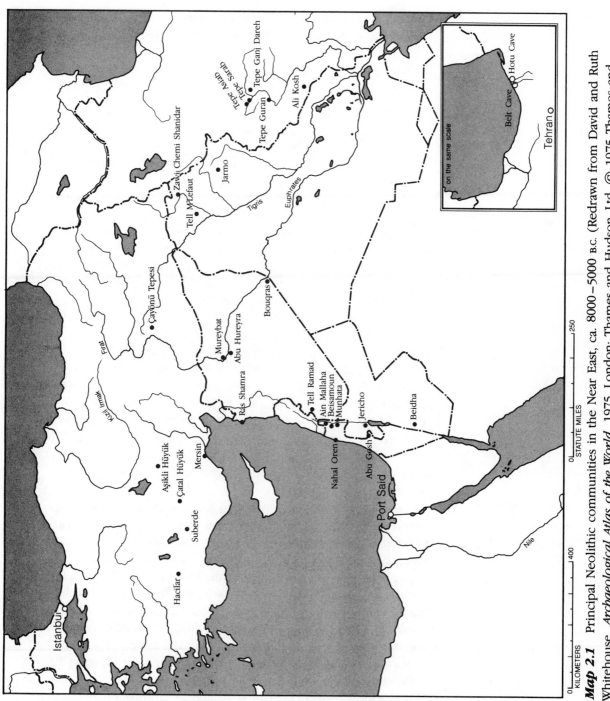

Map 2.1 Principal Neolithic communities in the Near East, ca. 8000–5000 B.C. (Redrawn from David and Ruth Whitehouse, *Archaeological Atlas of the World.* 1975. London: Thames and Hudson Ltd. © 1975 Thames and Hudson Ltd.)

us from two distinct protoneolithic cultures: the Natufian of Palestine and the Karim Shahirian of the Zagros Mountains of Iraq.

THE NATUFIAN CULTURE

While most of our knowledge of the Natufian comes from the upper levels of a number of caves in Palestine, the influence of this culture was apparently quite widespread. Its characteristic flint industry has been identified in Syria, Lebanon, and even at Beldibi, a cave on the south-central coast of Turkey. In Palestine, where the Natufian is best explored, radiocarbon dates span the two millennia from 10,000 to 8000 B.C.

The Natufian people lived in caves as well as open-air sites. In their most famous cave setting at Mount Carmel, in present-day Israel, Natufian folk lived in the cave and built low stone walls along its terrace. There is little beyond these walls, and the hearths, and stone-paved floors inside the caves, which can pass as architecture. In the more recently reported Natufian open-air sites, of which Mallaha in Israel is the best known, stone foundations of round houses have been excavated.

Most Natufian artifacts consist of flint—tiny blades with geometric forms. Of these, the presence of the sickle blade is of special interest, for the characteristic sheen or polish on its cutting edge may have resulted from cutting grasses or grain. At the Mount Carmel site, excavators have made another significant find: straight bone handles in which a number of flint sickles were set in a line to form a cutting edge. These provide a prototype for a scythe.[10]

The animal bones from Natufian levels indicate the presence of a modern fauna: gazelle, deer, hyena, bear, wild boar, leopard, and dog. None of the animals were domesticated, though all were exploited as a food source, most particularly the gazelle.

The Natufian people utilized bone, like flint, for the production of tools: these include harpoons, awls, and fishhooks, as well as beads. Other artifacts have been found besides those used as tools. The dead at Mount Carmel and Mallaha were buried with offerings placed in their graves. At Mount Carmel, two skulls had elaborate headdresses of shell beads adorning the deceased.

Evidence from Natufian sites indicates beginnings of a trend toward food production. The presence of large open-air settlements with architectural foundations; the discovery of agricultural tools such as sickles; the uncovering of mortars and pestles used for milling grains; the apparent attention to burials—all provide inferential evidence for both a degree of permanence in settlement and initial attempts to manipulate new food sources.

THE KARIM SHAHIR ASSEMBLAGE

The Karim Shahir assemblage, like the Natufian, appears in both open-air and cave encampments. Karim Shahir itself lies on top of a bluff in the Kurdish hill country of northeastern Iraq, about 350 miles from the closest Natufian sites. Two dates are available for this assemblage: the open-air site of Zawi Chemi Shanidar is dated at 8900±300 B.C.; the nearby cave site of Shanidar is probably somewhat more recent—8650±300 B.C.

As in the Natufian sites, the great bulk of objects recovered from Karim Shahir were chipped flints of geometric form and microlithic bladelets. These were produced by different techniques than their Natufian counterparts. The sickle blade, however, is all but absent, as are milling stones of both mortar and pestle.

While Karim Shahir has not yielded direct evidence for the manipulation of plant foods, there are considerable accumulations of bones of wild animals that were capable of domestication—sheep, goats, cattle, horses, and wolves. This evidence is noteworthy, for fewer of these remains have been found at earlier cave sites in the same area.

While our understanding of the beginning Neolithic Revolution is still sketchy, we can at least infer that the groundwork was being laid by 8000 B.C. in two distinctive environmental zones of the Near East: the Palestinian Levant and the Zagros Mountains of Iraq. Even if full-scale agriculture had not yet begun in both these areas, adaptations were being directed toward the manipulation of animal and plant resources.

INCIPIENT CULTIVATION: SOME CHARACTERISTICS

It is almost impossible to identify traits that are "characteristic" of all villages or cultures during the period of incipient cultivation. Above all, the evidence is incomplete. For reasons described above, we still are not sure just how far many early cultures had progressed in producing their own food. Moreover, it appears that there are actually very few common traits to identify. Food production began in many different areas with varying food resources, environments, and settlement patterns.

Early Settlement Patterns

Settlement patterns during the period of incipient cultivation may have consisted of permanent "base camps" as well as "exploitation camps"—periodic settlements for the exploitation of seasonal resources. The presence of exploitation camps has been given some support by recent field research showing that a family of five can harvest sufficient wild grains (still growing in quantity in southeastern Turkey) in three weeks to provide a year's supply of food.[11] Theoretically at least, a small band of individuals could have migrated to an area rich in wild grains and remained there until they had harvested a sufficient supply to fill their needs before returning to their permanent settlement.

Evidence for the presence of permanent villages by 7500 B.C. may seem surprising, particularly in light of theories like Childe's that viewed food production as a necessary precursor of settled communities. Yet it seems likely that in at least some permanent villages of this era, domestication of plants and animals may have been absent.

An example of such a village is the site of Mureybit on the Middle Euphrates, 80 kilometers east of Aleppo, Syria. A convincing cluster of radiocarbon dates places the earliest settlement of Mureybit from 8500 to 8000 B.C.[12] Excavations have uncovered evidence of permanent settlement in the form of round houses constructed of mud-clay and wood. Also present are ground stone tools and traces of wild cereals and wild cattle, onager (wild ass), and gazelle. The wild wheat found at Mureybit is well south of its present range of distribution, indicating either its artificial transport to the south or differing climatic conditions that allowed for its more southerly distribution at that period.

The Mureybit site is not the only evidence of permanent settlements without agriculture, nor is it the first. This new picture was first suggested by Jean Perrot in 1960, who suggested that "village sites" and domestication were two

Plate 2.1 The Neolithic mound of Ganj-dareh in northwestern Iran.

independent attributes. At Mallaha, Perrot pointed out the absence of any evidence for domestication within this permanently settled year-round village site.[13] Other sites recently discovered in the Near East suggest the existence of permanent settlements before the development of agriculture.

"Borderline" Villages

We must still infer a great deal about climatic, demographic, and social change during this period of incipient cultivation. There must have been numerous villages on the borderline between incipient cultivation and effective village farming.

One such site is Ganj-dareh in the Zagros Mountains of Iran, a small mound of 1 or 2 acres. Its earliest settlement appears to be an encampment of the last centuries of the ninth millennium, above which a community of the early eighth millennium built two-story houses. Evidence from this site has suffered a good deal of damage: the mud-brick structures were burned in a fire of such intensity as to obliterate any traces of seed; and other organic materials were also charred beyond recognition. Yet from the impressions of sheep or goat hoofprints in the brick, we can infer the domestication of one or the other of these animals, for neither wild sheep nor wild goats would be in such proximity to the village as to step onto wet bricks laid out to dry.

Plate 2.2   Aerial photograph of the excavations at Çayönü Tepesi. (Courtesy of the Oriental Institute, University of Chicago.)

Plate 2.3   Stone foundation of a domestic house in Area EF2 at Çayönü Tepesi. The "grill plan" foundation of the walls is visible as are the plastered room floors, ca. 7000 B.C. (Courtesy of the Oriental Institute, University of Chicago.)

The Ali Kosh site is in a wholly different environmental zone from Ganj-dareh, which is located in the semiarid piedmont in the Zagros region. This excavated mound dates from the mid-eighth millennium, and it, too, suggests an incipient adaptation to food production. Unlike Ganj-dareh, this site yielded no evidence from its earliest occupation for domesticated animals, though wild gazelle, onager, wild ox, boar, and yearling goats must have been hunted. But traces of domesticated emmer

Plate 2.4 Stone foundation of a domestic house at Çayönü Tepesi, ca. 7000 B.C. (Courtesy of the Oriental Institute, University of Chicago.)

(a cereal grain) have been found in hearths, together with carbonized wild legumes and barley.

In yet a third distinctive region, on the Tauros piedmont in southeastern Turkey, the site of Çayönü Tepesi has yielded domesticated cereals and pulses (leguminous plants such as peas, beans, lentils). Bones of domesticated dogs as well as wild animals have also been found at this site. Each of these sites—Ganj-dareh, Ali Kosh, and Cayönü Tepesi—has substantial houses, as illustrated for Çayönü in Plates 2.3 and 2.4. All are believed to be permanent year-round settlements. All have radiocarbon age determinations to at least the mid-eighth millennium, and all are in different environmental zones. Each of the sites has yielded evidence of some food production—but the foods produced suggest regional variations.

INCIPIENT CULTIVATION: SOME CONCLUSIONS

What all this means is that many of the past explanations for the beginnings of food production simply do not stand up against archaeological evidence. We can no longer accept a single site as responsible for the "invention" of food production; nor for that matter can we point to a single environmental zone or "nuclear area" as responsible for the development of food production. Indeed, there may not even be a single pattern of development that led to domestication in the several early centers.

The evidence is clear that following 8000 B.C., several villages had developed simple but effective means of food production. Just what the adaptive mechanisms were which led ever-increasing numbers of people to adopt the agricultural mode of subsistence remains one of the most intriguing archaeological questions. The transition from hunter and gatherer to agriculturist was by no means rapid or uniform. There are communities in the Near East which did not adopt a full dependence on domesticated animals and plants for a thousand years after their introduction, while the spread of agriculture reached distant Western European communities four thousand years after its inception in the Near East.

It is not unreasonable to infer from the increasing number of sites that there was a gradual population increase after 8000 B.C.[14] The developments between 8000 and 6000 B.C. represent a transformation to fully developed villages and towns, with considerable diversity and regional differences throughout the Near East. This transformation could not have come about without effective food production and settled village-farming life—developments which provided the cornerstone for the subsequent rise of civilization in this area.

Evidence of Sedentary Food Production

By the eighth millennium, populations were beginning to manipulate their environment in different ways. From the archaeological evidence that now exists, it is reasonable to suggest that this development took either of two paths. Certain populations specialized in sedentary food production, eventually within agricultural villages, while other groups specialized in animal herding, adopting nomadic patterns of existence.

Within the Near East, the first village farming community to be excavated for the specific purpose of documenting the transition to food production was Jarmo. Since the initiation of the Jarmo project in 1948, dozens of sites dating between 8000 and 5000 B.C. have also been excavated. In fact, the majority of archaeological research in the Near East since World War II has been directed toward these earliest farming villages. Since it is not possible to summarize them all, we will look here at four sites that are representative of distinctive environmental regions and evolved equally distinctive cultural traditions: Jarmo, in the Zagros Mountains (an area which was earlier the location of the Karim Shahirian tradition); Jericho (where the earliest occupation was of the Natufian tradition) on the floor of the Dead Sea Valley in Jordan; Çatal Hüyük on the Konya Plain of south-central Turkey; and the pre-Sumerian cultures on the alluvial plains of the Tigris and the Euphrates.

THE MOUNTAIN VILLAGE OF JARMO

Robert Braidwood's excavation of the primary village farming community of Jarmo was the first site specifically excavated to test V. G. Childe's hypothesis about the origins of the neolithic revolution.[15] The village dates from the mid-seventh millennium to the end of the sixth, and it offers clear evidence of permanent settlement and early food production.

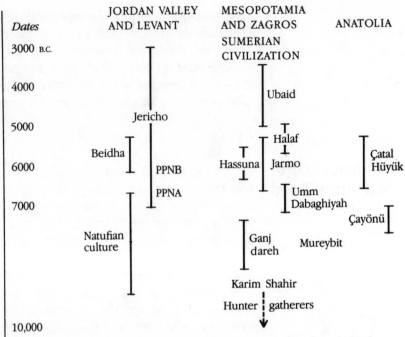

Figure 2.1 Chronological chart of the principal archaeological communities, 10,000–3000 B.C.

Jarmo's population is a matter of conjecture, as only a small portion of the site has been excavated. The inhabited area of 3.2 acres is believed to have contained between twenty-five and fifty houses: with an average of six persons per household, that population would have been between 150 and 300. After three seasons of excavation, in 1948, 1950–1951, and 1954–1955, Braidwood uncovered nearly 1400 square meters of the settlement. From his findings, we have a good idea of what the village looked like and how its inhabitants lived.

Settlement Profile and Cultural Achievements

Housing Patterns Jarmo's architecture was representative of its era. Houses were made of sun-dried mudbricks, the principal material used for construction in the Neolithic Near East. (Earlier houses of ninth-millennium Ganj-dareh had already been constructed of mudbricks made without molds.) Jarmo's houses of mudbrick were constructed over stone foundations and contained multiple rooms: we assume the larger rooms (about 5.6 by 2.2 meters) were living areas and the

Plate 2.5 Aerial photograph of the excavations at Jarmo. (Courtesy of the Oriental Institute, University of Chicago.)

Plate 2.6 Stone foundation of a domestic house at Jarmo, ca. 6000 B.C. (Courtesy of the Oriental Institute, University of Chicago.)

smaller ones (2 by 1.5 meters) were used for storage (see Plate 2.6). Floors were made of clean mud placed over a bed of reeds, while wall foundations were buttressed by stone. Roofs, like those in other seventh-millennium sites, were typically flat wooden beams stretched across the ceilings to support mud and reed thatching. As in other early village communities in the Zagros, there is no suggestion of conscious planning; nor are any structures indicative of centralized communal activities.

Tools, Technology, and Trade   Almost half the stone tools at Jarmo were made from obsidian, a hard volcanic glass which produces an extremely sharp cutting edge. The popularity of obsidian is evident in almost all Neolithic sites in Western Asia; the major source in the Near East is the Lake Van area of eastern Turkey, about 250 miles away. Chemical analysis of obsidian from seventh-millennium Neolithic communities proves that Anatolian obsidian was traded as far south as Beidha in Jordan and to Ali

Plate 2.7   Painted pottery sherds from Jarmo, ca. 6500 B.C. (Courtesy of the Oriental Institute, University of Chicago.)

Kosh in southwestern Iran—although here less than 1% of the stone tools were produced of Anatolian obsidian. The further away from the Anatolian source area the less this resource was utilized. Yet its presence on sites over a thousand miles away from its source indicates an active trade in this desirable commodity—and a trade that began well before Neolithic times. The use of Anatolian obsidian is already attested at Shanidar Cave (Iraq) in levels dating to Neanderthal times, as far back as 30,000 B.C.

Early farming communities like Jarmo also reveal signs of a significant ceramic technology. Ceramics have been found in the earliest levels of Ganj-dareh (ca. 8500 B.C., two millennia before the initial occupation at Jarmo—further evidence against Childe's argument that sedentism and ceramic production are interrelated phenomena attesting to the presence of agriculture; clearly, pottery could have contained wild as well as domesticated cereals, and it seems quite likely that it did.) The inhabitants of Jarmo produced and used ceramic containers as indicated from the fragment depicted in Plate 2.8; they also made baskets out of woven mats and waterproofed them with bitumen.

While no metal implements have been found at Jarmo, this does not indicate that the use of metals was unknown to early

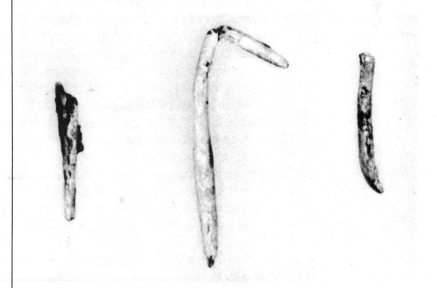

Plate 2.8 Copper pins from Çayönü Tepesi, ca. 7200 B.C. (Courtesy of the Oriental Institute, University of Chicago.)

food-producing villages. The earliest metal artifacts found in the Near East are of copper. Of these, the oldest comes from Shanidar Cave. It is a perforated pendant dated to 8700 B.C.

By Jarmo's time in the seventh millennium, copper objects appear on a number of sites, in the form of both decorative items and small tools. A small copper tube, hammered into shape, has been discovered at Ali Kosh in southwestern Iran. It dates to about 6500 B.C.. And Professor Braidwood has recovered several copper objects at Çayönü in southeastern Turkey, as illustrated in Plate 2.8 These include small round beads, a reamer, pins, and three fragments of oxidized "wire," all dated to around 7200 B.C. The majority of the metal implements from these sites appear to be decorative trinkets. Certainly no large functional tools or weapons of metal are known from these early villages.

Are we to interpret the appearance of these metal objects as independent inventions or as the result of diffusion from a single center of development? The evidence is far too scattered to weigh in favor of any one view. It is apparent that the development of metallurgy was a slow, cumulative process. Copper minerals were manipulated from at least 8000 B.C. solely for the production of small objects like trinkets; the separate technology involved in the production of larger utilitarian goods (like knives, containers, plows, and weapons) did not appear until 4500 B.C. After the initial discovery of copper's malleability by hammering and heating, millennia passed before the technological innovations of melting, casting, and alloying were discovered and put to use by full-time specialized artisans.

While no metal trinkets have been found at Jarmo itself, other types of personal ornaments were used. These include beads, pendants, and bracelets manufactured of stone, bone, and clay. Neither at Jarmo nor on any of the other Neolithic sites in the Zagros is there clear evidence for the specialization of crafts or for the production of food beyond the needs of the local community. Excavations at Jarmo, as well as other early agricultural sites in the Zagros (including Ganj-dareh, Sarab, and Tepe Guran), support the view that each community was self-sufficient in its own agricultural production. The evidence, though, is not conclusive: excavations at Jarmo represent the first attempt to derive an understanding of the economic subsistence patterns within the villages of the Zagros Mountains.

Evidence of Food Production

There is both indirect and direct evidence of at least some domestication of plants and animals in Jarmo. Indirect evidence for cultivation consists of sickles, polished stone celts (axes), hoes, mortars, pestles, and querns. This is complemented by direct evidence in the form of domesticated cereal seeds. Two types of wheat especially resemble their modern counterparts; also present are barley, field peas, and lentils. Osteological evidence indicates the domestication of goats and quite possibly pigs. Jarmo's inhabitants must have supplemented their diet with wild foods. Wild pig, sheep, and gazelle were hunted; pistachios and acorns were collected. In all, the picture suggested is one of a mixed economy based on hunting, food collecting, and limited animal and plant domestication.

Jarmo is no longer the unique site it appeared to be in the early 1950s. Today, we know of dozens of comparable sites in the Zagros, including Tepe Guran, Shimshara, Sarab, Ganj-dareh, and Asiab. And excavations at the sites of Ali Kosh and Choga Sefid

Plate 2.9 Stone bowls, mortars, pestles, celts, and bracelet fragments from Jarmo, ca. 6500 B.C. (Courtesy of the Oriental Institute, University of Chicago.)

Figure 2.2 Clay figurines of wild boar and stylized female figurines from Tepe Sarab, ca. 6500 B.C. (Reproduced from *Handbuch der Vorgeschichte,* C. H. Beck Verlag, courtesy of H. Müller-Karpe.)

have linked developments in southwest Iran (Khuzistan) as contemporaneous and related to those of sites in the Zagros group.

Even more recently, excavations at Umm Dabaghiyah in Iraq link the earlier Jarmo culture with the succeeding Hassuna culture of northern Mesopotamia (see the discussion at the end of this chapter). The excavator of Umm Dabaghiyah has suggested that in the early sixth millennium it functioned as a center for the hunting of onager and the production of leather goods.[16] Though relatively late in the Neolithic, this site is rare in indicating a specialized function in its productive economy. Only two other Neolithic settlements have been interpreted as having an entirely specialized function: Suberde in Turkey (ca. 6500 B.C.), believed to be a hunting village entirely dependent on securing supplies of wild animals; and Tepe Tula'i in southwestern Iran (ca. 6250 – 6000 B.C.), believed to be the first excavated nomadic encampment.

Jarmo and the other self-sufficient communities in the Zagros all share a number of common characteristics. There is a similarity in the technology of producing stone tools as well as in exploiting and using similar resources, such as obsidian for tools and alabaster for decorative bowls and bracelets. The size of the villages appears to be uniformly small, perhaps with populations not exceeding 500 people. This size provides a marked contrast to Neolithic-time developments in another region, the Dead Sea Valley in Jordan. Just as the environment of Jarmo differs from that of Jericho, so do the stone tool technology, the distinctive resources exploited, and, above all, the size of the community, which in contemporary times (ca. 6500) would have been fivefold larger in Jericho.

THE OASIS VILLAGE OF JERICHO

The oval mound representing ancient Jericho has been familiar to antiquarians for over a century, and its prominent role in Biblical history has attracted archaeologists to undertake excavations on this large and important site.

Biblical Jericho was discovered and identified by Charles Warren in 1868. The first systematic excavations were undertaken in 1907 – 1909, by Ernst Sellin and Thomas Watzinger, and resumed by John Garstang in 1930 – 1936. It was Garstang

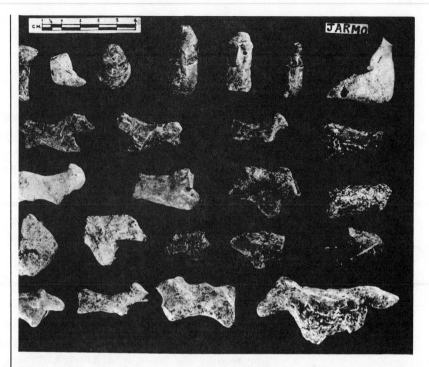

Plate 2.10 Clay figurines of animal and human forms from Jarmo, ca. 6500 B.C. (Courtesy of the Oriental Institute, University of Chicago.)

who first reached the Neolithic levels of the Jericho site, although he did not fully recognize their significance.

The earliest settlement of Jericho belongs to the Natufian culture, conventionally dated from about 10,000 to 8000 B.C. The significance of Jericho's great antiquity, especially when coupled with its food-producing achievements, was first brought to light in the third wave of excavations. Dame Kathleen M. Kenyon's seven field seasons at Jericho, from 1952 to 1958, transformed our thinking about the nature of Neolithic communities at the same time they documented the sequence from Neolithic all the way down to the Iron Age (ca. 1000 B.C.).[17]

Jericho and the Oasis Debate

Because of its long and almost continuous occupation since very early times, Jericho has afforded an unusually good opportunity to study the transformation to a food-producing economy. Kenyon explains Jericho's persistent settlement:

The oasis stands out as a patch of brilliant green in the dazzling white-
ness of the rest of the Jordan Valley. Its luxuriant vegetation is
nourished by a perennial spring which wells out at the foot of the
mound which marks the site of the ancient city, and which was the
reason why man first settled there.[18]

Jericho's rise on an oasis helped provide fuel for debate
between Professors Braidwood and Kenyon during the early
1950s. At the heart of the argument was the question of the
original location of the Neolithic Revolution. Braidwood
championed the hilly flanks of the Zagros as the "nuclear area" for
the origins of food production. He argued that the dramatic
events which led to the domestication of plants and animals had
to take place in an area where people lived in proximity to wild
plants and animals, for this would lead naturally to their
exploitation. Professor Kenyon advanced an "oasis theory" for
the origins of the Neolithic Revolution. As Childe has argued,
people would have been forced to domesticate animals and
plants to maintain the subsistence of growing populations. Each
excavator argued for the chronological priority of their own site
as well as the environmental determinant their excavation
seemed to support.

Today, with dozens of Neolithic sites known in Palestine and in
the Zagros, the uniqueness of both sites and the determinant
role of the environment are seen as gross oversimplifications. We
now know that one cause cannot be singled out as the "only"
cause; we also know that there was no single nuclear center from
which the Neolithic Revolution "spread" to the rest of the area.
One point of debate does remain, and that centers on the
extraordinary nature of Jericho. Was early eighth-millennium
Jericho a village (which it seemed more than), or was it a city
(which it seemed less than)? The evidence is ambiguous.

To the southwest of the Natufian settlement at Jericho is a small
mound consisting of innumerable floors and eroded clay walls
built one upon the other. No architectural plan has been
discerned in these ruins, but the depth of deposit (4 meters)
suggests frequent occupation near the Jericho spring. This is the
protoneolithic (literally, "giving rise to the neolithic")
occupation, dating from ca. 10,000 to 8350 B.C. Here there is no
evidence of grain or mortars and pestles: only wild species of
plants and animals have been recovered.

Directly above these 4 meters of occupational debris is

evidence of a remarkable change. A vast agglomeration of round houses spreading over 10 acres engulfed the small proto-Neolithic mound. This agglomeration spans a period of a thousand years (ca. 8350–7350 B.C.), and this period of remarkable growth is referred to by the excavator as *Prepottery Neolithic A* (or PPNA). This PPNA culture was the first of two distinctive prepottery Neolithic settlements at Jericho, and it was to be succeeded by what the excavator calls the "prepottery Neolithic B" (PPNB) culture.

Jericho in the PPNA

The architecture of the PPNA culture is perhaps the most remarkable achievement of early Jericho. The earliest PPNA settlement at Jericho was not surrounded by a defensive wall, but by about 7200 B.C. (carbon-14 dated), a stone wall, 3 meters thick and 4 meters high, was constructed with an articulating round tower as illustrated in Plate 2.11. That tower is a massive architectural achievement. It is 10 meters in diameter and 8.5 meters high, with a 22-step staircase in its solid stone core providing access from the bottom of the tower to the top. The wall has been partially excavated on the northern and southern limits of the settlement: it may have encircled the entire 10 acres of Jericho.

Just precisely why the community was fortified is an elusive question. It is apparent from archaeological survey that a considerable number of contemporary PPNA sites existed in Palestine, and it is not unreasonable to assume that increasing demographic pressures led to competition, hostility, and warfare as well as the need for social institutions to control and allocate the growing demands for available resources.

While we may not know why the massive fortification and lookout tower were built, they do suggest a picture of PPNA Jericho's social structure. Apparently, the community had developed a good degree of specialization in its social structure and probably in its economy. In order to build the wall, Jericho needed to call upon considerable communal manpower. That would have required both leaders who could organize public works and an economy that could support such a communal undertaking. Moreover, Jericho's size alone indicates that it was an important center within that area today incorporating Israel, Jordan, and Syria.

Plate 2.11   Jericho Pre-pottery Neolithic A fortification tower, ca. 7000 B.C. (Jericho Excavation Fund.)

It has been suggested that trade and the control of resources were responsible for Jericho's preeminent status.[19] The material inventory at Jericho, however, does not show great wealth, let alone the presence of a single commodity which could have served as barter. Salt, sulfur, and asphalt, all products of the Dead Sea, may have played a role in Jericho's rise. But these materials are not uncommon throughout Palestine.

The chief source of Jericho's wealth must have been agricultural produce. Surplus food, seed corn, and horticultural knowledge

Plate 2.12 Jericho Pre-pottery Neolithic A: a view of the deep sounding and super-imposed walls. (Jericho Excavation Fund.)

must have been far more valuable than other commodities. Settlement pattern studies indicate a good reason for this. Populations were increasing at the time of Jericho's rise, and environmental studies indicate that this was also a period of increasing aridity.[20] In such times, the planting of domesticated seed corn could easily explain Jericho's preeminence. Surplus crops could have necessitated the construction of communal building projects to protect excess seed corn. (Storage areas are associated with the fortification system.) Such surpluses would also have allowed for the development of social institutions by freeing individuals from the food quest and thus permitting the differentiation of labor, leadership, and craft specialization. Exactly how much specialization actually existed is still a matter of conjecture. Art of any kind is lacking, as is evidence for specialized activity areas such as cult places or administrative buildings.

While there is considerable evidence that plants were grown for crops, there is nothing to confirm the domestication of animals. The hunting of wild gazelle, cattle, goat, and boar provided the principal source of meat. The great achievement of Jericho during the PPNA lies in the evidence for plant domestication. Barley and wheat were clearly domesticated, and lentils and figs have also been found among carbonized seeds.

Other communities contemporary with PPNA Jericho have also been excavated. One of the most important is Mureybit in northern Syria, described earlier in this chapter. Mureybit's size and its occupation throughout the eighth millennium B.C. strongly suggest that, as in Jericho, we are witnessing the beginnings of farming.

To what extent were villages like Mureybit, Ganj-dareh, and Jericho in communication, sharing experiences which led to greater control over their environment? The majority of the architecture, material inventory, and technology is superficially distinctive—thus arguing for isolation and independent invention. On the other hand, the close contemporaneity of such sites as Jericho and Ganj-dareh (to mention a few in distinctive, geographically distant environments) argues for a process beyond the mere coincidence of independent inventions. It is apparent that there was some communication of information, if only from the fact that both these sites (and Mureybit and Mallaha as well) utilized Anatolian obsidian to produce similar tools.

Ideas and information were as much involved in the technology of obsidian production as they were in the manipulation of the environment for food resources: if one technology was disseminated from one center to the next, then it stands to reason that the other would be, too.

While it seems likely that the various PPNA sites traded information as well as obsidian, salt, and bitumen, the Neolithic Revolution did not spread uniformly throughout the eighth-millennium Near East. Not all communities of the eighth millennium participated in the new subsistence strategies leading toward domestication. Some continued hunting and gathering for several millennia before beginning to produce their own food. Technological changes were not uniformly adopted within a culture, let alone between different cultures, any more than they are today.

PPNA Jericho was abandoned around 7300 B.C. There is no evidence of any military confrontation or any catastrophic event; whatever reason caused the community's abandonment still eludes archaeologists.

Jericho in the PPNB

Directly over the PPNA levels at Jericho rests the *Prepottery Neolithic B (PPNB)* site, dated between 6800 and 6000 B.C. Whatever cause there was for the abandonment of the PPNA culture, it appears that after an occupational gap of a few centuries (one cannot be certain as to how many) the advantageous position of the Jericho springs brought new populations to settle.

The origin and the extent of the distribution of the PPNB culture remain subject to considerable debate. Some archaeologists contend persuasively that the sites of Mureybit (in northern Syria) and Çayönü (in southern Turkey) provide the bases for the formation of the PPNB culture. Their view argues for an invasion of northerners to account for the development of the PPNB culture in Palestine. Other archaeologists see in the more recently excavated sites, such as Beidha in Jordan and Tell Ramad in Syria, the presence of many PPNA cultural features surviving into the PPNB culture. Such a view suggests a continuation of local PPNA developments, perhaps only fertilized by new ideas from the north. The origins of the PPNB remain unresolved, as does the cause for the decline of the PPNA culture. It is interesting to note, however, that one of the reasons suspected for the demise of the PPNA culture is environmental change: an increasingly severe aridity which caused a locational shift in human settlement.[21] If such is suspected for the PPNA it is argued as almost certain that climatic oscillation around 6000 B.C. played a major role in the collapse of the agricultural settlements of the PPNB culture.[22]

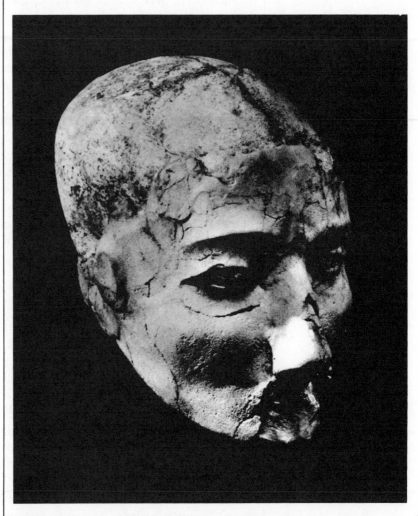

Plate 2.13 Plastered skull from Jericho Pre-pottery Neolithic B, ca. 6500 B.C. (Jericho Excavation Fund.)

Settlement sites of the PPNB are found throughout Palestine, Lebanon, and Syria. And with archaeological exploration beginning in Saudi Arabia there are suggestions that major PPNB sites will be discovered there, too. In all these areas, save for the sites of Jericho and Wadi Fellah in Israel, PPNB settlements lie on virgin soil.

There can be little doubt that PPNB times were ones of considerable economic and cultural advance. In comparison with the PPNA period, a far greater degree of cultural interaction is evident in the distribution of specific resources exchanged. At Jericho, trade in Anatolian obsidian was continued during the PPNB, while at Tell Ramad in Syria and Beidha south of Jericho in Jordan, obsidian from different regional sources of Anatolia is present.

Many materials other than obsidian were exchanged over distant areas to Jericho. These included turquoise from the southwestern Sinai and greenstone or jadeite from northern Syria. Red Sea cowries and Mediterranean shells are present as well; so are ochre, malachite, and hematite, found in ingotlike blocks. The main material traded throughout the PPNB period was flint—in many different varieties and from several geographical points. Different types of flint have characteristic properties and so are specifically adapted to the production of different types of tools. A close study of flint sources would greatly increase our knowledge of early exchange systems.

As we saw earlier, metal was still not widely used during the PPNB period. A simple native copper bead from Tell Ramad in Syria is the only attested example of metal in the PPNB culture. Though metal pins, hooks, and bracelets were utilized at Çayönü in southeastern Turkey as early as 7200 B.C., even small metal objects requiring little technology were far from common even a thousand years later—and it was close to three thousand years before large, utilitarian metal tools were produced.

From Jericho and other sites, it is evident that food production was becoming more important and more versatile during the PPNB. At Beidha in Jordan, inhabitants cultivated wheat and especially barley. Gallons of pistachio nuts and acorns have also been found here, as well as two kinds of lentil, vetch, and various other leguminous plants. The excavator of Beidha has suggested that cultivation would not have been possible without the practice of rudimentary irrigation techniques.[23] Such evidence suggests

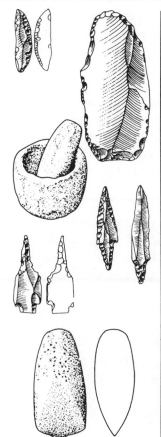

Figure 2.3 Stone tools, axes, and mortar and pestle from Beidha, Jordan, ca. 6300 B.C. (Reproduced from *Handbuch der Vorgeschichte,* C. H. Beck Verlag, courtesy of H. Müller-Karpe.)

an early experimentation with irrigation two millennia before its widespread adoption by the Sumerian city-states.

The PPNB culture distributed inland and along the coast of the eastern Mediterranean was economically dependent on hunting and agriculture. A balanced diet could readily be attained from domesticated cereals, collected pistachios and acorns, domesticated peas and lentils, and domestic goats, herded gazelle, or other hunted game. Birds and fish are conspicuously absent. The extent of nomadism, dependent on domestic herds of sheep and goats, during this period is wholly unknown.

Although the PPNB culture marked advances in both trade and agriculture, it did not last very long. Around 6000 B.C., the culture disappeared with the widespread desertion of sites in Palestine and the Syrian steppe. Only in the very north of Palestine, in the Damascus basin and along the coast, did significant settlements continue. As with the PPNA site in Jericho, nowhere does the abandonment of settlement seem to have been accompanied by destruction or violence. Excavators have had to look elsewhere for a cause.

The most convincing explanation to date comes from the study of pollen cores derived from the Dead Sea, Lake Huleh, and Lake Tiberius. These cores indicate sharp decreases in tree pollen around 6000 B.C. This evidence has been used to postulate a climatic deterioration, a desiccation which caused some change in the vegetation.[24] This may in turn have forced a transformation of the PPNB culture.

There is some corroboration for this interpretation from other areas. Similar signs of environmental stress appear to exist in the Mesopotamian steppe, for instance, where a decline of agricultural productivity is noted at Ali Kosh in southwestern Iran at about the same time.

As we saw in Chapter 1, environmental factors causing massive population shifts, settlement abandonment, and general cultural decline have long been a favored explanation for cultural change. Too often, such explanations are derived without the benefit of evidence for climatic conditions. In this instance, however, several lines of evidence tend to converge to support a theory of environmental desiccation. If the cause remains unclear, the effects are all too apparent in the archaeological record: over three-quarters of the PPNB settlements were abandoned.

The theory also provides a reasonable explanation for the sudden change in settlement patterns. Communities which had just learned to manipulate their environment would be particularly vulnerable to shifts in rain or wind patterns: their marginal agricultural activities would quickly succumb to detrimental changes in the environment. Water shortages force animals to migrate and plants to cluster in ever-diminishing optimum areas. Faced by dwindling food supplies, people move elsewhere. Only favored areas of the Mediterranean littoral would have continued to offer viable conditions for sustained occupation—and this is where evidence indicates that new centers arose.

With previous patterns of agriculture destroyed, some groups apparently emigrated northward and westward into the more productive Mediterranean forest zone. There settlements were established for the first time in about 6000 B.C. Groups that remained in Palestine and Syria turned more to seminomadic pastoralism and stockbreeding.

These conditions prevailed for over half a millennium until at last, around 5500 B.C., populations began to filter back into Palestine. Here they expanded, enriched by new ideas and technological achievements. But a significant change had taken place. As a result of the cultural breakdown after PPNB times, Palestine lost its erstwhile preeminence; it was destined to become an appendix to Syrian and Mesopotamian developments for millennia.

ÇATAL HÜYÜK AND THE ANATOLIAN NEOLITHIC

As recently as the mid-1950s, it was possible for an eminent archaeologist to write that Anatolia did not participate in the principal developments of the Near Eastern Neolithic.[25] But the site of Çatal Hüyük, excavated by James Mellaart in 1961–1963, points to the inaccuracy of this statement.[26] The exceptional discoveries at Çatal Hüyük, dated from 6500 to 5400 B.C., have led some archaeologists to refer to the site as a "city"; others have even conferred the word "civilization" upon it.

Definitions aside, this extraordinary Neolithic community provides a ready contrast to the contemporary sites of Jarmo in the Zagros and the PPNB culture in the Syro-Palestinian Levant.

Indeed, the evidence at Çatal Hüyük provides strong support for the presence of regional areas of Neolithic development rather than a single "nuclear area." Contrasts among Jericho, Çatal Hüyük, Jarmo, and Umm Dabaghiyah—all about 6000 B.C.—suggest a considerable regionalization within widely scattered Neolithic communities of the Near East.

A Profile of Çatal Hüyük

With a few minor exceptions, the Bronze Age (3000–1000 B.C.) occupation of Anatolia, in the western plateau lands of Turkey, was confined to the southern half of the region. The site of Çatal Hüyük is 11 kilometers north of Çumra, in the Konya Plain of central Turkey. The site itself covers 32 acres, making it the largest known Neolithic settlement in the Near East. How much of this community was inhabited at one time is unknown: fourteen building levels in an area representing only one-thirtieth of the mound have been excavated. The date of first settlement is unknown, too. The more than thirty radiocarbon dates span a time from 6500 to 5400 B.C., but the lowest levels of earliest habitation have not yet been excavated.

Plate 2.14 General view of the excavations at Çatal Hüyük. (Courtesy of J. A. Mellaart.)

Architecture and Demography While excavation of Çatal Hüyük is still far from complete, the findings we have provide an unusually clear picture of a Neolithic community, in terms of both physical characteristics and activities of its inhabitants.

Houses at Çatal Hüyük were built to a standardized rectangular plan, covering 25 square meters of floor space, including a large livingroom and smaller storeroom. Access into houses was by ladder, through a hole in the roof. Houses were closely built, one against the other: there were no streets, lanes or alleys. All communication must have taken place either at roof level or in communal courtyards which offered some open space (see Figure 2.4). Ruined or abandoned houses also provided extra

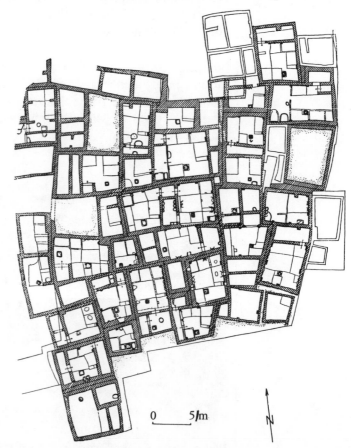

0   5 m

N

Figure 2.4 Plans of domestic houses from Çatal Hüyük, ca. 6500 B.C. (Reproduced from *Handbuch der Vorgeschichte,* C. H. Beck Verlag, courtesy of H. Müller-Karpe.)

space, but these seem to have served mainly as rubbish disposal sites or as toilets. Furniture in the houses was built of mudbrick and consisted of platforms for work or sleeping. At one end of the room a hearth, a flat-domed oven, and wall niches provided the essentials of a kitchen.

The presence of numerous burials at Çatal Hüyük afford the best view of Neolithic demography. The average lifespan was 34.3 years for men and 29.8 years for women. Some individuals were buried at ages over 60, however: they would have been the elders, maintaining the continuous traditions of the community. Statistics provide a sort of "family profile" for Çatal Hüyük: the average number of children born per woman was 4.2; and as the death rate was 1.8 per mother, the surviving ratio was 2.4 children per family.

In terms of population growth, this rate of survival would have represented a population boom if unchecked—an increase of at least 528 times over eight hundred years. If Çatal Hüyük had begun with 50 people in the earliest excavated level, there would have been over 25,000 by the last settlement. But this is not the case. There is evidence for significant increases, but the population of Çatal Hüyük never exceeded 5000 or 6000.

Agriculture, Trade, and Industry   Çatal Hüyük's economy was well-advanced Neolithic, based on simple irrigation agriculture, cattle breeding, trade, and industry. Of importance is the evidence for cereal hybridization of breadwheat and six-row naked barley, whose seeds may have been enlarged by the practice of irrigation.

Agriculture and animal domestication produced a wide range of nutrients. Domestic emmer and einkorn provided starch; legumes such as peas, vetch, and vetchling provided protein; and crucifers, acorns, pistachios, and almonds yielded vegetable fats. Dogs and cattle had been domesticated by the time of the earliest excavated levels. Sheep were also commonly present, but they were still morphologically wild. (Goats were not native to the region, and they are rarely present.)

The foods produced in Çatal Hüyük, Jericho, and Jarmo are each distinct and representative of a different environment. Specific adaptations within different environments set the conditions for domesticating and utilizing resources in the earliest Neolithic communities. Goats and barley have been found throughout the

Palestinian Levant, and sheep and goats provided the principal meat supply in the Zagros Mountains. Çatal Hüyük and other Neolithic sites of Anatolia relied on cattle and wheat as the dominant domesticates. The importance of cattle at Çatal Hüyük can be seen from decorations on the interior walls of houses, where elaborate bulls' heads project from, are carved into, or are painted onto wall surfaces.

A rich variety of plants and animals were utilized beyond those cultivated or domesticated. Many animals were hunted for skins or to provide a dietary change from beef. These included onager, half-ass, boar, red roe deer, fallow deer, bear, wolf, and lion or leopard; freshwater fish and birds (including griffon vultures) and eggshells were also included in the diet. Some of the fruits we know were used are crabapple, juniper berries, and hackberry. It also seems reasonable to assume some foods were used that leave no archaeological trace: dairy products like milk, butter, cheese, and yogurt; green and root vegetables; onions; beverages like fruit juices, hackberry wine, and beer; and also grapes, pears, walnuts, figs, and pomegranates, all of which grow wild in Anatolia.

Anatolia's economy must have depended heavily upon trade as well as agriculture. As we have seen, Anatolian obsidian was used throughout much of the Near East for the production of stone implements. Two groups of obsidian-producing volcanoes dominate the Anatolian plateau: a central Anatolian group at the northeastern end of the Konya Plain and an eastern Anatolian group around Lake Van. This clearly desirable material for the production of stone implements found its way across the Taurus Mountains of eastern Turkey as early as the Upper Paleolithic. By 6500 B.C., trade in obsidian provides an excellent case for the presence of regional exchange in a single commodity.

Anatolian obsidian was only one article of exchange. Perishables such as foodstuffs, skins, and textiles must also have been traded, and another important commodity exchanged was information. Within each of the three major spheres of interaction—Anatolia, Palestine, and the Zagros—food-producing technology as well as religious concepts were shared. Information also traveled well beyond regional boundaries. The developments in these principal spheres affected the more distant regions of North Africa and Soviet Turkmenistan, where sites from about 6500 B.C. suggest at least secondary influence, if

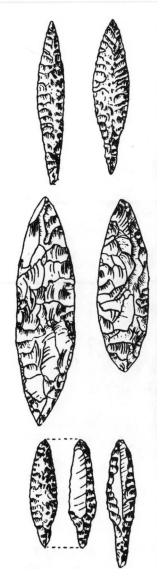

Figure 2.5 The chipped stone industry from Çatal Hüyük Level II, ca. 5800 B.C. (Reproduced from *Handbuch der Vorges-chichte*, C. H. Beck Verlag, courtesy of H. Müller-Karpe.)

not direct contact with these three areas of primary development.

Besides being the center of production for the raw material needed for stone tools, Anatolia also developed a notable technology for using this resource. The chipped stone industry of Çatal Hüyük, illustrated in Figure 2.5, was easily the most elegant in the Near East. Over fifty types of implements have been identified, including arrowheads with tangs and barbs, flint daggers, and obsidian mirrors. The bone industry is equally rich and varied: finds have included awls, needles, beads, pendants, and elaborately carved dagger hafts, fishhooks, hairpins, and belt buckles.

The ceramic products of the earliest inhabitants (ca. 6500) consist of simple oval bowls, handled jars, and flat-based vessels. Many shapes betray their ancestry in basket and wood prototypes. The ceramics are handmade, burnished to a dark polish, or covered with a red wash. A single piece of the distinctive "white ware" of the limestone variety so typical of Tell Ramad indicates contact with Syria by about 6000 B.C.

Along with the chipped-stone and ceramic technologies, Çatal Hüyük also developed a metallurgy. Lead pendants occur by 6000 B.C., copper beads by 5800 B.C.; and slag from a later level indicates smelting and extraction of copper from ore by 5500 B.C. The use of azurite and malachite for painting indicates the manipulation of minerals for cosmetic and decorative purposes.

Trade and industry, with specialized part-time craftsmen (metal, architecture, weaving, flint and obsidian, woodcarving, beadmaking, and production of clay and stone statuettes), were all clearly features of Çatal Hüyük. It is not likely, however, that the craftsmen at Çatal Hüyük were full-time specialists. It is worthwhile distinguishing between part-time and full-time specialization of labor. Full-time specialists earn their subsistence by labor expended in the production of nonagricultural activities. The products of their labor, nevertheless, assure the exchange of work for subsistence goods (above all, food).

At Çatal Hüyük, it is unlikely that the subsistence base allowed for the production of an agricultural surplus large enough to support full-time craftsmen. It seems more reasonable to assume that artisans skilled in the production of particular goods were able to enhance their economic position through their trade while still depending largely on their own agricultural productivity. The evidence at Çatal Hüyük suggests that the economy had

Plate 2.15   Clay statue of the so-called "Mistress of the Animals" from Çatal Hüyük, ca. 6500 B.C. (Courtesy of *Propyläen Verlag Berlin.*)

progressed beyond kin-organized production but had not yet specialized in either surplus agricultural production or full-time commodity production. There is good reason, however, to suspect that Çatal Hüyük owed its importance to more than its material and worldly prosperity; it may well have served as a spiritual center for a wide geographical area.

"Shrines" and Evidence of a Belief System   The numerous "shrines" at Çatal Hüyük depicting painted scenes and plaster reliefs elude our ready understanding (see Plate 2.16). The

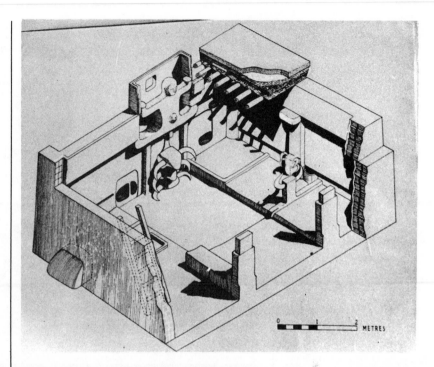

Plate 2.16   Isometric view of one of the "shrines" at Çatal Hüyük, ca. 6000 B.C. (Courtesy of J. A. Mellaart.)

excavator has suggested that these shrines were places where cultic practices were undertaken by "priests" in a separate quarter of the community.[27]

Benches and platforms, often holding one to seven pair of auroch horns, are set against the plaster walls of the shrines. In some instances, bulls' horns molded over with plaster protrude from the walls. Scenes in the shrines depict women giving birth to bulls' or rams' heads. Modeled plaster reliefs depict female forms, possibly deities, while male counterparts are represented by symbols: the bull, the ram, and less commonly the stag, leopard and boar, as illustrated in Plate 2.17. There are other forms of symbolism: female breasts containing lower jaws of boars; fox and weasel skulls; or reproductions of griffon vultures— scavenger animals associated with death. It has been suggested that the scenes represent a concentration of symbolism dealing with aspects of fertility, fecundity, and death. That explanation seems reasonable.[28] It is not difficult to imagine an

Plate 2.17 From the houses at Çatal Hüyük, ca. 6000 B.C.: two spotted leopards and two bulls in relief decorating the interior of rooms. (Courtesy of J. A. Mellaart.)

Plate 2.18   View of the interior of two houses at Çatal Hüyük, ca. 6000 B.C. Two common motifs are depicted: bulls and vultures above headless humans, ca. 6000 B.C. (Courtesy of J. A. Mellaart.)

early farming community concerned with the primary aspects of fertility, both human and agricultural.

Wall paintings within the shrines are executed in monochrome or polychrome mineral- and vegetable-base paints. They vary from decorative panels of textilelike patterns to scenes of vultures flying over headless human corpses (see Plate 2.18); there are also landscape scenes with erupting volcanoes and scenes of the chase in which deer are hunted with bow and arrow by men wearing leopard-skin clothes. The evidence indicates that the same shrine rooms were used over a span of several years. In

Plate 2.19 Reconstruction of hunt scenes from the walls of houses at Çatal Hüyük, ca. 6000 B.C. (Courtesy of J. A. Mellaart.)

many cases, paintings had been renewed by fresh plaster and new scenes.

Further signs of a rich belief system come from the burial practices of Çatal Hüyük. The dead were buried either in communal graves beneath the floors or platforms of their houses or in shrines. Burial practices were unusual, for it seems that the dead were exposed to vultures, insects, and rodents prior to their final interment. After excarnation, the skeletal remains were wrapped in cloth, mats, or baskets and interred beneath the floor of the houses. While most bodies were not provided with burial gifts, the dead were adorned with their personal ornaments: necklaces, armlets, bracelets, and wristlets of stone, shell, lead, or copper beads; with the males there were weapons. Red ochre was often washed over the bones prior to interment. Special attention was given to the skull, which was often separated from the body and placed against the wall in some of the shrines.

Communal graves beneath the floors of the houses were often reopened to admit a new burial. The corpses were disturbed, but disarticulated skulls were carefully arranged within the chamber. One had cowries set into the eyesockets, a detail directly reminiscent of practices at Tell Ramad and Jericho.

Evidence for class differentiation as well as differential accumulation of wealth comes from the graves of the dead associated with the shrines. Unlike the bodies found under houses, the dead found in shrines were often buried with valuable objects: ceremonial flint daggers, polished stone bowls, cosmetic sets and obsidian mirrors (indicating that females too achieved high status), bone belt fasteners, polished maceheads and arrow quivers, wooden boxes, baskets, metal beads, and rings.

Çatal Hüyük provides an unusually broad-based picture of the cultural system of a Neolithic community. To date, it is the only site preserved in the archaeological record of a Neolithic agricultural community extending its symbolic belief systems in so rich a manner. For us to interpret those beliefs correctly, though, is another matter.

More answers may lie in future excavations, both at Çatal Hüyük and at other sites. Since the earliest levels at Çatal Hüyük are as yet unexplored, it is not known whether they will provide evidence of the transition from hunting and gathering to domestication, of the first production of ceramics, or of the indigenous development of the elaborate belief system so evident in the later shrines. The presence of irrigation agriculture at Çatal Hüyük, its developed ceramic tradition, its stone technology, its apparent cult practices, and its general subsistence pattern all argue for a local Anatolian Neolithic tradition that was independent of its neighbors in the Zagros, the Levant, and northern Mesopotamia—or, at the very least, not greatly influenced by them.

THE SPREAD OF THE NEOLITHIC

Contemporaneous with the end of settlement at Çatal Hüyük are numerous other sites in Anatolia and beyond. Combined these offer a relatively complete picture of the sixth and fifth millennia as an extension of Neolithic traditions of the seventh millennium over a broad geographical area. Among the most important excavations are Aceramic Khirokitia on Cyprus, a Neolithic community contemporary with the PPNB of Palestine. The presence of widespread Neolithic communities around 6500 B.C. can be documented from Nea Nikomedia in Greek Macedonia to Djeitun in Soviet Turkmenistan. And the discovery of sites dated back to 7000 B.C. or so in the Sudan indicates agricultural settlement in yet another direction.

Archaeologists have become accustomed to the ever expanding range of Neolithic communities throughout the Near East and eastern Mediterranean. A greater surprise has been the recent discovery of an entirely independent agricultural revolution in Southeast Asia. In Thailand the site of Spirit Cave excavated by Chester F. Gorman has yielded fragmentary remains of several plant genera, some of which are believed to have been cultivated at a very early date.[29] Plants that were apparently cultivated included butternut, almond, betel nut, pepper, and candlenut; other plants, including cucumber, pea, bean, broadbean, and soybean, may also have been cultivated. The occupation of the cave spanned a period of four thousand years, with the earliest strata dated by radiocarbon to 11,000 B.C. As yet, no sites discovered in this part of Asia show signs of permanent architecture. The important point is that an independent center of agricultural production was developing in Southeast Asia. By 10,000 B.C. people were experimenting and beginning to cultivate different kinds of wild plants. At some point, conceivably as early as 10,000 B.C. in the northern reaches of this region, experiments culminated in the domestication of certain plants.

The significance of the Spirit Cave findings, as well as separate excavations within the Near East and surrounding regions, has had the effect of reversing archaeological theory in the time since Childe first described the Neolithic Revolution. With an independent center of agricultural origins in Southeast Asia, it is also entirely possible that regions such as the Sudan, southeastern Europe, and even areas directly within the Near East took individual and independent steps toward horticulture. The archaeological record has made the search for the origins of a Neolithic Revolution within a single "nuclear area" entirely untenable.

Agricultural developments along the Nile Valley and the Tigris-Euphrates lowlands do not appear until well after the Near Eastern Neolithic had already got underway. It was several millennia after animals and plants were fully domesticated, and technological innovations such as irrigation, metallurgy, and ceramics were accomplished before settlements were established in the areas which would give birth to two of the world's earliest civilizations.

The Mesopotamian Lowlands

It is in the Mesopotamian lowlands—the Tigris and Euphrates floodplains—that one can trace the antecedent developments which led to the Sumerian, Babylonian, and Assyrian civilizations. In this region, one can trace a nearly unbroken record of archaeological cultures from late Neolithic villages (ca. 5500 B.C.) to the era of townships and, finally, to the urban, literate world of the Sumerians (ca. 2500 B.C.). Even though archaeological work in this area has a tradition of over a hundred years, new discoveries continue to bring about wholly new understandings of the process which led to the rise of civilization. Here we can only summarize briefly the principal sites, point to unresolved problems, and relate this area to wider developments in distant geographical areas. While the Neolithic sites discussed earlier contributed greatly to developments throughout the Near East, it is only in the Mesopotamian lowlands that Neolithic advances led to the foundation of literate civilizations.

Mesopotamian cultures can be divided into two geographical zones: the lowland area, including the Assyrian steppes of northern Syria and Iraq, and the southern Mesopotamian alluvium. The lowland area includes the Umm Dabaghiyah, the

Hassuna and Samarra, and the Halaf cultures; the other zone includes the Ubaid and Susiana cultures. With the exception of Susiana, which represents a somewhat different story from our concern in this text, we will take each of these cultures in turn and summarize both their principal contributions and their relationship to other Neolithic cultures.

THE UMM DABAGHIYAH CULTURE

The Umm Dabaghiyah is the earliest culture discovered in northern Mesopotamia: it is dated to the mid-seventh millennium. The earliest occupation consists of oval gypsum-lined basins cut into virgin soil. These may represent temporary shelters or storage areas. Interestingly, the earliest settlements on a number of sites (Ganj-dareh, Ramad, Beidha) consist of similar lined pits without associated architecture. It is possible that these pits were storage facilities that were once covered with now–eroded mat and reed architecture.

Above this early occupation were three well-preserved levels of architecture. In these levels are the ruins of domestic houses consisting of a living room, kitchen, and one or two associated small rooms. The houses have internal buttresses forming arched or square doorways. The houses provided more than minimal shelter: niches in walls served as cupboards, plaster boxes for storage were sunk into floors, and round plastered windows served for ventilation. They also must have been subject to some interior decoration. Traces of red paint are present on the preserved floors, and in the latest two levels, paintings of onager hunts were discovered on house walls. The wall paintings were done in red, black, and yellow paint. Scenes were separated by white plaster, a technique similar to that used in contemporary Çatal Hüyük.

The paintings of hunt scenes, together with what excavator Dr. Diane Kirkbride has interpreted as "storage blocks" (plastered cubicles, set along corridors and entered through trapdoors in the roof, which appear to have been used for cold storage of onager hides and meat), have caused the excavator to suggest that this Neolithic community specialized in onager hunting and hide preparation.[30] The high percentage of wild onager bones (68.4% of animal remains) is unparalleled on any other Near Eastern site—a strong corroboration for Kirkbride's conclusion.

Perhaps the surplus production of hides was the basis for trade. They may have been exchanged for Lake Van obsidian, present in abundance, or for Syrian-type arrowheads, which would point to western contacts.

Aside from the specialization of onager hunting, the economy of Umm Dabaghiyah shows other peculiarities. There is mixed evidence for food production. Morphologically domestic sheep, goats, cattle, pigs, and dogs have been found, with the first two species dominating. But as we saw earlier in this chapter, signs of agricultural production are very scanty—perhaps the result of living in a region marginal to dry farming. There is limited evidence for the cultivation of cereals and barley. White pea, lentil, and breadwheat must have been imported, for they could not have grown in the treeless steppe environment where Umm Dabaghiyah is located.

The great innovation at Umm Dabaghiyah is in the widespread use of pottery, even at the earliest levels of the site. Most ceramics are primitive: vessels were built up from coils and heavily tempered with straw, then baked at low temperatures. The majority of the vessels are undecorated, though red ochre occasionally was applied to produce simple geometric motifs.

The origins of this ceramic tradition are still unknown. Ancestral to the Umm Dabaghiyah culture must lie an as yet undiscovered aceramic culture, probably contemporary with earlier PPNB times. There are elements at Umm Dabaghiyah which indicate links both to Syrian sites like Tell Ramad and to sites like Jarmo in the Zagros Mountains. Umm Dabaghiyah's ceramic tradition, however, is sufficiently distinctive as to disallow its origin from either area. Furthermore, its wall paintings, architecture, and painted ceramics reveal distant parallels to a third style—that of Çatal Hüyük.

This apparent hybridization of ceramic traditions, together with the presence of such a specialized hunting community as Umm Dabaghiyah, further accentuates the degree of specialization that must have existed both within and between such contemporary communities as Jericho, Çatal Hüyük, Çayönü, and Jarmo—all by the mid-seventh millennium. Each of the communities was fully adapted to its own environmental zone and each produced distinctive tools for its own use. But there also must have existed a network of at least indirect communication as these centers exchanged resources native to their area.

Though Umm Dabaghiyah was contemporary with and influenced by many of the sites discussed in this chapter, it takes on special significance as the first in a new and important succession of cultures. After the end of the Umm Dabaghiyah culture around 6000 B.C., the classic trio of the Hassuna, Samarra, and Halaf cultures provides a chronological sequence spanning one millennium and a settlement pattern which expands over the entirety of northern Mesopotamia. This succession takes us beyond the consideration of small rural villages for the first time. A slow, cumulative growth in population becomes evident in the increase of archaeological sites and in the widespread distribution of these cultures. Certainly by Halaf times (5500 B.C.), political and economic integration points to a level of development beyond that of individual village organization. Sites increase in

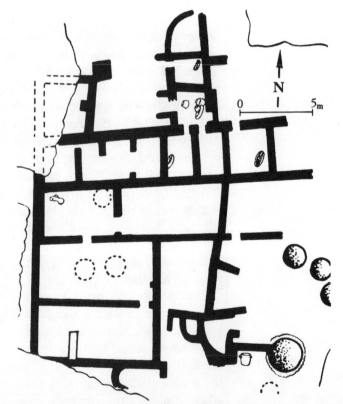

Figure 2.6 Architectural plan of the latest building level at Tell Hassuna, ca. 5500 B.C. (Reproduced from *Handbuch der Vorgeschichte,* C. H. Beck Verlag, courtesy of H. Müller-Karpe.)

both size and number, supporting a view that embryonic political and economic structures were developing that would further unite geographical areas. In the succession following Umm Dabaghiyah, there are clear indications of specialization of labor and also differential wealth within the community—in short, a class structure. This is an important milestone, for the development of class structure is essential to the formation of the state.

We cannot credibly suggest that Samarra or Halaf was at the state level of organization. We can, however, hypothesize that they were involved in incipient state formation, territorial demarcations, and specialization of community function. Traditionally, state formation is assumed to have occurred around 3500 to 3000 B.C. in the ancient Near East. Yet at 5000 B.C., the communities reviewed below (most especially Tell-es Sawaan) indicate a considerable population with economic wealth far exceeding that of an egalitarian agricultural village and with an early form of political integration. Such developments at Tell-es Sawaan should come as no great surprise when one considers the existence of Çatal Hüyük and Jericho some one to two millennia earlier. We turn now to the substantive evidence that suggests the extent of social transformations within the Hassuna, Samarra, and Halaf cultures.

THE HASSUNA CULTURE

The Hassuna culture (6000–5250 B.C.) takes its name from the mound of Tell Hassuna located southwest of Mosul in northwestern Iraq. The mound contains six superimposed building levels. The last level in 5500 B.C. is illustrated in Figure 2.6. It, and a recently excavated mound by Soviet archaeologists called Yarim Tepe, have provided us with a picture of agricultural villages in the first half of the sixth millennium. They are not by any means the only sites of this date excavated. A number of sites in Iran, Turkey, and Palestine have been uncovered which are contemporary to the Hassuna culture, centered in northern Iraq.

The distribution of Hassuna sites in northern Iraq indicates that populations had expanded and settlements were established in virtually all fertile zones. Hassuna sites are not large, however. Hassuna itself is 200 by 150 meters, while Yarim Tepe is but 100 meters in diameter. It is doubtful whether many Hassuna communities had populations beyond 500.

Yarim Tepe level VI (ca. 5500 B.C.) provides the fullest view of a Hassuna-period village. Passages and courtyards separate multiroomed houses with interior courtyards. Doorways have both pivot stones and thresholds, and buttresses were used to strengthen construction for the raising of flat roofs. There is no evidence of second stories. At the northern limit of settlement, there is a single large structure which the excavator believes to be a "communal" storage facility;[31] no other community buildings are indicated.

The ceramics of Hassuna, which first appear in the second building level of that site, resemble the coarse wares of Umm

Plate 2.20 Shallow bowl with antelope motif from Hassuna, Samarra culture, ca. 5000 B.C. (Hirmer Fotoarchiv.)

Dabaghiyah. Pottery of the same style has been found in many other Hassuna sites, marking it as a separate tradition. Toward the end of the Hassuna culture the ceramics of the Samarra culture make their initial appearance. This superior ceramic, once thought to be a Hassuna luxury ware, is today recognized as a diagnostic ceramic of the distinctive Samarra culture.

The economy of the Hassuna culture is best documented at Yarim Tepe. As in the earlier community of Umm Dabaghiyah, sheep, goats, and pigs were the main domesticated animals. Farm produce included domesticated einkorn, breadwheat, and barley. Local flint and small quantities of Anatolian obsidian were utilized for tools. There are fine beads of marble, chalcedony, turquoise, and carnelian, small toilet sticks of stone, and small stone seals with hatched designs. Copper ore and beads found at Yarim Tepe provide the first evidence of metallurgy in the Mesopotamian lowlands.

The Hassuna culture conveys a picture of rustic simplicity. Houses and furnishings are simple; luxury materials are minimal and not distributed in a manner indicative of great class

Plate 2.21   Neck of a bottle-like vessel from Hassuna, Samarra culture, ca. 5000 B.C. (Hirmer Fotoarchiv.)

distinctions or differential wealth. Architectural exposures have not uncovered any evidence for administrative or religious centers. Yet the wide distribution of Hassuna and Hassuna-like ceramics points to a certain integration of these independent farming villages. It is not unreasonable to suggest that the integration of these villages was based on a tribal organization structured by kinship. Greater differentiation within villages, and greater integration among communities, were to mark succeeding cultures.

THE SAMARRA CULTURE

The site of Tell-es Sawaan, on the east bank of the Tigris about 60 miles north of Baghdad, provides us with the clearest picture (indeed, practically the only solid picture) of the succeeding Samarra culture. Although the site itself is no larger than that of Hassuna (220 by 110 meters, compared to Hassuna's 200 by 150

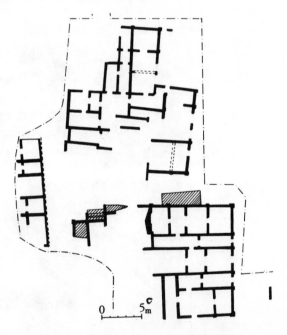

Figure 2.7 Architectural plan of the houses at Tell-es Sawaan, ca. 5600 B.C. (Reproduced from *Handbuch der Vorgeschichte,* C. H. Beck Verlag, courtesy of H. Müller-Karpe.)

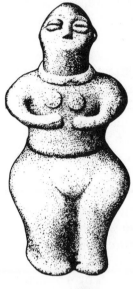

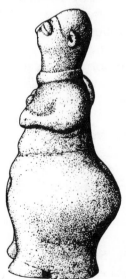

Figure 2.8 Alabaster figurine of a female from Tell-es Sawaan, ca. 5400 B.C. (Reproduced from *Handbuch der Vorgeschichte,* C. H. Beck Verlag, courtesy of H. Müller-Karpe.)

meters), excavations at Tell-es Sawaan have indicated a measure of cultural complexity and technological achievement previously unsuspected for this period of time in the Mesopotamian lowlands.[32]

The earliest settlement at Tell-es Sawaan dates from around 5500 B.C. It was defended by a ditch dug around the rectangular settled area. The earliest buildings were rectangular, swept clear of household goods and lacking internal appointments like hearths or benches. The buildings are all large, containing as many as fifteen rooms. As in Yarim Tepe, walls were reinforced by buttresses to support beams for flat roofs. The structures were built of mudbrick cast in molds—the first appearance of this building material in Mesopotamia.

Much of our information about the Samarra culture comes from burial sites at Tell-es Sawaan. The dead were covered with ochre, tightly contracted, and wrapped in matting. Buried with them were a variety of goods that indicate considerable wealth in some cases.

The materials placed in the graves also suggest a high technological and aesthetic level of production, as well as the existence of trade. The dead were buried with a variety of personal ornaments: alabaster, greenstone, turquoise, carnelian, and copper beads were strung together with shells for necklaces and bracelets. Numerous alabaster female figurines were placed around the burial as illustrated in Figure 2.8. Phalli and headless squatting females, together with a variety of alabaster bowls, jars, ladles, and palettes, were also placed in the tombs. The presence of obsidian, turquoise, and carnelian indicates the existence of an exchange mechanism to procure these resources from distant areas. Copper is present only in the form of jewelry: functional tools are entirely absent.

Most of the burials found at the site (over 130 graves, mostly infants) were positioned beneath a single building; it has been suggested that this building was a shrine.[33] Whether a shrine or not, it is certain that this building was distinguished from others by the presence of this rich cemetery.

The people of the earliest settlement herded domestic sheep and goats and kept dogs. Hunting appears to have been relatively unimportant, as few wild animal bones have been found in the settlement. Agriculture, on the other hand, was well developed. Carbonized plant material indicates that the Samarra culture was already practicing irrigation, evidence not available for their northern Hassuna neighbors. Hybrid barley and breadwheat were developed by mutation, and large-seeded flax, used for weaving linen, was also developed at Tell-es Sawaan. None of these crops could have been developed without irrigation, for rainfall in this area is insufficient for dry farming. Irrigation had reclaimed the otherwise unproductive lands of Mesopotamia for settlement by the middle of the sixth millennium. Within a thousand years, cities would exist in areas wholly dependent on an agricultural produce gained from irrigation technology.

In the Middle Samarran phase at Tell-es Sawaan (ca. 5400 B.C.) a buttressed fortification wall was raised along the course of the earlier ditch. Within this fortification, buildings were constructed either in a T shape or as rectangular structures with external buttresses. The rectangular structures were houses. They varied in size from 9 by 7 meters with twelve rooms to 8 by 4.5 meters with eight rooms. In some of the houses, excavators recovered clay figurines of females wearing elaborate coiffures and colored garments, complete with nose and ear plugs and tatoos.

The T-shaped buildings are of importance not only because they served as storehouses for agricultural produce but also because of their distinctive architectural style. The storage function of these buildings suggests that seed as well as grain was communally owned. Such a situation, if true, would argue for the communal ownership of land as well as the pooling of labor products in communal storehouses.

Equally significant may be the fact that the T-shaped buildings provide convincing prototypes for the later Sumerian T-shaped temples—which they do in fact resemble. Samarran times are at least 1500 years earlier than the era legitimately called Sumerian. The formation, ancestry, and evolution of the Sumerian civilization has been a topic of long debate and heated controversy, and very few scholars would accept in Samarran times the presence of traits or complexes later to become part of the Sumerian world order. Yet the Samarran T-shaped communal storehouses do provide a certain evolutionary base for the formation of the Sumerian T-shaped temples, which we know did control a significant amount of the agricultural produce of the community. It is clear that we have a good deal more to learn about the Samarra culture, its influence and relations with the dispersed agricultural communities of the Iranian plateau and Syro-Palestine, as well as its relation to the Hassuna and the later Halaf culture, to which we now turn.

THE HALAF CULTURE

We know very little about the Halaf culture: most of our information comes from research undertaken prior to World War II at the site of Arpachiyah (east of the Tigris and north of Nineveh in Iraq), save for the ongoing excavations of the Soviets on Yarim Tepe II in Iraq.

Perhaps the exceptional aspect of the Halaf, as of the Hassuna, is the wide geographical expanse in which its distinctive ceramics have been found. The Halaf culture was centered in northern Syria, southeastern Turkey, and northwestern Iraq, but it appears to have expanded or, at the very least, influenced cultures in more distant areas. Halaf ceramics have been found from Iran to the Mediterranean coast as far south as Palestine. It is clear that the long duration of the Halaf (5500–4700 B.C.) was a time of increasing contacts, communication, and acculturation of distinctive cultures. This does not mean that the Halaf was directly ancestral to the later great civilization of Sumeria. Southern Mesopotamia (south of Baghdad), the later heartland of this civilization, appears to have been still entirely uninhabited during Halaf times.

The earliest levels of Halaf settlement at Arpachiyah consist of insubstantial houses. Domestic houses, however, are not the only architectural forms recovered from Halaf sites. Excavations at a number of other sites have consistently uncovered enigmatic structures referred to as *tholoi*. The tholoi are round structures, often with an attached rectangular annex, antechamber, or open courtyard, producing a typical "keyhole" plan. They seem to have been used as storage facilities. If this attribution is correct, there is clear evidence for substantial production of grain and seed storage.

Another function beyond storage has also been suggested for the tholoi. At Arpachiyah, a number of human burials accompanied by clay figurines and pots were found in the tholoi. This association has caused some archaeologists to argue that the structures were religious sanctuaries for the burial of important people.

The tholoi remain the only architectural forms on Halaf sites indicating specialized functions and activities. Precisely what their function was, nevertheless, remains elusive. Some of the tholoi contain burials; others do not. None of the burials in the tholoi contained metal artifacts or other luxury items. Halaf sites, in fact, are surprisingly devoid of metal objects, though occasional fragments are recovered from habitations which attest to the Halaf peoples' knowledge of metals.

The Halaf Economy

Evidence of the Halaf economy, and for other elements of the Halaf culture, is scanty. From the little information available, archaeologists infer that Halaf agriculture was based on the production of cereals by dry farming (there is no evidence for irrigation) and stockbreeding (a favored motif of Halaf pottery was the depiction of bulls' heads and horns). It remains an unfortunate fact that our understanding of the Halaf culture is derived from excavations undertaken years ago when botanical and zoological remains were not collected. Consequently, we have only the vaguest notion of their economic subsistence patterns. We have somewhat more information about Halaf industry and trade, although almost all of this understanding is inferred from the remains of a single technology—ceramics.

Ceramics are surprisingly uniform in their production and decoration. Halaf pottery is exceptionally attractive, a luxury ware which must have been greatly sought after. Indeed, the evidence shows that it was traded to great distances. In the south, Halaf ceramics have been found in later levels at Tell-es Sawaan, in the north at Tilki Tepe near Lake Van in Turkey, and on the Mediterranean coast at Ras Shamra in Lebanon.

The uniformity and quality of the ceramic production and the elaboration of painted motifs argue for its production by specialists in a limited number of areas. The intricate textilelike motifs on Halaf pottery clearly resemble weaving, stitching, or embroidery, and it is not impossible that the important later Mesopotamian textile production had already begun during Halaf times. Precise and neat, minute and repetitive, the intricate Halaf patterns on ceramics provide a ready contrast to the bold,

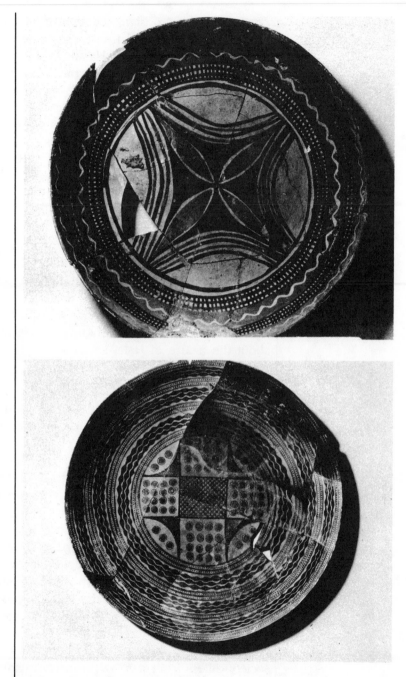

Plate 2.22 Two shallow bowls from Arpachiyah, Halaf culture, ca. 5000 B.C. (Hirmer Fotoarchiv.)

open, naturalistic designs painted on contemporary pottery in the villages of Anatolia and Iran or with the simple and unimaginative production of Hassuna.

This admittedly fragmentary picture of the Halaf economy is enriched by the wide geographical distribution of their material culture. The large territory influenced by the Halaf culture must have played a major role in the communication of ideas.

The distribution of Halaf ceramics over a wide geographical area suggests trade in Halaf ceramics. And even more important, it implies a process of acculturation. This process brought the Halaf culture into contact with different cultures, allowing one, for the first time, to trace its distribution over an area ranging from its center in northern Mesopotamia to the Mediterranean coast in the west and southeastern Turkey in the north. In some of these areas there existed small villages of agriculturists maintaining either the older traditions of the Hassuna culture or cultures contemporary with the Halaf but unexplored by the archaeologist. The precise character of these cultures and their contacts with the Halaf is unknown; little more is understood about the nature of Halaf society.

Halaf Social Organization

It has been suggested that Halaf social organization was structured on a tribal base.[34] This highly conjectural statement requires amplification.

The evolution of social organization is thought to have progressed through three major stages. In the societies of hunters and gatherers, and in the earliest village communities, social organization was *egalitarian*. In such societies, political structures do not adhere to any formal system—social organization is based on shifting patterns of leadership wherein all members of the society share equal access to power and resources. Leadership in group activities (such as the hunt) depends on the success of the chosen leader and frequently changes hands. This basically egalitarian structure of social organization is believed to have also characterized early farming villages, such as Mureybit, Jarmo, and Hassuna. An egalitarian society differs from a *tribal* form of organization in the latter's greater formalization of political and social structure. Members of a tribe all trace themselves to a common, often mythical, ancestor and follow a common leader: a chief. The last stage in the evolution of society, the origin of the *state,* is a step that will be discussed in Chapter 3.

The evidence for the tribal aspect of Halaf culture is inferential and based entirely on ceramics. It has been argued that within specific geographical areas Halaf ceramics have a greater

Plate 2.23 Three painted bowls from Arpachiyah, Halaf culture, ca. 5000 B.C. (Hirmer Fotoarchiv.)

Figure 2.9 Elaborate Halaf bowl with intricate stylized bulls, ca. 5500 B.C. (Reproduced from *Handbuch der Vorgeschichte,* C. H. Beck Verlag, courtesy of H. Müller-Karpe.)

incidence of shared motifs painted on the pottery. The segregation of specific geographical areas with their specific motifs is interpreted as the separation of tribal areas—a fact indicative of a chiefdom level of society.[35] Such an analysis based on ceramics alone is entirely tentative; it has been made additionally so in a recent analysis of Halaf pottery that indicates the presence of regional centers in the manufacture of Halaf pottery and its subsequent exportation to larger areas.[36] This last evidence would certainly suggest specialization of production, but it would not necessarily indicate the presence or absence of tribes.

Halaf settlements do not indicate the presence of administrative structures: the communities are rarely larger than 3 to 4 acres in size, and there is little to demonstrate a hierarchy of settlement size. The absence of buildings suggestive of administrative control and settlements suggestive of different functions tends to make it difficult to prove that the Halaf culture had reached the chieftain stage of cultural evolution. It is as likely that at Çatal Hüyük one is dealing with tribal chiefdoms as at Halaf. The archaeological problem lies in devising a method which can conclusively indicate the nature of social organization within an archaeological site. Such methods have not yet been fully developed, and so doubt remains in dealing with the nature of their society.

In numerous sites, ceramics of the Halaf culture have been found alongside those of the late Samarran—evidence that the two cultures overlapped in time. But while there was clear contact between the contemporary cultures, there was evidently little assimilation. Perhaps one may interpret this as further evidence for tribal organization, which would have reinforced each community's obstinate maintenance of its own styles and traditions as well as its own ethnic boundaries.

The origins of the Halaf culture are obscure. It is possible that the beginnings of Halaf are contemporary with late Çatal Hüyük, and it is perhaps from this direction that the Halaf culture derived its interest in depicting bulls and bull horns. The discovery of the Umm Dabaghiyah culture, however, allows for a view of Halaf origins of a somewhat different nature. Here is a culture, contemporary with Çatal Hüyük, with plaster floors, animal heads in relief, and painted ceramics that could easily have given rise to the early Halaf. Similarities are undeniable. It has also been suggested that the Halaf culture, which was located just south of the Anatolian resource, controlled aspects of the obsidian trade which offered them an opportunity for enrichment and expansion.[37] This may well be. If so, it can only be documented by evidence derived from excavation—which for the Halaf culture is sorely needed.

The cultures of Umm Dabaghiyah, Hassuna, Samarra, and Halaf are all representative of important advances from earlier Neolithic cultures—in terms of population growth, economic and political integration, and the development of a class structure. But none of these northern cultures holds strong claim to the direct line of descent of the later Sumerian civilization to the south. Toward the end of the period when these cultures flourished, developments were beginning to take place in the Tigris-Euphrates delta of southern Mesopotamia that would soon mark a turning point in the slow evolution we have traced in this chapter. It is to these developments, and the Ubaid culture, that we now turn.

THE UBAID CULTURE

By 4500 B.C., southern Mesopotamia's population was still small in comparison to the regions in the north, and settlement was sparse—less than half a dozen sites are recorded. These facts might not be noteworthy except that this area gave birth to the great urban centers of the Sumerian civilization less than a thousand years later.

The Search for Origins

The first settlements in southern Mesopotamia that we are able to associate with one another date from 4500 to 3500 B.C. They are referred to collectively as the Ubaid culture, named after the small archaeological mound of al-'Ubaid, 4 miles from Ur of the Chaldees, south of modern Baghdad. Just why nobody settled there sooner has been the object of much conjecture. Some archaeologists believe that this landmass south of Baghdad was submerged beneath the Persian Gulf until Ubaid times. Others argue that pre-Ubaid sites do exist, but are buried beneath the Mesopotamian alluvium, with all traces of human settlement effectively buried beneath silt. Recent geological and archaeological research contradicts both these theses, suggesting that the present shoreline at the delta of the Tigris-Euphrates has remained essentially unchanged.[38] The answer this suggests is that in this area culture developed late for some other reason—the most likely being the inhospitable climate and the dearth of resources compared to areas in the north and east. Full evidence is not available to resolve the conflicting points of view.

Other questions about the Ubaid are also unanswered, among them the origin of the Ubaid culture. If there was no previous settlement in this area, where did the Ubaid culture come from? In the past, archaeologists have tried to derive the Ubaid from places as distant as India or Palestine, though Iran has remained the favored area of origin. To test this last thesis, virtually all corners of the Iranian plateau have been explored. Findings have not been fruitful. It is the informed archaeological wisdom today that the Ubaid culture did not originate in Iran or, most certainly, in India, Palestine, or Turkey.

Other areas have also been searched in the hunt for Ubaid's origins. Within the past three years, the Kingdom of Saudi Arabia has launched the first archaeological survey of that country. At first, the discovery of Ubaid sites in the Eastern Province of Saudi Arabia excited great interest and suggested the possibility that the "homeland" of the Ubaid had been found at last.[39] The Ubaid sites of Saudi Arabia, approximately fifty in number, are distributed along or close to the shores of the Persian Gulf. The sites are small, all less than an acre in size. Exploratory excavations indicate a dependency on cattle and marine resources. None of these sites, however, is earlier than the Ubaid sites of southern Mesopotamia; in fact, the contrary is indicated. The problem of the origin of the Ubaid remains.

Development of the Culture

While we do not know where the Ubaid settlers came from, or why the culture arose when it did, we do have an approximate idea of how the culture developed and how its society functioned. During the period when the Halaf culture was flourishing in the north, Ubaid farmers began to settle on the Mesopotamian floodplain. This region, the southern delta of the Tigris and Euphrates rivers, lacked animals and plants suitable for domestication. In fact, the region was a far cry from what one might describe as a Near Eastern Garden of Eden. Searing heat through the summer months, an entirely unpredictable and unreliable rainfall, and severe cold in the winter set almost impossible conditions for agriculture: only limited cultivation was possible along the banks of the major rivers, lagoons, and tributaries. Added to these harsh conditions was the lack of resources. Neither stones nor wood were available for construction; also absent were ores for metal production and precious stones for the production of jewelry or statuary.

The birth of civilization in Mesopotamia illustrates Toynbee's concept of "challenge and response."[40] In a hostile and difficult environment, human settlement must accept a severe challenge to its existence. If the energy exerted to overcome the challenge exceeds the severity of that challenge, the result is an advance in the development of the social institutions. Toynbee notes that many of the earliest civilizations evolved in hostile environments. Here the environmental challenge was met by a cultural response—the formation of a social order to overcome the environment. By 3500 B.C. the resource-poor urban centers of Mesopotamia were rich with imported goods.

Challenging it must have been; and in response, the Ubaid settlers at first took the path of least resistance. They settled along the banks of the rivers and took advantage of the natural drainage patterns for agricultural production. Robert Adams, in his extensive settlement surveys of lower Mesopotamia, has shown that there is little evidence for any more sophisticated plan in the earliest settlement patterns. The Ubaid sites were loosely scattered over the unmodified alluvial plain, with little indication of centralization of political control within territorial units. All this was soon to change.

Settlement Patterns

The millennium between 4000 and 3000 B.C. saw the rapid growth of towns and small cities in southern Mesopotamia. In following this growth, Adams' hierarchy of settlement sizes provides a useful means of measurement.[41] Using size as the major factor, he distinguishes between villages, towns, and urban centers. Thus "villages" range from 0.1 to 6.0 hectares; "towns" from 6.1 to 25 hectares; and "urban centers" from 50 hectares on up.

Figure 2.10 The earliest so-called temple from Mesopotamia at Eridu Level XVII, ca. 4500 B.C. (Reproduced from *Handbuch der Vorgeschichte,* C. H. Beck Verlag, courtesy of H. Müller-Karpe.)

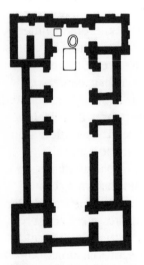

Figure 2.11 Plans of the temple at Eridu, ca. 3500 B.C., built directly over that illustrated in Figure 2.10 but separated by 11 intervening temples built one above the other. (Reproduced from *Handbuch der Vorgeschichte,* C. H. Beck Verlag, courtesy of H. Müller-Karpe.)

Our knowledge of many of the earlier villages is limited, especially where later Sumerian or Babylonian cities were built on top of the earlier village ruins. Although excavations at the sites of Eridu, Ur, Telloh, Uqair, Uruk, and Susa reached the lowest Ubaid levels, deep soundings at the bases of these large mounds provide only limited information. Quantities of fishbone at Eridu, for example, indicate little beyond the village's dependence on marine life. Likewise, excavations of Ubaid levels at the small village sites of Ras al-Amiya (where evidence for early cereal cultivation is present) and Hajji Mohammed reveal an incomplete picture of life in the rural areas.

A better idea of the Ubaid village pattern is provided by the site of al-'Ubaid itself, which dates from 4500 B.C. Excavations here have uncovered houses of mudbrick and reeds. Animal and plant remains indicate that economic subsistence was broad-based. Food was provided through fishing, hunting of gazelles and horses, herding of cattle and goats on the alluvial plain, and cultivation of cereal crops. Craft specialization was present in the production of ceramics and most likely in the manufacture of beads and stone tools. Metallurgy was entirely absent. There is no indication of centralized administrative functions, elaborate religious structures, or accumulated wealth in the hands of an elite.

Excavations at the contemporary site of Eridu provide an interesting contrast to al-'Ubaid. Eridu was first settled in about 4800 B.C., while the Halaf culture was still producing its familiar painted pottery in the north and while al-'Ubaid was still an undifferentiated village. But here excavations have revealed not only mudbrick houses but also a mudbrick structure identified by the excavators as a "temple," which is illustrated in Figure 2.10. Clustering around the temple were the houses of the elite. Craftsmen lived a short distance from the elite, while still further from the temple were the houses of farmers. Even at this early date, Eridu's total population probably exceeded 5,000, in comparison to al-'Ubaid's likely population of 750.

The settlement pattern shown by Eridu's earliest levels indicates a centralizing role of the temple. This role was to increase in importance. By 3500 B.C., the temple, rebuilt several times over the millennium, had grown to monumental proportions, and not just at Eridu (see Figure 2.11). The temple complex served as an administrative center in every major Ubaid settlement.

Typically, the temples were the largest and best-constructed buildings in the community. At Eridu and other Ubaid sites, a religious architectural tradition was maintained on the same spot for over a thousand years. This extraordinary continuity of specific locations for the temples suggests the concept of a sacred precinct. The Sumerian city-state evolved from the shrine of its principal temple. Paul Wheatley has argued that *all* cities evolved from "ceremonial centers."[42] The rise of Mesopotamian cities would seem to support his thesis. By late Ubaid times, the temple had already become the central focus of economic and social activity in the large cities.

Trade and Cultural Contacts

Other changes had taken place over the same millennium. Ubaid society had grown in complexity and spread over a considerable geographical expanse. By 4000 B.C., the Ubaid culture had extended to northern Mesopotamia, replacing the Halaf culture. The north retained a number of cultural elements distinctive from those of the southern Ubaid. In Tepe Gawra, for instance, a site in northern Iraq, the dead were buried in inhumation pits, while at Eridu they were placed in brick-vaulted tombs. In addition, Tepe Gawra's excavation yielded many terra-cotta painted Mother Goddesses which have not been found in the south.

Despite some important regional differences, though, the emergent picture suggests a peaceful acculturation of the Ubaid people with the descendants of the Halaf culture, even though the latter still represented a majority of the population in the north. This fundamental unity was not to last long. An increasing gap between the cultures of the north and the south began to emerge by 3500–3000 B.C., as the south took the lead in developing a major civilization.

By 3500 B.C., the Ubaid people were living along the Tigris and Euphrates rivers reaching into northern Syria and even Cilicia in Turkey. The Ubaid boundaries were defined by the Taurus Mountains to the northwest and the Zagros Mountains to the east, though commercial intercourse reached even more distant areas. The extent of Ubaid trade is attested through findings of amazonite (a semiprecious stone from India) at Ur, north Anatolian obsidian at several sites, and imported ores and metals at Tepe Gawra.

Figure 2.12 Ubaid painted pottery from Tepe Gawra, ca. 4500 B.C. (Reproduced from *Handbuch der Vorgeschichte,* C. H. Beck Verlag, courtesy of H. Müller-Karpe.)

In addition to well-developed trade and the existence of specialized crafts, settlement survey analysis indicates a thriving economy. Agriculture was productive. Food supplies were sufficient to support a fast-growing population, though there is no evidence to support the contention that even the later Ubaid culture practiced anything beyond a simple basin irrigation technology.

Both the society and intersocietal contacts were becoming more complex. The growing population led to new settlements, mostly along river banks. These settlements were not isolated; they maintained contact by boat. And within that network of communities, differential settlement size suggests that there was a hierarchical arrangement of towns and villages.[43] Within individual Ubaid communities the increasing size of the temples clearly indicates a growing centralization of authority in the hands of the priests.

The centralization of authority in the temple was typical throughout the range of the later Ubaid culture. At Tepe Gawra to the north, archaeologists have recovered a complex of three temples situated around a central courtyard. This "acropolis" of late Ubaid date has temples similar in design to those of Eridu—further evidence of a single culture that spread from the northernmost parts of Syria all the way south to the delta lowlands.

The Meaning of the Ubaid

It may be premature to refer to the Ubaid culture as Sumerian, but it certainly must have prepared the ground for the principal developments of the Sumerian civilization. The evolution of social differentiation and trade specialization, the growth of population accompanied by the settlement of new villages and towns, the signs of a growing centralization of authority not only within each community but also within groups of communities—all indicate a new trend that separates the Ubaid culture from earlier Neolithic cultures: a cumulative process of cultural growth.

Even further evidence comes from the location of Ubaid settlements, which often rest directly beneath later Sumerian and Babylonian cities. These early sites have been reached only at the bottom of narrow sounding pits, and consequently there is little horizontal exposure to shed light on town planning or the

Plate 2.24 Terracotta male figurine from Eridu, early Uruk period, ca. 3700 B.C. (1 ft 5½ in.). (Hirmer Fotoarchiv.)

internal social, political, and economic organization of the community. While the Sumerian culture may not have been the direct lineal descendant of the Ubaid, it seems apparent that all the principal cities of ancient Sumer were to evolve from these Ubaid communities.

Summary

Not too many years ago, archaeologists perceived the Neolithic Revolution as a singular event resulting from the invention of the domestication of plants and animals. Some even argued that such an event was to be discovered through archaeological excavation of a particular site within a specific geographic-ecological area.

Archaeological research over the past thirty years has exposed the naivete of this view. Today we recognize the Neolithic revolution as a process which began by at least 10,000 B.C. and lasted in some areas of the Near East until after 5000 B.C. The Neolithic Revolution is best seen as an adaptive process of long duration. Some communities in the Near East, as Nahal Oren in Israel, were manipulating cereals and animals as early as 12,000 B.C.; other communities (including Suberde in Anatolia and Tepe Asiab in Iran) still consisted of temporary encampments of hunters and nomadic herders by 6500 B.C. and even later.

Over the past three decades, archaeologists in the Near East have turned a great deal of attention and energy toward understanding the Neolithic. The dozens of excavated sites in Palestine, Anatolia, the highland mountains of the Zagros in Iran, and other areas indicate the great diversity of these Neolithic communities. This diversity rests in such factors as:

1. *Population and size:* Population varied tremendously in Neolithic sites, from the large towns of Çatal Hüyük and Jericho to the smaller contemporary villages of Jarmo and Mureybit.

2. *Environment and subsistence pattern:* Each community adapted to its own ecological system, utilizing and specializing in the exploitation of specific resources which differed substantially from community to community. Agriculture and sedentism were not necessarily the norm: some communities continued to depend on hunting and gathering, others appear as nomadic encampments, while still others adapted to a sustained agricultural dependence.

3. *Technology and production:* The communities of the Neolithic show as great a variation in subsistence pattern as they do in technological achievement. A few Neolithic communities began experimentation with metallurgy by 7000 B.C.; others began using metals millennia later. The extent of technological experimentation and achievement varied greatly between Neolithic communities, whether one is speaking of architecture or of the pyrotechnologies of ceramic and metal production.

4. *Trade and exchange systems:* That the Neolithic communities were in contact with each other is more than substantiated by the presence of nonindigenous resources within the communities. To such resources as obsidian, turquoise, carnelian, and metal, which have survived the archaeological record, one must add the exchange of less durable goods, including textiles and, as Umm Dabaghiyah indicates, leather.

5. *Social organization:* The diversity of population and varying intensity of settlement, the extent and dependency on trade, and the specialization in certain aspects of production were all characterized by varying patterns of social organization. The extent of interaction between the settled communities and nomadic herders remains archaeologically little understood. The "defensive" walls about Jericho, the richness of the murals at Çatal Hüyük, and the ever present female figurines in Neolithic communities all imply rich and varied ideological systems embedded within specific and seemingly different systems of social organization.

The specific social framework of the Neolithic communities is debatable. Most archaeologists would argue for a system of tribal organization, but the specific structure and geographical limits of the tribes remain unknown. The Halaf culture, it has recently been proposed, is representative of a chiefdom, while archaeologists have claimed that such communities as Jarmo represent an egalitarian village social organization. The social organization of Neolithic communities in the Near East, it must be admitted, remains a great enigma.

Each of these five factors is fundamental to an understanding of the Neolithic communities of 10,000 to 5000 B.C. But it is just as important to recognize that while each of these factors played a basic role in the cultural developments that took place during this time, they did not play identical roles in all (perhaps in any) of the cultures we know of. The study of population growth and settlement size, environment and subsistence patterns, technology and production, trade and exchange, and social organization clearly shows the great diversity of communities and cultures—not only in the Old World but in the New World as well.

In this chapter, we have begun to see that both qualitative and quantitative changes were starting to take place during the end of the sixth millennium B.C. These changes, dealt with at length in Chapter 3, resulted in the transformation of earlier Neolithic communities; they culminated, moreover, in the urban world of Mesopotamia.

Notes

1. Isaac (1975:77–103).
2. Childe (1925, 1928).
3. Zeuner (1963:192).
4. Braidwood (1974:92).
5. Braidwood (1974:102ff).
6. Sauer (1952:24ff).
7. Flannery (1969:73–101).
8. Binford (1968:313–336).
9. Flannery (1969:94ff).
10. Garrod (1957:211ff).
11. Harlan (1967:197–201).
12. Mellaart (1975:283–284).
13. Braidwood (1974:118).
14. Cohen (1977:Chapters 2,7).
15. Braidwood and Howe (1960).
16. Kirkbride (1974:85–92).
17. Kenyon (1957).
18. Kenyon (1957:33).
19. Anati (1962:273ff).
20. Smith (1976:19ff).
21. Legge (1977:64).
22. Mellaart (1975:68).
23. Kirkbride (1966:61–66).
24. Moore (1973:39–41).
25. Lloyd (1956:74).
26. Mellaart (1967).
27. Mellaart (1967:77–130).

28. *Ibid.*
29. Gorman (1972:79–110).
30. Kirkbride (1973:1–8).
31. Lloyd and Safar (1945:277–278).
32. Oates (1966); El-Wailly and Abu-Soof (1965).
33. *Ibid.*
34. Watson and Le Blanc (1973:117–133).
35. *Ibid.*
36. Davidson and McKerrell (1976:45–56).
37. Mellaart (1975:170).
38. Larsen (1975:176ff).
39. Masry (1974).
40. Toynbee (1947:111–118).
41. Adams (1972:17–19).
42. Wheatley (1971).
43. Adams (1972).

3. The Rise of Civilization: Egypt, Sumer, and the Indus

Prior to the rise of city-states in Mesopotamia, the geographical focus of settlement is limited almost entirely to the "Fertile Crescent." As we saw in Chapter 2, this half circle which extends from the plains and foothills of the Zagros Mountains in Iraq to the Taurus and Amanus ranges and down to Lebanon on the west was the site of the first early agricultural villages. These plains and foothills had sufficient rainfall for agriculture as well as the wild ancestors of domesticated species of animals and plants: sheep, pigs, goats, emmer, barley, and einkorn.

In contrast to the early settlements of the Fertile Crescent, the later cities of southern Iraq, as well as Pharaonic Egypt and the Indus civilization, depended upon irrigation. Each required an agricultural surplus to feed growing populations and support the specialization of labor within a more sophisticated economy. Clearly, transformations not only in scale but also in kind separated the urbanized civilizations that arose in the third millennium from the Neolithic settlements that preceded them. These changes, and the pressures that brought them about, will be the focus of this chapter.

The Ecological Basis: Contrasts and Consistencies

The basic commonalities among the earliest civilizations hide many contrasts. To this day, in Egypt, a sail up the river Nile reveals that the major cities were restricted to either side of a river that has not changed its course for millennia. In the Indus region, many of the principal sites of the Harappan civilization are situated along, but not restricted to, the banks of the Indus River.

The major urban centers of Sumer in the Mesopotamian lowlands, though, are situated on the banks of neither the Tigris nor the Euphrates. Mesopotamian civilization, unlike that of Egypt, was subject to the erratic behavior of the Tigris and Euphrates riverine systems. These two great rivers, which brought the country's life-giving water, were liable to unpredictable floods or inadequate flow. Even more disastrous, the Tigris and Euphrates could alter their courses so radically that within a generation a flourishing city, once astride one of the great rivers, was reduced to an isolated ruin in the middle of the desert. The great Sumerian cities of Kish, Nippur, Uruk, and Ur, built along major channels of the Euphrates, now appear as ruins within a desiccated environment beyond the river's view.

In the three civilizations of Egypt, Mesopotamia, and the Indus we meet with varying degrees of dependence on the annual flooding along the banks of the principal rivers to sustain their agricultural production. The riverine system of Mesopotamia, unlike that of Egypt, was not as subject to annual inundation but provided the water source for the development of complex irrigation systems. The Harappan civilization, distributed over an area far larger than either the Egyptian or Mesopotamian, exploited riverine (the Indus River), coastal (the Indian Ocean), and intermontane valleys of Pakistan and northwest India. It would be wrong to argue that the formation of these three civilizations was brought about through similar ecological conditions resulting from their dependency on the riverine system, for in each case that dependency took on a distinct and individual character.

THE MESOPOTAMIAN LOWLANDS

Written texts inform us that the great Mesopotamian cities of Nippur, Shuruppak, Larsa, Uruk, and Ur were once all connected by a major course of the Euphrates. These sites were in turn connected with other communities by small irrigation channels which crisscrossed the deep alluvial soils of southern Iraq. Mesopotamia's dependency on the two great rivers was important well before the rise of the Sumerian civilization. Already during the prehistoric Ubaid period, these earliest inhabitants were directing the waters of the river into their fields. Their dependency on water channels presents one of Mesopotamia's chicken-or-egg choices: Did the existence of canals attract settlers, or did the growth of settlement necessitate a canal for increased agricultural production?

Sumer's canals were important for more than agricultural irrigation: they were also essential as trade routes. Settlements along water canals allowed for boat transport, connecting communities and facilitating exchange. Sumer entirely lacked resources. Metals, timber, stone (carnelian, turquoise, lapis lazuli)—all had to be imported from the mountainous regions of the north or from the Iranian Plateau. The need to import these natural resources required considerable exchange and contact with distant peoples, not just by water but overland as well. The extensive canal system of Sumer facilitated the internal distribution of these materials.

The climate of the southern alluvium of Mesopotamia is one of extreme harshness, characterized by excessive heat in the long summer months, rare and irregular rainfall in late autumn and winter, and extreme cold in winter months. Southeast of Mesopotamia is modern Khuzistan, the ancient Susiana or Elam, where climatic conditions are similar, except near the hills and mountains where there was sufficient rainfall for agriculture.

These territorial pockets in the mountains are cut off from one another; as a result, they have rarely coalesced into major political units. There are a few passes through the mountains to the north and east, and these facilitate contact with Mesopotamia and the Armenian and Iranian highlands. Nomadic groups form a major part of the highland population, and their interaction with the urbanized, settled population of the Mesopotamian alluvium is a recurring phenomenon throughout the history of the area.

In Sumer itself, the geographical setting was far from an environmental continuum. The canals and the surrounding areas were fertile indeed, and not just as farmland. When waters from a canal flowed onto low ground, swamps or even lakes were created, forming large marshes which abounded in food staples like fish and waterfowl. Another staple provided by the swamplands was reed: the basic construction material not only for baskets, but also for houses and boats. Thickets around the canals were so dense that wild boars and even lions were a constant threat to the livestock. Away from the water, the land was quite different. Between the thickets and lagoons lay large expanses of desert. Unreached by irrigation canals, the land here was entirely uninhabited and of no economic value to the settled communities.

There is no clear evidence that ecological conditions in Mesopotamia during the last ten millennia differed greatly from those of today. It is doubtful, too, whether the climate of the better-watered areas of the Fertile Crescent has changed significantly since ancient times. This does not mean that there have been no fluctuations in climate. There is no doubt that there were good and bad years, and even these minor fluctuations would have had profound ecological effects on human settlement in the marginally productive areas of southern Mesopotamia.

EGYPT'S FLOODPLAINS

Like the Tigris and Euphrates of Mesopotamia, the Nile moves across a large alluvial floodplain. Unlike the Mesopotamian rivers, though, the Nile provided a more dependable source of irrigation. Agriculturists could rely on the same annual cycle that characterizes the Nile today. With the summer monsoon in Ethiopia, the river rises to flood the alluvial flats, depositing rich silt over the levees. These levees were distinctly inviting to early settlement, as they were flooded only for short periods at the crest of the annual inundation.

This simple picture of a natural floodplain is fundamental to understanding the settlement of Egypt. Settlement from Predynastic to modern times has been largely restricted to the levees or low desert regions where seeds could be sown in the rich wet mud left from the annual flood and where cattle could graze on the herbaceous and brush vegetation which flourished there. The inhabitants of the Nile were far more dependent on the annual flood than were the Mesopotamians for their agricultural productivity. The natural floodplain produced the rich agricultural fields which in Mesopotamia were created by constructed irrigation canals.

As in Mesopotamia the peoples inhabiting the Nile Valley were greatly dependent on trade to obtain their resources. We read of organized expeditions in Old Kingdom times (ca. 2500 B.C.) to obtain gold, turquoise, wood, and copper—all of which must be got considerable distances from the Nile Valley. The presence of these resources by the end of the fourth millennium indicates that the settled communities along the Nile were already trading with other communities beyond the Nile Valley. The Nile Valley is a single fertile strip surrounded by desert. This condition isolates the inhabitants of the Nile to a greater degree than the people of Mesopotamia. The interaction of the settled populations of the

Mesopotamian alluvium with the settled populations of the highlands, on the one hand, as well as with nomadic elements, on the other, provided a more complex network of cultural communication than existed within the more isolated communities along the Nile.

In comparison to Mesopotamia, where ecological conditions over the past ten millennia have not drastically altered, the Nile Valley has undergone distinct change. During Predynastic times, the land and climate around the Nile were far more favorable for agriculture than they are today. Geological deposits indicate that there was a greater abundance of water in the desert streams beyond the Nile; tree roots of acacias, tamarisks, and sycamores found beyond the current reach of floodwaters attest to the existence of earlier, wetter conditions in desert areas of today.

Further evidence of changed environmental conditions comes from ancient artwork found in the eastern desert and highlands of the central Sahara. Rock drawings dated prior to 4000 B.C. show a magnificent array of animals, including the elephant, giraffe, ibex, hartebeest, barbary sheep, donkey, cattle, deer, hyena, various cats, and ostrich. The many individualistic local styles of rock art strongly suggest the existence of ethnic groups within specific habitats.

From such pictorial evidence, verified in some instances by paleontological evidence of animal remains, one can reconstruct the living conditions as reflected in modern distributions of animal species and rainfall. The absolute ecological change was rather small, even when compared with today. But the presence of semidesert and grassland belts of 50 to 150 miles on either side of the Nile and a concomitant contraction of the Sahara provide a reasonable explanation for the wide distribution of Neolithic sites in what are today uninhabitable deserts in eastern Egypt and Libya.

THE VARIED TOPOGRAPHY OF THE INDUS

The region of the Indus Valley provides a third geographical setting for the rise of an early civilization. Unlike Egypt and Mesopotamia the civilization along the Indus was not restricted to the alluvial plains of the riverine valleys. The Indus, or Harappan, civilization has a far greater geographical distribution than that of

Egypt or Mesopotamia. The Indus civilization, moreover, exploited a far wider range of ecological areas: riverine, intermontane, and coastal settlements were neither as isolated nor as dependent on either annual flooding or irrigation technology as were the Mesopotamian villages. Communities of the Harappan civilization inhabited both the highlands and the lowlands. Its geographical distribution from the modern border of Iran extends eastward along the Indian Ocean to the Gujarat peninsula of India toward New Delhi; to the north of the coastal plain it extends northward to Lahore along the Indus and even reaches the Oxus River of northern Afghanistan. Within such a vast geographical area it is obvious that the Harappan civilization exploited a far greater range of environmental conditions than either Egypt or Mesopotamia. Its great geographical distribution and cultural uniformity, within areas of indigenous non-Harappan populations, provide conditions very different from those of Egypt and Mesopotamia. The equally distinctive nature of its civilization, sometimes referred to as an "empire," will be dealt with later in this chapter.

While the ecological settings of the three great civilizations differed in climate, resources, and topography, one geographical feature was shared by all three. Sumer, Egypt, and the Indus (and the Shang dynasty in China, as well) all flourished on alluvial plains that permitted irrigation practices—which in turn resulted in surplus agricultural production.

Beyond irrigation, though, innumerable factors contributed to the rise of civilization, and a number of problems still confound the task of identifying all these factors—not just in these three areas, but in Mesoamerica as well. Of these problems, the most persistent is still the lack of information, both from archaeological data and from written records. While writing first appeared at the end of the fourth millennium, about the time that civilizations arose in the Old World, the earliest written records have not only been difficult—or impossible, in the case of the Indus civilization—to translate, but often they tell us nothing about ancient events or the nature of their institutions.

By far the most extensive excavations of the first urban sites have taken place in lowland Mesopotamia, in what is now southern Iraq. Translations of Sumerian texts, moreover, have been the most thorough. For this reason, we understand more of the rise of civilization in Sumer than in the other early centers. While this chapter will look at Egypt, Sumer, the Indus, and the cultures of the Iranian Plateau between Sumer and the Indus, its focus will be on Sumer where our understanding is most extensive.

The Egyptian Civilization

EARLY SETTLEMENTS AND THE PREDYNASTIC PERIOD

Because relatively little archaeological research has been undertaken in Egypt to illuminate the time before 3000 B.C., we have only the sketchiest picture of the emergence of the pharaonic state. Recent work, mostly salvage programs undertaken during the construction of the Aswan Dam, has shown a virtually uninterrupted sequence of occupation from the Paleolithic to the Mesolithic in southern Egypt—that is, from about 30,000 to 10,000 B.C.

Recent archaeological research indicates the reaping and grinding of wild grains in Upper Egypt and Nubia as early as 12,500 B.C. Although there is an absence of direct evidence, it is plausible that domestication of cattle and seed grasses was attempted prior to 5000 B.C., when they are first documented in the archaeological record. In the main, however, it appears that broad-spectrum hunting and gathering were sufficiently successful on the Nile floodplain so that full-scale dependence on domesticates did not come before 5000 B.C. The result was a series of predynastic cultures from 5000 to 3000 B.C. with considerable individuality. Pastoral nomads tended sheep, goats, and cattle. Even in settled communities along the Nile, fishing, fowling, and big game hunting often far outweighed the cultivation of cereal.

The time period from 5000 to 3100 B.C. was characterized by the gradual adaptation to an agricultural way of life in both northern (Lower) Egypt and southern (Upper) Egypt. Evidence from Fayum and Merimde to the north, and Tasa, Badari, Naqada, and Abydos to the south, indicates that dogs, sheep, goats, cattle, geese, pigs, and cereals were fully domesticated by about 4000 B.C.

At this point, our knowledge of the subsistence patterns of Predynastic Egypt is incomplete. Our understanding of the early village farming communities of the north and the south Nile Valley comes mostly from excavations undertaken

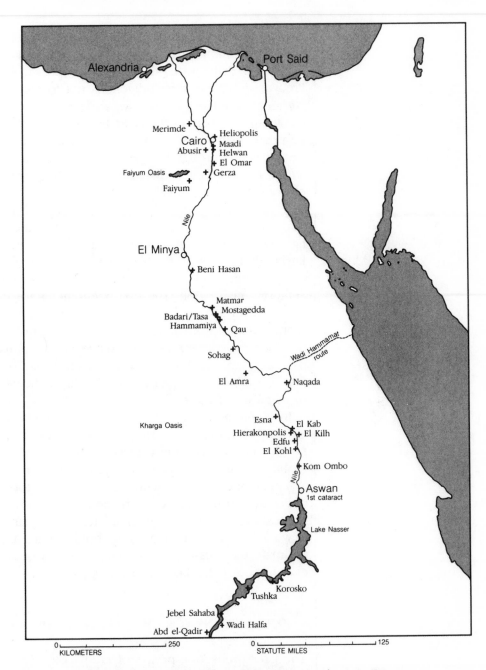

Map 3.1 Distribution of settlements in Predynastic Egypt, ca. 5000–3000 B.C. (Redrawn from David and Ruth Whitehouse, *Archaeological Atlas of the World.* 1975. London: Thames and Hudson Ltd. © 1975 Thames and Hudson Ltd.)

prior to World War II. We do know that many of the domesticated plants and animals (including emmer and einkorn, sheep and goats) that formed the economic subsistence base for Predynastic Egypt were indigenous not to the Nile Valley but to Western Asia. The evidence for earlier domestication of these plants and animals in the Near East suggests that the earliest Egyptian agriculturists may have learned these subsistence strategies not through independent invention but by the process of *diffusion* —that is, the dissemination of the ideas and technology of domestication from the Near East to Egypt.

If diffusion played a role in the development of agriculture, it also seems to have been at least a factor in the formation of the Egyptian state. The appearance of the pharaonic state in Egypt, shortly before the end of the fourth millennium, was contemporary with the rise of the great city-states of the Sumerian civilization. The two phenomena are intimately linked, the result of a broadly based cultural evolution that had characterized the Near East and northeastern Africa during the previous millennia. (The appearance of the Indus civilization, probably some half a millennium later, is also seen as related to this broad-based cultural evolution. But it did not derive directly from either of the earlier civilizations.)

In addition to cultural diffusion, indigenous aspects (the environment, the settlement patterns, and the cultural traditions present in each area) also played a part in the development of civilization in each center. At this stage in our research, we are just beginning to understand the relevant factors which lead to civilization in these three areas and other early centers. The process is slow: data are incomplete, and explanations that seem to work for one area often do not hold true for another. Some of the main theories explaining the rise of civilization in Egypt are examined in the following paragraphs.

EXPLANATIONS FOR THE RISE OF EGYPTIAN CIVILIZATION

The later prehistoric period of Predynastic Egypt (ca. 3500–3000 B.C.) is one of far-reaching change. These changes were so extensive, in fact, that until recently it was believed that they were brought about by incursions of peoples from Western Asia. Many authors believed in the existence of an "Asiatic invasion" which transformed the earlier "African culture" and established the foundations on which the dynastic state was based.[1]

This view has no support in the archaeological record. There is little doubt that cultural relations between Egypt and Western Asia, especially the Syro-Palestinian Levant, were greatly intensified over these five hundred years: such innovations as writing and the use of cylinder seals must have resulted at least in part from increased contact brought about by the development of sturdier seagoing ships. But there is no reason to infer a sudden immigration of "Asiatics."

Another explanation for the rise of civilization in Egypt, and in Mesopotamia as well, is the "irrigation hypothesis" (discussed in Chapter 1 and also later in this chapter). According to this theory, most effectively put forth by Karl Wittfogel, the development of irrigation technology in Egypt and in Mesopotamia led to numerous other developments: the competition for water resources; an increased labor efficiency; intensified irrigation systems; the development of a bureaucracy to manage the labor force; and, ultimately, the rise of a state superstructure. This picture may be valid in some early stages; unfortunately, it does not fit with the recent understanding of the role of irrigation in Egypt. More recent evidence suggests that flood control and irrigation projects were in the local administrative domains, so these enterprises would not have contributed to the development of a statewide power system.[2]

Another recent explanation has centered on the role of trade in the development of civilization.[3] This view seems to have some validity in both the Old World (Mesopotamia) and the New World (Maya) civilization. Trade was present in Egypt, too: periodic markets may have existed there, and the evidence is more than sufficient to argue for the existence of an effective method of internal trade and exchange during the predynastic period. It would be pressing the evidence, however, to suggest that the growth of an urban structure in Egypt was dependent on the methods for the distribution of goods.

In fact, in the view of Wolfgang Helck, long-distance trade was restricted in Egypt compared to other early states, limited to only a few points where goods entered Egypt by sea from the Syro-Palestinian coast or where east-west trade crossed the Nile Valley through western oases to the Red Sea.[4] The limitation of long-distance trade, along with the immigration of nomadic peoples who settled in small villages along the Nile Valley, is seen by Helck as working against the development of large towns instead of stimulating their growth.

Helck's theory shows the influence of the earlier views of John Wilson of the University of Chicago. In a provocative paper entitled "Egypt through the New Kingdom: Civilization without Cities," Wilson (1960) contrasted the urban centers of Mesopotamia with the scattered villages and administrative centers of Egypt. The Mesopotamian centers, he said, were true cities, but this was not the case for the Egyptian centers. Wilson and Helck based this argument on a limited definition of the city. Because the few centers of population that existed in ancient Egypt were limited to ceremonial or managerial functions only, they did not exhibit the diversification of crafts and labor or differentiation of class structure that normally characterize cities. Because of this single dimensionality, Wilson did not consider these centers to be cities in the true sense of the term.

Wilson's concept typifies the traditional view of Egypt's settlement pattern. For years, archaeologists believed that throughout not just the predynastic period, but during the dynastic period as well, Egypt had conformed to a *primate distribution* of settlement: there existed only a few large towns restricted to administrative or priestly functions, surrounded by numerous small villages of a purely agricultural nature. This settlement pattern was seen as distinctive from that of Mesopotamia with its *rank-size distribution:* a hierarchical pattern of villages, towns, and cities covering a full range of settlement sizes from large to small.

The primate interpretation was based in large part on evidence from ancient texts. More recently, this view has been directly challenged by scholars like Kemp (1977) and Butzer (1976), who turn their attention more toward the archaeological record.

The evidence we have of early settlements suggests that there were population concentrations in the narrower floodplains of both the far south and the northern delta regions of the Nile Valley during the time period from 6000 to 5000 B.C. Moreover, recent research indicates that even in predynastic times the evolution from a primate to a rank-size settlement pattern was beginning to take place, and Dynastic Egypt was characterized by the latter pattern.[5] It seems that Predynastic Egypt was distinguished by a

THE EGYPTIAN CIVILIZATION

large number of primate settlements on the desert edge, but by the First Dynasty (ca. 3100 B.C.) many of these sites had been abandoned, indicating a direct nucleation of previously scattered populations and the formation of a rank-size distribution pattern with a distinct hierarchy of settlements. Just why this development occurred still eludes us. We do, however, have an emerging, if sketchy, picture of some of the processes that marked the Nile Valley's transformation from a series of scattered settlements to a pharaonic state.

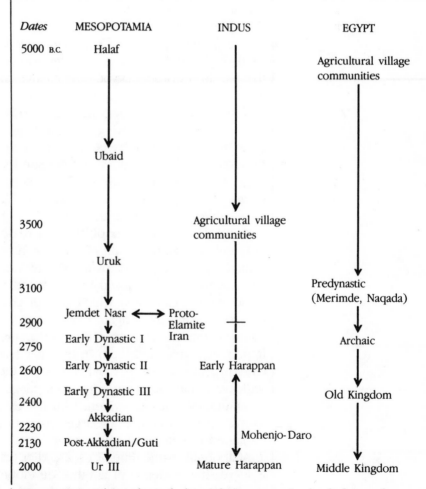

Figure 3.1 Chronological chart of Mesopotamia, the Indus, and Egyptian civilizations.

EVOLUTION OF THE PHARAONIC STATE

Evidence from both historical tradition and archaeological excavation suggests a thumbnail outline of the emergence of the Egyptian city and state. As we have seen, for much of the predynastic period (the millennium prior to 3100 B.C.) settlement distribution was strongly primate. Only two major concentrations of population are currently known: Naqada, 100 miles north of Aswan, and Hierakonopolis, about 50 miles north of Aswan. The majority of the population lived in small villages subsisting on broad-spectrum patterns of hunting, gathering, cultivation of cereals, and pastoralism (the herding of domesticated animals like sheep, goats, and cattle).

The primate pattern of settlement persisted until about 3200–3100 B.C. At this time, two developments began to take place that would transform Egypt. One change was the abandonment of many of the small settlements that had surrounded the larger settlements of Hierakonopolis and Naqada, with populations of the smaller villages moving into the larger towns. This apparent migration has made it exceedingly difficult to pinpoint the role of demographic change. Is the increased size of some of the larger towns the full result of the abandonment of small villages, or was there a population increase as well? At this point, it is impossible to be certain, though most archaeologists would contend that a gradual population increase was taking place.

In either case, the result of population changes coincides with a change in the nature of towns. The two towns of Hierakonopolis and Naqada were enclosed by walls, and in both communities a cemetery was excavated which is referred to as "royal" on the evidence of the extravagance of both grave goods and tomb construction. The character of both these walled communities, the importance attributed them in the later historical record, and the existence in each of a "royal" cemetery indicate that the two settlements had become more than villages.[6] In these two communities, one has evidence for the existence of early primate towns—political centers of larger areas in which populations remained in dispersed small villages.

At about the same time or even earlier (ca. 3400–3200 B.C.) there is increasing evidence of another development—a struggle for predominance between Upper and Lower Egypt. An Upper Egyptian state was formed: Naqada may well have been the first capital; but for reasons poorly understood, Hierakonopolis soon took over the role of principal capital and became still larger. Toward the end of the fourth millennium, in about 3100 B.C., the two regions were unified by the first pharaoh, Menes (alias Narmer, the Scorpion King), and with Menes begins the Archaic period of Dynastic Egypt.

In this early picture, we can trace the emergence of a situation that occurs over and over again in Egyptian history: the more developed and cosmopolitan centers of the northern delta resisting membership in a corporate whole. From the south, an ambitious prince (as Menes most certainly must have been) terminates a period of anarchy and rivalry by conquering the north, placing it under his sway, and so creating one state out of a congeries of rival powers.

Figure 3.2 Painted ceramic vessel from Naqada illustrating an oared vessel and an ivory figurine from the cemetery of Naqada, ca. 3500 B.C. (Reproduced from *Handbuch der Vorgeschichte*, C. H. Beck Verlag. Courtesy of H. Müller-Karpe.)

The evidence for the political ferment which produced the unification of Pharaonic Egypt is depicted on a number of votive objects excavated at Hierakonopolis, capital of this earliest dynastic tradition. Such objects depict scenes of the subjection of one person to another resulting from acts of violence, as illustrated in Figure 3.3. If our picture were more complete, the transition from Predynastic to Pharaonic Egypt might appear more gradual than the sudden efflorescence which the distance of time and absence of evidence suggest. As it is, the formation of Pharaonic Egypt under a single god-king who assumes in his person the character of a god ruling over a unified state, his magical powers controlling the annual inundation of the harvest-giving Nile, seems to arise suddenly, almost out of nowhere.

How did this transformation take place? Along with the presence of divine kingship and the political unification of Egypt, two

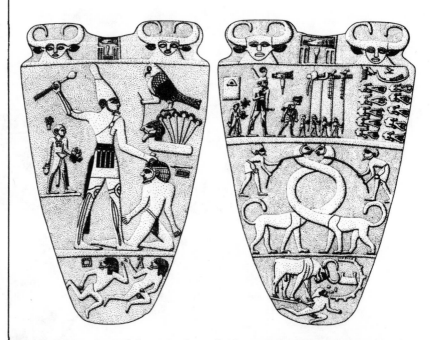

Figure 3.3 Carved "votive plaque" of stone depicting a man wearing the crown of Upper Egypt and subjugating an individual. The opposite side has carved on the upper register a man wearing the combined crowns of Upper and Lower Egypt marching behind standard bearers before rows of decapitated individuals. The object is from Hierakonopolis, ca. 3200 B.C. (Reproduced from *Handbuch der Vorgeschichte,* C. H. Beck Verlag. Courtesy of H. Müller-Karpe.)

other factors stand out. One of these was the development of writing.

Writing is believed to have first appeared in Mesopotamia a century or two before its beginning in Egypt. Was the origin of writing in both places entirely independent, or does Mesopotamian priority indicate that its invention was diffused and adapted in Egypt? If the former is true it is a remarkable coincidence that the independent invention of writing was so nearly simultaneous in both areas. If the latter is true, then why are Egyptian hieroglyphs so totally different from the Mesopotamian cuneiform style of writing as is so readily apparent in Figure 3.4? It is possible to reconcile these contradictions by accepting the indigenous development of both writing systems within a broader pattern of evolution and communication between both regions. Thus the development of writing may have evolved independently in both areas as a result of the convergence of parallel evolution. Within Egypt and Mesopotamia the origin of the hieroglyph and cuneiform style of writing remains little known. If the system of writing was entirely distinctive in both areas, so too was its function. The earliest hieroglyphs dating from around 3100 B.C. record proper names

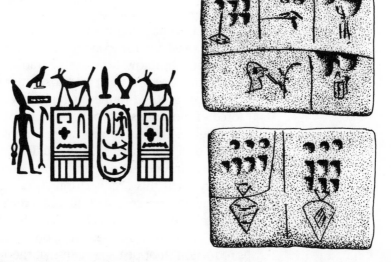

Figure 3.4   Early form of Egyptian hieroglyphics from Abydos, ca. 3000 B.C., and Mesopotamian pictographs and cuneiform from Uruk, ca. 3300 B.C. (Reproduced from *Handbuch der Vorgeschichte*, C. H. Beck Verlag. Courtesy of H. Müller-Karpe.)

and establish kinship relations and authority over property; the first tablets of Sumer are economic accounts. A third development took place at roughly the same time as the appearance of writing and political unification. This was the escalation of courtly burials, which in turn led to the building of the pyramids, the construction of temples, and the formation of local administrative and redistributive centers. The presence of a multitiered economy is clearly suggested in both the monumental architecture of the Early Dynastic Period of Mesopotamia and the written records of the Old Kingdom in Egypt.

Egypt built the first unified nation state system in history. It has been suggested that the "building" in itself—the construction of the remarkable pyramids—assisted in the formation and maintenance of the Egyptian state. According to Kurt Mendelssohn (1974), agricultural work was at a standstill in the villages during the annual three-month flood season. This period enabled the pharaoh to harness thousands of peasants to quarry, transport, and construct his pyramid. The grain that fed the workers was derived from the accumulated surpluses of the villagers. This in turn made the populations of the Nile more dependent on each other as well as on the state bureaucracy to redistribute food and organize labor. The construction of such huge monuments allowed the pharaoh to ascend to heaven, it was thought. Perhaps more significant, it allowed for the formation of a new structure of human organization—one in which state-directed labor could be deployed for the construction of state works.

We do not know how the pharaoh recruited the great labor forces that erected the pyramids. The Great Pyramid alone covers 13.1 acres and is 140 meters high: it would have required a labor force of thousands. Egyptian sources of later date do not inform us whether these laborers were volunteers or slaves, and in the absence of evidence, opinions differ.

The monumental pyramids were constructed for only about a century; then this architectural style was abandoned. But the construction process had already created an economic and political situation, claims Mendelssohn, that allowed subsequent rulers to control the peasant labor and surplus agricultural production. It appears certain that the building of pyramids was essential and pragmatic for organizing and institutionalizing the Egyptian state. Mendelssohn's argument centers on Egypt, but it may provide an explanation in other cultures. The presence of monumental architecture in almost every formative civilization—including the Maya, Sumer, and the Indus—is suggestive of a pattern in the development of the state and its control over the labor force.

THE EGYPTIAN STATE

The First Dynasty (ca. 2900 B.C.) saw further political change and, with it, the founding of a new political capital in the Nile delta: Merimde. Local factors—resource availability, subsistence strategies, and relationship to the centralized state—now began to influence the growth of towns, and this in turn resulted in a rank-size distribution of settlement.

Even in the process of urbanization, the state remained specifically Egyptian. The growth of populations and settlements accommodated sufficient local variation, but this did not lead to the fragmentation of the state (except for a brief period at the end of the third millennium) throughout the three thousand years of its existence. In this respect, Egypt is almost alone in not having shared the most common form of organization in the ancient world, whether Mesopotamian or Mayan—that of the *city-state* in which an extensive territory is divided into a host of neighboring cities, autonomous or semiautonomous, governing their agricultural hinterlands. In contrast, the Egyptian state remained unified under a single pharaoh.

The pharaoh ruled the whole countryside with his massive bureaucracy. The state was divided into specifically defined geographical entities called *nomes*, not unlike the manorial estates of medieval Europe which were ruled by the nobility under the charge of the king. These nomes were administered by the pharaoh's governors, but they remained firmly under the pharaoh's rule. The Egyptian state collected taxes, enlisted ranks for the army (which at times reached 20,000 men), maintained scribes to keep state records, and employed hundreds of craftsmen to embellish the royal palaces, ornament the royal persons, and prepare the pharaoh's tomb. The thousands of state-controlled workers were provided daily rations of food and work. By the middle of the third millennium, Egypt (far less

Sumer) became dependent on slave labor for the construction of public works and for domestic service. In fact, it is difficult to find any exception to the rule that slaves were a fundamental presence in the labor force of all early civilizations.

The Egyptian state differed in many ways from the Sumerian city-state and from that of the Indus civilization. Pharaohs were divine gods who ruled without the constraints of written law; in Sumer the mortal kings ruled by divine right and were guided by codified laws. Since matrilineal inheritance was the rule, women of the pharaoh's family enjoyed great power. Both the eldest son of the pharaoh and his eldest daughter, whose dowry was the kingdom, were the royal heirs—an arrangement that required the eldest brother and sister to marry in order to perpetuate their divine though incestuous rule.

The achievements of Pharaonic Egypt, technological and cultural, were directly inspired by the centralized state. The appointed officials, members of the priesthood, and nobility acted as patrons in sponsoring the production of works of art in metal and stone as well as the construction of large administrative and religious structures.

Such state-inspired production resulted in a uniformity of architectural and artifactual styles. The majority of specialized craftsmen were employed for the production of materials to aggrandize the person involved in running the state. Their products of metal, stone, and wood represent a masterful control over these resources, many of which had to be imported from distant areas. State expeditions were organized to procure these materials.

The pharaoh of Egypt ruled over distant lands blessed with abundant resources. From Nubia and Arabia came gold; from the Sinai came copper and turquoise; from the deserts and mountains closer to the Nile Valley came a wealth of minerals. But the basic stability of Pharaonic Egypt, which far exceeded that of the rest of the Near Eastern kingdoms, came from something more important than its riches. With the support of an efficient staff of hereditary officials who controlled state affairs by the weight of both tradition and precedent, the pharaoh's reign was to continue effectively for three thousand years. In Sumer in the Mesopotamian lowlands, there was no parallel to the uniformity nor the longevity of the Egyptian kingdom.

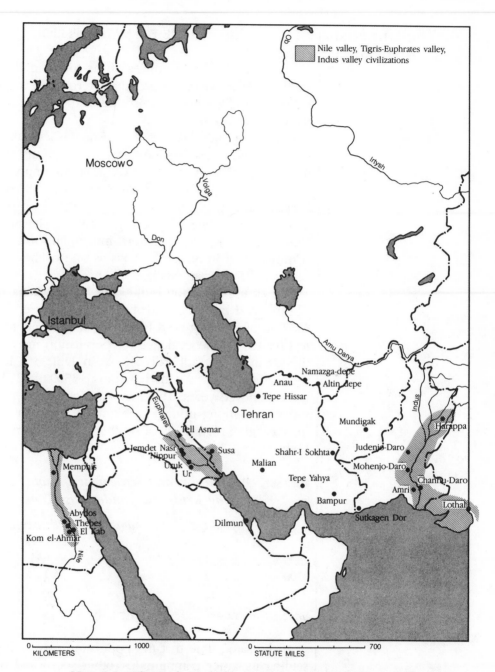

Map 3.2 The early civilizations: Mesopotamia, Egypt, and the Indus Valley. (Redrawn from David and Ruth Whitehouse, *Archaeological Atlas of the World.* 1975. London: Thames and Hudson Ltd. © 1975 Thames and Hudson Ltd.)

The Sumerian Civilization

THE FORMATIVE PERIOD

As in Egypt, the last centuries of the fourth millennium B.C. in southern Mesopotamia were characterized by a quickening of cultural development, culminating in the clear definition of the Sumerian civilization.

One of the key features that distinguished this period from earlier Ubaid times was the development of urban centers. The period resulting from the new conditions imposed by an urban state is referred to as the *Uruk Period* (ca. 3500–3100 B.C.). It takes its names from the site of Uruk, which remains the most important and extensively excavated site in southern Mesopotamia. In the later third millennium this city is acknowledged in Sumerian texts as one of the five principal centers of Sumerian civilization.

The clear population buildup in Mesopotamia has been well documented by Robert Adams and Hans Nissen.[7] Following his division of a three-tiered hierarchy of settlement (outlined earlier in Chapter 2), the evidence for population increase and urban development is graphically shown in Table 3.1. It is obvious that the population greatly increased from 3500 to 3200 B.C., a period of three hundred years. This may have been due to an increasing sedentism among nomads, emigration from rural to the increasingly urban areas of southern Mesopotamia, or, most likely, both.

TABLE 3.1   *Population and Settlement Growth during Uruk and Jemdet Nasr Times*

Era	Villages	Towns	Small urban centers	Cities
3500 B.C.	17	3	1(?)	0
3200 B.C.	112	10	1	0
2900 B.C.	124	20	20	1

Source: From Adams and Nissen (1972:18).

At the same time that the population was multiplying and settling in larger communities, other social and technological changes were taking place. These had the cumulative effect of changing the essentially rural Ubaid society into a more unified culture in which we can recognize the roots of the Sumerian civilization: Childe's "urban revolution" was slowly evolving.

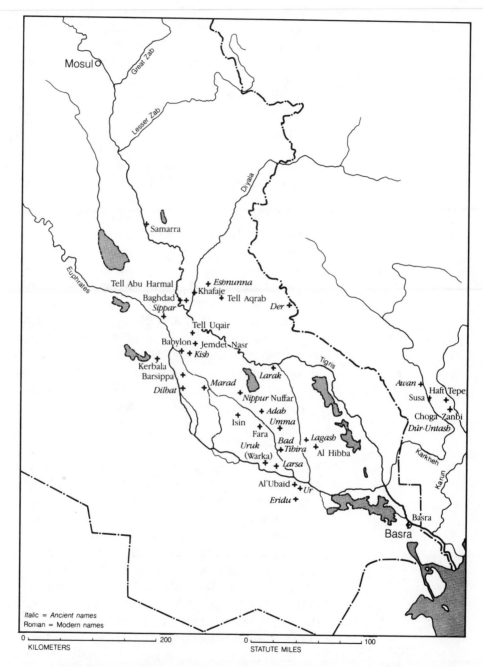

Map 3.3 The principal sites of Sumer and Elam. (Redrawn from David and Ruth Whitehouse, *Archaeological Atlas of the World*. 1975. London: Thames and Hudson Ltd. © 1975 Thames and Hudson Ltd.)

Changes were broad-based. As in Egypt, they included the appearance of writing and the development of a monumental architectural style, here most impressively expressed in the temples.

Other changes were the growing differentiation of social rank as well as job specialization. People involved with production and administration were concentrated in the temple area: priests of various rank, artisans, and shopkeepers. Moreover, political and religious power gradually became the organizing force of society. Kinship ties, which had previously dictated the patterns of tribal leadership and unity, slowly broke down. The laws, rights, and privileges inherent in any kinship system were eventually replaced by the laws of nontribal, state-ordered administrative systems.

The urban revolution—the transformation from village to city—was not as rapid as many writers would have us believe. It was not the revolutionary act of spontaneous generation which V. G. Childe's concept and phrase imply.[8] The revolution was centuries in the making. Out of it came a more sophisticated metallurgical technology, complex irrigation techniques, and major architectural innovations. With the concomitant population increase, these archaeologically visible changes attest to the institutional transformation of the social order.

Explaining the Urban Revolution

What caused the transformation that took place in southern Mesopotamia at the close of the fourth millennium? Many explanations have been offered.

A minority of scholars have theorized that changes in southern Mesopotamia, as in Egypt, were so rapid that the invisible hand of an invading culture must have been responsible. Too many developments took place at once: the move from villages to cities; the appearance of new forms of pottery; the development of the cylinder seal as an instrument of proprietary ownership; and the invention of writing in about 3200 B.C.

But as in explanations of the Egyptian urban formation, here too it is far too easy (and wholly inadequate) to presume major social change to be the result of foreign invasions. In fact, close examination reveals evidence for direct continuity in social organization: there was no real break in architectural or technological traditions from the earliest Ubaid times.

Another explanation centers on the role irrigation played in the development of complex societies. This theory has been a subject of great debate. In his *Oriental Despotism* (1957), Karl Wittfogel argued that the development of irrigation technology implies the presence of a strong coordinating authority to provide the necessary labor for the building and care of the canals. Basing his argument on evidence for the rise of civilization in Asia, Wittfogel further claimed that the presence of the completed irrigation system also worked toward maintaining differentiation, for it led to the concentration of power and wealth in the hands of the few who controlled the overall development of water rights in the entire agricultural system. According to Wittfogel's explanation, Mesopotamia's irrigation system was the key to the development of its urban civilization.

Wittfogel's theory has met with criticism. Robert Adams has shown that complex political and economic institutions had existed in Mesopotamia prior to the presence of complex irrigation networks.[9] It seems reasonable that irrigation was one of several factors which brought about the Sumerian city-state, though not necessarily the prime mover.

Plate 3.1 Typical Near Eastern archaeological mound built up of accumulated cultural debris. The date of this mound, Tepe Yahya, is 5000 B.C. at its base and 500 A.D. at the top. (Peabody Museum, Harvard University.)

Another explanation for the rise of civilization lies in the interaction between the villagers and nomads of the Meso-potamian region. If not a sole cause, this interaction must certainly have acted as a catalyst in the formation of the state.

The desert environment, rivers, and canals isolated the settled communities of southern Mesopotamia from the northern highland nomads. As we saw in Chapter 2, the relationship between nomads and farmers must have provided an important cultural motif in Mesopotamia from Neolithic times. There is little direct evidence of the interrelations between these distinctive subsistence patterns. If we project from textual sources written several hundred years later, it is apparent that relations between the nomadic and sedentary communities were built upon suspicion, if not open hostility. This relationship, described in Sumerian texts five thousand years ago, continued until recent times.

Yet despite hostility, the mobility of the nomads plus their pastoral livelihood must have made them indispensable to the villagers for communication, trade, and livestock production, particularly of sheep and goats. The nomads controlled valuable information. Their migratory movements led them to a knowledge of available resource zones and an awareness of political developments in different areas. These movements enabled them, moreover, to act as intermediaries in the exchange of materials and ideas between settled peoples in the highlands and Mesopotamia. The importance of the nomadic element in the formation of Mesopotamian civilization is one aspect in which the process of urbanization in the Near East differs fundamentally from that of the New World, where nomadism was absent.

The factors which brought about the urban form in Egypt, the Indus or China, Mesopotamia, and Mesoamerica—whether irrigation, trade, population increase, or warfare—remain subjects of continuing debate. All these factors have been suggested, and it is likely that all were involved in differing degrees, depending on specific circumstances and conditions in each area. While we have no clear answer as to "why" urbanization took place, we do have growing evidence of the chronology of cultural developments and the important factors involved. The clearest picture to emerge in the Old World for what some authors regard as the first civilization comes from southern Mesopotamia. The first stage in that development is most clearly documented on the site of Uruk and other communities of the same period.

The Uruk City-State: A Profile

The archaeological ruins of Uruk (the Biblical city of Erech) are among the most impressive in the Sumerian world. The site lies halfway between Baghdad and Basrah, in present-day Iraq, in a desert environment irrigated by canals from branches of the Euphrates River. German archaeologists have been digging at Uruk since 1928; it is through their excavations that the best picture of a Sumerian city emerges.

Uruk was first settled around 4200 B.C. by the Ubaid people, and at the lower levels it seems to be a characteristically Ubaid site. But beginning around 3500 B.C., there is evidence of major changes which some archaeologists believe were characteristic of a new culture and others believe represented an indigenous evolution of the "Ubaidians." In either case, and the latter seems more convincing, the changes are all documented at Uruk as well as at other sites.

It was during the Uruk Period that the basic expression of Sumerian society was formulated. This is most evident in three main developments seen at Uruk: the construction of monumental temples, the masterful production of cylinder seals, and the evolution of cuneiform writing.

Many temples were built in Uruk itself, and they are reminiscent of those of the Ubaid period at Eridu (see Chapter 2). The similarity of buttressed façades and a long central room surrounded by small rooms testifies to the persistence of both architectural traditions and belief systems. The city of Uruk, like all Sumerian cities, was dedicated to a specific deity. Uruk was dedicated to the two great Sumerian gods Anu (the sky god) and E-Anna (Ishtar in Babylonian texts), the goddess of love.

The magnificent architecture of the many temples at Uruk tends to overshadow other forms of art. A number of Uruk Period temples have been excavated, including six temples dedicated to the goddess E-Anna and the remarkable Limestone Temple. The Limestone Temple measured 86 by 33 meters and was constructed of ashlar (dressed stone) masonry rather than the more usual mudbrick. The walls of the courtyard, as well as the columns and the platform on which the columns rested, were decorated by

Plate 3.2   Aerial view of the city state of Uruk depicting areas of excavation. (Courtesy of Georg Gerster.)

mosaic arrangements framed by flat ends of terra-cotta cones painted in black, red, or white and stuck into the mud plaster of the walls.

All the temples built in Sumerian cities were constructed over low brick platforms, as were those of Ubaid date, and were rebuilt over the same site. With the passing of time and the repeated rebuilding of new temples on top of older ones, the height of the temples eventually exceeded all other buildings in the city. Here, in all probability, is the origin of the Mesopotamian *ziggurat,* the stepped tower topped by a shrine, so typical of each of the Sumerian cities. The evolution of the temple complex is well illustrated by the Anu Temple in Uruk. Six temples were constructed, one above the other. By 3000 B.C., after five hundred years of rebuilding, a monumental brick platform rose 16 meters above the community. The sanctuary known as the White Temple was constructed on this platform.

The Sumerians built monumental temples not just in Uruk, but in each of the four other principal cities—Nippur, Kish, Eridu, and Ur. At the same time, smaller communities to the north were building smaller temples such as the one at Tepe Gawra in Syria. All these temples were built with an enormous expenditure of organized, communal labor. They served not only as centers of worship but also as storerooms for surplus agricultural produce and administrative centers for the redistribution of temple goods. The hundreds of temple laborers and craftsmen (who formed a distinctive class within the tightly stratified society) were supported by agricultural surplus. While this surplus must have come from agricultural communities outside the urban center, there is little evidence to suggest that during Uruk times political (temple) authority and centralization extended beyond the villages immediately adjacent to the cities.

The Uruk temples had clear precursors in the temples of the Ubaid culture. Another basic Sumerian element to emerge during the Uruk Period—this one seemingly for the first time—was the cylinder seal. The seal impressions of the Uruk Period are miniature masterpieces. They were small cylinders made of ordinary or semiprecious stone, like lapis lazuli, ranging from 2.5 to 7.5 centimeters in length and varying in thickness from that of a thumb to that of a pencil. The cylinders were pierced lengthwise so they could be hung around the neck or waist. Designs were engraved on their surface, so that when the cylinder was rolled over wet clay, the scene could be repeated ad infinitum. The seals were masterfully carved and depicted scenes of daily life or mythological subjects performing ceremonies of unknown significance.

From its beginning in about 3500 B.C., the art of cylinder seal manufacture had an unbroken tradition in Mesopotamia for almost four thousand years. While a great artistic tradition, the elaboration of seals did not represent the creation of an art form as an end in itself. The function of the seal varied somewhat over this long period of time, but its primary purpose was to indicate ownership, and this remained unchanged. If one wanted to lock or secure a room, one had simply to roll a seal over the soft clay. If that seal were tampered with or broken, it would be immediately recognized. Similarly, merchandise could be transported in vessels or wrapped in reed bundles, tied securely, and sealed to prevent theft or interference en route to its destination.

Beyond the aesthetic quality and distinctive function the seals must have served for the Sumerians, they tell us a number of things about the Uruk culture. They indicate the existence of private property, extensive commercial trade between communities, and the specialization of labor.

The artistic sense of the Uruk was evident not only in their temples and cylinder seals but also in the lavish appointments of their public buildings and in their sculpture, carved stone vases, and jewelry. Aesthetic advances were not universal, though. Compared to the earlier handmade painted ceramics of the Ubaid culture the Uruk pottery comes off second best. Some Uruk shapes, believed to be copies of metal forms, are elegant and simple, but the majority of the wares are undecorated and singularly common. Perhaps the greater availability of bronze and a technological mastery of alloying and casting vessels, tools, and jewelry, as well as the use of the potter's wheel, which enabled mass production, were responsible for the decadence of ceramic art during this period.

The evolution of the great temples and the appearance of the cylinder seal are clearly significant developments of the Uruk culture. A third development, though, might even be described as epoch-making, for it set the Uruk Period apart from all others which preceded it. This invention, one of the greatest in human history, is often taken as the single criterion which separated the stage of barbarism from that of civilization. It was the invention of writing.

Like the Neolithic Revolution and the Urban Revolution, writing must be placed in its proper perspective. It was not a revolutionary invention born of a single person's genius. Symbolic motifs were used to communicate shared ideas even in Paleolithic times. It was suggested recently that the ever present ceramic cones, balls, and cubes found in Neolithic villages were

Plate 3.3 Two impressions of characteristic Akkadian cylinder seals, (ca. 2300 B.C.). Both seals portray a procession of deities presenting gifts to a seated god (lower register) and to a god holding a knife (upper register). In both, one of the deities holds a sacrificial animal while the cylinder sealing in the lower register contains an inscription before the deity holding the knife. (Courtesy of Edith Porada, Pierpoint Morgan Library.)

mathematical counters.[10] Once dismissed as gaming pieces, it is now argued that they represent a notational system which formed the basis for the development of writing.

Writing appears for the first time in the archaic temples of E-Anna at Uruk toward the end of the fourth millennium. Undertaken by professional scribes, the writing consisted of incised pictographs. The scribe took a lump of fine clay, shaped it into a smooth cushion a few inches square, and with the end of a reed stalk etched the pictographs on the tablet as illustrated in Figure 3.5. The tablet was then made virtually indestructible either by oven-baking or by slow drying in the sun.

Over the course of the next five hundred years, the technique of writing continued to develop, changing constantly. By the mid-third millennium the evolution was complete and true *cuneiform* writing (from Latin *cuneus:* wedge, nail) appeared. The principle of writing was quite simple: one object or idea equaled one sound which in turn equaled one sign. Because some of the signs incised on the tablets were positioned in a sequence known only to the scribe, and because some signs used in the earliest period were abandoned with their phonetic values unknown, linguists are unable to read many of the

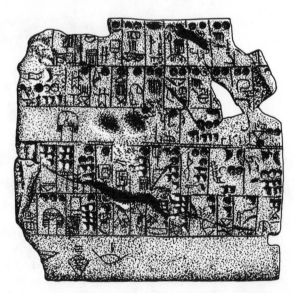

Figure 3.5 Early tablet from Uruk, ca. 3200 B.C. (Reproduced from *Handbuch der Vorgeschichte,* C. H. Beck Verlag. Courtesy of H. Müller-Karpe.)

earliest texts. Although we cannot read these texts, we can recognize what they are about. All have the characteristics of economic accounts; they are lists of workers, goods, receipts, transactions, or deeds of ownership. They do not inform us of historical events. It is a chastening, if not disappointing, thought that the invention of writing had little to do with poetry, epics, legends, history, or what we would call "literature." Its invention was strictly for administrative purposes.

While changes in the script through time complicate efforts to decipher old texts, they do assist in another way, by enabling the paleographer to date a text as accurately as archaeologists can date a piece of ceramic. The earliest texts in our possession were written in Sumerian. The Sumerian language belongs to its own family and is not related to Semitic, Indo-Aryan, or any other modern language. It is, like its civilization, extinct.

Until the close of the Uruk Period, the developments in Mesopotamia indicate higher levels of achievement than those in Egypt, the Iranian Plateau, and the Indus Valley. In the subsequent Jemdet Nasr Period (ca. 3100–2900 B.C.), the archaeological evidence suggests for the first time a period of internationalism: increasing cultural contact bringing together Egypt, Mesopotamia, and points east.

THE PROTOLITERATE PERIOD

The material culture that existed in southern Mesopotamia during the Protoliterate Period (literally, the start of writing) is named Jemdet Nasr, after the village site between Baghdad and Babylon where distinctive painted pottery from this period was first excavated. The Jemdet Nasr Period existed from about 3100 to 2900 B.C. and did not differ fundamentally from the Uruk. Religious and secular themes depicted on cylinder seals were identical; the monumental architecture retained its earlier function and interior decor; and the bulk of ceramics continued the traditions established in Uruk times. Only the painted ceramic motifs showed the new influence of contact with Iran, and this distinguished the pottery from the Uruk style. In terms of cultural achievement, the Jemdet Nasr Period was marked not by innovations but by progressive developments in the techniques of metallurgy, art, writing, and bureaucracy—all readily identifiable characteristics of a mature civilization, and undeniably Sumerian.

In terms of population growth and distribution, too, the Protoliterate Period was marked by a continuation (if speeded up) of trends already identifiable in the Uruk. As we saw in Table 3-1, towns and villages almost doubled in both number and size within a short three hundred years. Whether this population increase resulted from the rapid sedentism of nomads, the immigration of peoples into Sumer, an increased birthrate, or a combination of these factors remains an unresolved question.

In one area, though, the Protoliterate Period represents a marked change from previous Uruk times. That is the beginning of an age of "internationalism," with the development of another third-millennium civilization that not only rivaled the Sumerian culture in achievements but was also in close contact with it. This civilization, known as the Elamite, was centered in southwestern Iran where its capital city Susa has been the scene of French-directed excavations for decades.

It is evident that trade between the two civilizations was widespread, for Jemdet Nasr–related ceramics and seals have been found at Tepe Yahya on the Iranian Plateau—over a thousand miles east of Uruk. Of even greater significance, though, is the presence of written tablets on numerous sites of the Iranian Plateau in a language distinctive from the Sumerian. These tablets, first discovered in Susa and dating from 3200 B.C., are referred to as *Proto-Elamite* (see Figure 3.6), in the belief that they were written by the precursors of the Elamite civilization. The Elamite language, like its Sumerian contemporary, is extinct,

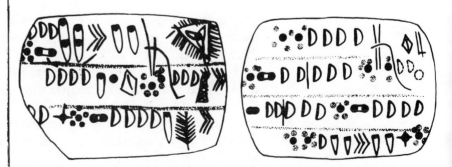

Figure 3.6 Both sides of an inscribed tablet with Proto-Elamite writing from Tepe Yahya, ca. 3200 B.C. (2½ inches in length).

and it is unrelated to Sumerian or any modern language family.*
We can digress briefly to look at the cultural developments on the
Iranian Plateau that paralleled those in Sumer around the close
of the fourth millennium.

Sumer and the Proto-Elamite Culture

Proto-Elamite tablets recently have been found on sites in virtually
every corner of the Iranian Plateau: Yahya, Sialk, Shahr-i
Sokhta, and Hissar. Their range may have extended even further.
Soviet archaeologists have proposed, quite credibly, that signs
painted on figurines and fragmentary "tablets" found on sites in
Turkmenistan were derived from the Proto-Elamite signary.[11]

These distantly separated sites not only shared a written
language; they also used similar ceramics, cylinder seals, and
architecture. What are we to make of this distinctive Proto-Elamite
culture scattered over the Iranian Plateau, and what was its
relationship to the Sumerian civilization? How widely diffused
was this culture? What relationship did it have to the
development of the Indus civilization to the east? These questions
have absorbed the interest of many archaeologists in the past
decade.

There is little evidence to support the existence of a centralized,
coordinating authority on the Iranian Plateau prior to 3200 B.C.
The picture changes dramatically in Jemdet Nasr times, however,
with the emergence of a centralized Proto-Elamite state (ca.
3200–2900 B.C.). Arising in southwestern Iran, it developed only a
few centuries after the consolidation of the Sumerian state in
Mesopotamia. Within a short time, the Proto-Elamite state had
imposed its authority over distinctive cultures on such distant sites
as Tepe Yahya in southeastern Iran.

Explanations for the causes of this phenomenon vary. Perhaps
population increases in southwestern Iran, like those in Sumer, led
to the search for new resources and productive land. Perhaps
increasing competition between the Sumerians and Proto-

---

*In recent years, some have suggested that Elamite and Dravidian (the
language spoken in southern India today and in the regions of
Pakistan and northwest India in antiquity) may have stemmed from a
common Elamo-Dravidian ancestor. See McAlpin (1974).

Elamites for resources, populations, and markets brought about this eastward expansion. What is clear from the archaeological evidence is that by 3000 B.C. the extent of interaction within the Near Eastern world was far greater than ever before. There was interaction between Proto-Elamite and Sumerian communities, as attested in the similarities between cylinder seals and ceramics. There is also evidence of relations between the Proto-Elamites and cultures to the north (Soviet Turkmenistan), the south (on the Arabian peninsula), and the east (Baluchistan), as seen in the similarities of many aspects of material culture.

Settlement patterns around Proto-Elamite centers are poorly understood. Only in southwestern Iran does it appear there was a hierarchical arrangement of cities (Susa and Malyan were the major centers), towns, and smaller villages comparable to Sumer. The settlement pattern around the "colonies," those communities over which the Proto-Elamites extended their hegemony, has not been examined in detail. Tepe Yahya is the only Proto-Elamite colony, whose administrative complex is illustrated in Figure 3.7, where settlement surveys have been undertaken.[12] Settlements of earlier and later date at Yahya are larger in number and totally different from those during the Proto-Elamite settlement. This is entirely in keeping with what we would expect in a temporary situation of foreign colonization.

Speculations on the political and social structure of the Proto-Elamite state as compared to that of Sumer are of special interest, though admittedly conjectural. In each of the Proto-Elamite colonies, as well as in the major urban centers of southwestern Iran, excavations reveal a similar though limited inventory of material remains. Each community has an imposing "administrative building": a single, large structure containing cylinder seals, specialized ceramic forms, and tablets. The cylinder seals attest to the existence of long-distance trade. Cylinder seal impressions in clay found at Yahya are nearly identical to those of Susa some 500 miles away, providing tangible evidence not only for communication but also for exchange of sealed goods. More significant still, specialized ceramic forms such as beveled-rim bowls are identical to those of both Susa and Sumerian cities. It has been argued, still inconclusively, that this specialized ceramic form may have represented a standardized unit of volume, a ration bowl, or perhaps a votive offering bowl.

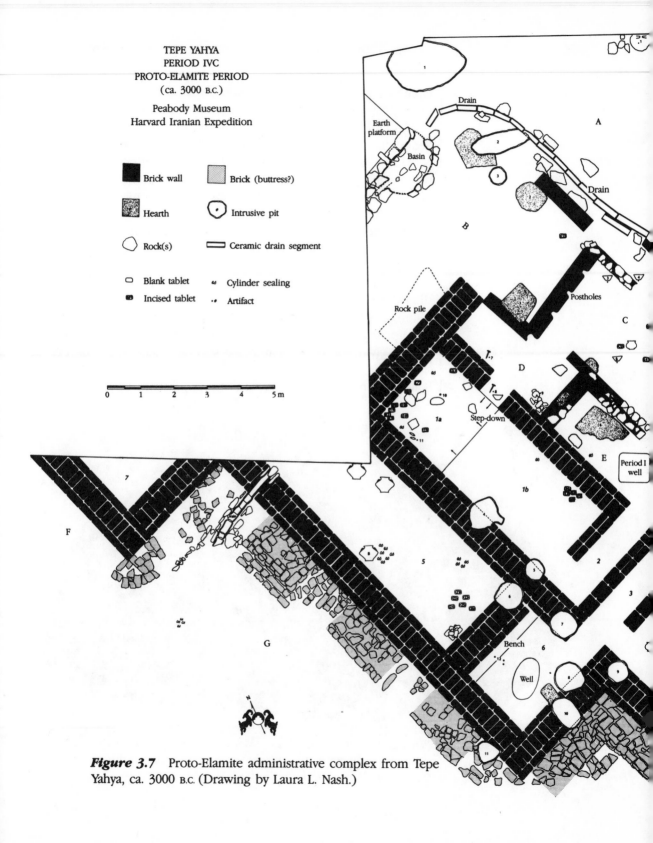

Figure 3.7 Proto-Elamite administrative complex from Tepe Yahya, ca. 3000 B.C. (Drawing by Laura L. Nash.)

Whatever its use, its identical nature on Sumerian and Proto-Elamite sites supports a common function.

The tablets found on Proto-Elamite sites are difficult to decipher, as are those of the earliest Sumerian communities. What is evident is that their function was exclusively economic, representing receipts of goods received, exported, produced, or consumed. Professor Meriggi, the foremost authority on Proto-Elamite tablets, has studied the corpus from Yahya. One tablet (dated from 3100 B.C.) may be selected to characterize this group. The inscription on one side of the tablet records the delivery of a specific ration of bread to a specified number of female slaves; the other side records a larger ration of bread for a single female foreman.[13]

Tablets like this, found in both Sumerian and Proto-Elamite sites, provide a glimpse into the social order of these earliest literate civilizations. They indicate several things: the presence of slavery, the existence of private property, as documented on the Blau Monument in Plate 3.4, and the importance of a centralized

Plate 3.4 The so-called Blau Monument, Sumerian, ca. 3400 B.C. It is shale and is believed to be a document pertaining to the sale and ownership of land. (width 6¼ in.). (Hirmer Fotoarchiv.)

authority in the distribution and control of production. The tablets of the Sumerian and Proto-Elamite communities are identical in suggesting that a centralized state authority organized through the temples controlled most of the production and allocated surplus resources. This form of economy, or mode of production, has been referred to as a *redistribution economy.* Its existence can be seen by 3000 B.C.; its classic Sumerian formulation, which is by the third millennium supported by ample textual documentation, will be discussed later.

Sumerian-Egyptian Relations

A picture is beginning to emerge of the interaction between the Sumerians of Mesopotamia and the highland Proto-Elamites of the Iranian Plateau; it is far more difficult to understand Egyptian-Sumerian relations. What were the geographical routes and cultural circumstances which led Egypt into direct contact with Sumer, and how extensive was that contact? There is little evidence around 3000 B.C. on the archaeological sites of the Syro-Palestinian Levant for Egyptian-Sumerian relations. It has been suggested, however, that such contact may have been by boat around Arabia or across the archaeologically unexplored routes of the Arabian desert. What is incontestable, despite the minimal evidence, is that relations did exist.

Typical Mesopotamian cylinder seals have been discovered in the Egyptian predynastic graves of Naqada (ca. 3100 B.C.) in southern Egypt. Several of these cylinder seals are of lapis lazuli, the precious "diamond" of the ancient Near East. There are no deposits of lapis lazuli in Africa, Europe, or the Near East. The closest source to the Egyptian and Mesopotamian civilizations is located in the high Pamir Mountains of Afghanistan (where 95% of the world's supply of lapis is still mined). It has long been recognized that the lapis of Protoliterate Mesopotamia came from Afghanistan, further evidence of the wide-reaching exchange networks within the ancient Near East.

The Mesopotamian-derived lapis lazuli cylinder seals in Egypt are not alone in signifying interaction with Sumer. Favored motifs such as hunting scenes, lions devouring beasts with intertwined necks, and heroes holding off lions were copied on plaques by Egyptian lapidaries from Mesopotamian prototypes. Interestingly, this evidence of contact, like the lapis cylinder seals, seems to belie more than single dimensionality in early international relations. Henri Frankfort, the distinguished Near Eastern archaeologist, suggested thirty years ago that these motifs indicate Elamite rather than Sumerian influence: He found their closest parallels at the site of Susa.[14] His thoughtful suggestion remains unresolved but more provocative in light of the recently understood expansion of the Proto-Elamites. Frankfort was first to note another sign of Sumerian-Egyptian relations. The Royal Tombs of the First-Dynasty Egyptian pharaohs use recessed façades in a manner nearly identical to their earlier counterparts on Mesopotamian temples. Still further evidence for contact between the two cultures is more inferential. The formation of state polity in Sumer and Elam, for instance, was only a few generations earlier than the unification of Egypt under a single pharaoh.

Mesopotamian influence on Egypt is clear, yet there is virtually no evidence for Egyptian influence in the city-states of Mesopotamia. Only at Tell Arad, in Israel, are there a number of vessels with Egyptian hieroglyphs—one including the name of Narmer, the victorious pharaoh who unified Upper and Lower Egypt and established the first dynastic reign. Beyond this, plus a few ceramic parallels, the archaeological record is silent. It comes as a surprise that contact between the two great centers of early civilization from 3000 B.C. to Roman times was so slight and so superficial, even though each was always aware of the other's presence. Unfortunately this situation has never been the subject of serious study.

The Mesopotamian Center

While the Sumerian state's influence was felt as far as a thousand miles to the east and across the Red Sea to Egypt, the hills of northern Mesopotamia and the north Syrian plain remained largely impervious to developments in the south during the early period of civilization. Only faint traces of Sumerian presence can be detected on north Mesopotamian sites. At Tell Brak in northern Iraq, Sir Max Mallowan recovered a typical Protoliterate temple built over a platform, the so-called Eye Temple, named after the numerous small, stylized human idols engraved with outsized eyes.[15] Such a settlement, together with the more recently excavated site of Habuba Kabira in northern Syria where early tablets have been found, may represent a colony of detached Sumerians in the north, as Yahya represents a Proto-Elamite colony.

More typical is the situation at Tepe´ Gawra, where throughout the Uruk and Protoliterate Periods there is no evidence of writing, pottery was handmade, stamp seals of unknown function continue in the absence of cylinder seals, and metal objects remain rare.

The gap between north and south that existed at the end of the fourth millennium was never entirely bridged. In fact, the whole of the Sumerian Early Dynastic Period (2900–2371 B.C.) would elapse in the south before the first written documents appeared in the north. Sumerian references to their northern neighbors describe them as not only foreign but culturally inferior.

The Protoliterate Period in the south serves as an introduction to Sumerian civilization, representing the formation of a literate, complex society. It is no easy task to capture what Spengler referred to as the "spirit" of a past civilization. In the following pages, we attempt merely a sketch of the economic, political, and social history of that chronologically distant and culturally foreign cosmos. It is to the legacy of Sumer that we owe one of the most precarious of human inventions: the formation of the city, organized not by kinship ties but by formal rules of law and state administration.

THE DYNASTIC TRADITION

One of the most important distinctions between the early civilizations of the New World and Old World is the presence of thousands of tablets in the Near East that are absent in the western hemisphere. They inform us of religious and economic attitudes, place before us the historical personages that ruled the city-states, and reveal foreign relations and productive technologies.

The history of Mesopotamia, like its prehistory, is divided into different periods. Unlike prehistory, however, where changes in the material culture are often believed to signify changes in culture itself, the periods after 3000 B.C. are understood and dictated by the known textual record.

The Chronology from Historical Texts

The very earliest written history was far from modern standards, and the precise order of events in the third millennium remains vague. Radiocarbon dates are unreliable in the Near East for constructing a chronology, and, unfortunately for us, the Sumerians did not chronicle their own history in the early part of the third millennium. None of their early writings dealt with historical events, or even less with analyses of the how and why of their institutions. After several centuries of exclusively economic texts, there begin to appear (ca. 2600 B.C.) a small percentage (surely less than 10%) of administrative and religious texts from which one may extract aspects of political and military importance. The information contained on these tablets is confirmed and expanded upon by inscriptions on monuments and on stone and metal artifacts, proclaiming the names of kings who built the structure, the gods and goddesses to whom it was dedicated, and the priests who superintended it (see Plate 3.5).

The most useful of "historical" documents is the Sumerian King List. This text, recording the sequence of kings and the length of their reigns, begins with pure fable (recording, for instance, individual reigns which lasted thousands of years). The King List includes mention of the four famous rulers of Uruk who figure prominently in the later Sumerian epic tales—Enmerkar, Lugulbanda, Dumuzi, and Gilgamesh. Like the heroes of Homeric epics, they emerge as historic figures lionized by subsequent generations.

While a good bit of legend is mixed with its ancient history, the King List provides a reliable chronicle in its recording of more "recent" events. If we accept the dates of 2371–2316 B.C. for Sargon of Akkad's reign, we can work backward to at least 2900 B.C. with a reasonable accuracy of named Sumerian kings.

The Early Dynastic Period, following the Protoliterate, extends from about 2900 to 2371 B.C. and is divided into three subperiods.* Throughout this period, archaeologists have uncovered exceptional architecture, the Royal Tombs, technological achievements, and written records allowing a basic understanding of their social and political organization. We turn first to the textual evidence.

---

*I -ca. 2900–2750 B.C. (Early Dynastic I).
 II -ca. 2750–2600 B.C. (Early Dynastic II).
 III-ca. 2600–2371 B.C. (Early Dynastic III).

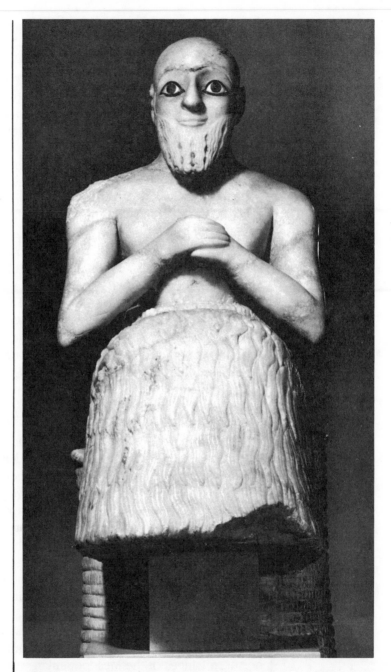

Plate 3.5 Seated alabaster statuette of Abikhil (identified by inscription placed on his back), superintendent of the temple at Mari, ca. 2800 to 2685 B.C. (height 20⅝ in.). (Hirmer Fotoarchiv.)

The Early Dynastic Period An analysis of the Sumerian King List indicates that throughout the Early Dynastic Period (2900–2371 B.C.) a number of independent city-states existed. In their continuous struggle for supremacy one of them would attempt to establish a tenuous hegemony that rarely lasted more than a short period. The King List records only the kings of those city-states which succeeded in controlling all of Sumer. We are informed that the cities of Kish, Uruk, Ur, and Lagash ruled over Sumer at different times, though only as *prima inter pares*. The text also documents the presence of the powerful foreigners who conquered Sumer at different times. During Early Dynastic II (ca. 2700 B.C.), for instance, the already familiar Elamite dynasty conquered Sumer for a short time.

At the very end of the Early Dynastic III period the king of Umma, Lugal-zagge-si, conquered Lagash and captured the rest of Sumer. If his own boastful inscriptions are to be believed, he even conquered lands beyond Sumer. His "empire," and with it Sumerian dominance in Mesopotamia, ended with his reign (2400–2371 B.C.) when the great Semitic king, Sargon of Agade (Akkad), conquered both south and north Mesopotamia. He proclaimed himself "King of the Four Quarters of the World, King of Sumer and Akkad," and he founded the first dynastic empire of the ancient Near East.

The Sargonid Period With the end of the Early Dynastic Period and the establishment of the Akkadian hegemony over Mesopotamia, our knowledge is on firmer ground. The Sargonid or Akkadian Period lasted just over 150 years, but it permanently altered the course of Mesopotamian history. There were five great kings of the Sargonid dynasty. The greatest of these were the founder, Sargon (2371–2316 B.C.), and his grandson, Naram-Sin (2291–2255 B.C.), fourth in the line of succession. These two rulers subdued all the Sumerian city-states, conquered northern Mesopotamia, and vanquished the Elamite dynasty at Susa.

Their own ascendancy was not so easy to maintain. The Akkadian dynasty was under continual attack, constantly threatened by internal revolt and nomadic raids from the northern fringes of the Mesopotamian world. It was one of these nomadic groups, the Guti from the northern Zagros Mountains, which finally brought down the Sargonid dynasty around 2200 B.C. The Guti's act of bringing the Akkadians to submission

Plate 3.6 Bronze head from Nineveh which is often identified as depicting Sargon the Great, ca. 2415 to 2290 B.C. (height 14⅜ in.). (Hirmer Fotoarchiv.)

continues to illustrate the major, and at times critical, role that the nomadic peoples played in the history of the ancient Near East. Despite its short life, the Sargonid dynasty had brought about political, economic, and cultural changes which had lasting impact on Mesopotamian society.

The recent excavations at Ebla in northern Syria shed new light on this period and underscore how little we know of northern Mesopotamia during Sargonid times. Prior to its destruction (before the establishment of the Sargonid dynasty there around 2300 B.C.), Ebla was the capital of an important independent kingdom in northern Syria. Excavations of the royal palace uncovered the royal archives, which included an administrative library of over fifteen thousand tablets dated to the Sargonid Period.[16] These texts are greater in number than the sum total of third-millennium texts discovered in Mesopotamia, and they shed light on many aspects of Sargonid economic, political, cultural, and literary traditions.

The majority of the tablets at Ebla are written, unexpectedly, in Sumerian. The texts from the royal archives, however, are written in Eblaite, a Semitic language previously unknown and having important analogies to Phoenician and Hebrew. The discovery of these texts pushes our evidence back a millennium for the existence of northwest Semitic dialects.

Reports of international trade in textiles and clothes constitute the most important part of the royal archives. Over fourteen thousand tablets are concerned with commercial, administrative, financial, lexical, historical, and literary information. Five hundred tablets deal specifically with agricultural productivity. Particularly interesting are abstracts of international treaties between Ebla and other Syrian, Mesopotamian, and Anatolian kingdoms. Complete translation of these royal archives will transform our understanding of the nature of international relations between disparate centers of power at the end of the third millennium.

The cause for, and the perpetuation of, the destruction of Ebla remain unclear. Excavations are continuing annually on this important site. It will be years before the textual sources are translated and understood. Archaeologists and philologists disagree as to the involvement of the Akkadians in the destruction of Ebla. The destruction of Ebla, though unrelated to the fall of the Akkadians some two centuries later, formed part of the social and political upheavals that characterized the end of the third millennium.

The Golden Age and Its Downfall   The arrival of the Guti and their conquest of the Akkadians around 2200 B.C. ushered in a period of anarchy. The Sumerian King List asks "Who was king? Who was not king?", recording twenty-one kings in a period of ninety-one years. The last of these kings was defeated by Utu-Legal, king of Uruk, in about 2120 B.C. In turn, Utu-Legal was overthrown by Ur-nammu, governor of Ur, who not only assumed the title "King of Ur" but constituted himself as "King of Sumer and Agade."

Ur-nammu founded the Third Dynasty of Ur which lasted just over a century (2113–2000 B.C.) and ushered in a Sumerian renaissance—a "Golden Age" which stands out as the most creative period in Mesopotamian history. It was during the reign of Ur-nammu that the most impressive temples—as that of the moon god, Nanna (see Plate 3.7)—and ziggurats were constructed and Sumerian literature reached its zenith. The earliest law code, preceding that of Hammurabi by three centuries, belongs to this period, too, as do many of the most memorable Sumerian myths and legends.

Plate 3.7   Ziggurat of the moon-god, Nanna, built by Ur-Nammu, King of Ur, ca. 2250 to 2233 B.C. (Hirmer Fotoarchiv.)

The Third Dynasty of Ur, the most creative centuries of the third millennium, was obliterated by Elamite invasions from the east and Amorite nomads from the west. For the next two hundred years, Mesopotamia floundered in a mosaic of small kingdoms dominated by the city-states of Isin and Larsa in Sumer and Assur and Eshnunna in the north. In the eighteenth century B.C., the political center of gravity shifted northward away from Isin and Larsa with the defeat of Rim-Sin, last of the kings of Larsa, by the great Babylonian King Hammurabi. Sumer met its final dissolution within a Babylonian kingdom.

Ironically, we owe much of our knowledge of the Sumerians to the Old Babylonian kingdom that conquered them, for the Babylonian literary tradition incorporated Sumerian traditions and preserved them throughout the dark ages of the later second

Plate 3.8 Aerial view of the city of Ur with the ziggurat of Nanna dominating the city. (Courtesy of Georg Gerster.)

and early first millennium. These traditions, revived again in the first millennium B.C. by Neo-Babylonian and Neo-Assyrian scribes, later formed important leitmotifs for the Biblical legends.

The Archaeological Evidence

The textual evidence has been fundamental to our understanding of the Sumerian world. Added to this important corpus is the invaluable information learned from extensive excavation.

Much of our information comes from "royal" tombs of the Early Dynastic Period. These contrast dramatically with private graves that have been excavated, providing abundant evidence of class distinctions and differential accumulation of wealth.

The tombs, like those of the earliest dynasty in Egypt, were subterranean chambers. In the "royal" tombs at Kish, where Sumerian legend tells us that kingship was bestowed as a gift of the gods, a form of ritual burial called *sati* appears which characterized the burials of the elite in both Sumer and Egypt. At the death of an important person, attendants (probably slaves) were immolated to accompany their master in the afterlife. Other evidence documents the belief in an afterlife. At Kish, corpses were interred with a chariot or a four-wheeled wagon (sometimes both) drawn by onager. Such vehicles, perhaps utilized as hearses, served as transport for commodities and as engines of warfare. They had solid wheels which turned on a fixed axle. Heavy and cumbersome as the vehicles were, they represented an expenditure which only the wealthy could afford.

The most dramatic expression of Early Dynastic funerary ritual came from the Royal Cemetery of Ur. Excavated in 1928, the cemetery of Ur contained over 1500 burials, of which less than twenty contained "royal" personages. These royal burials suggest a ritual and accumulation of wealth appropriate to the concept of kingship. The royal person was placed in a private chamber replete with the trappings of earthly power: objects of gold, jewelry of lapis lazuli, carnelian, and turquoise. As in Dynastic Egypt, there seems to have been little sex discrimination in burial honors accorded to noble personages. The excavation of Queen Shubad's (Puabi) tomb attests to the fact that ladies of the court were given the same gruesomely lavish attention as the males.

Burial chambers were erected at the bottoms of deep shafts. They were constructed of limestone blocks and baked bricks,

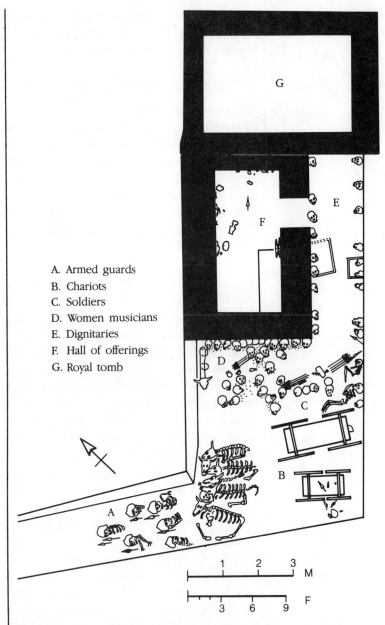

A. Armed guards
B. Chariots
C. Soldiers
D. Women musicians
E. Dignitaries
F. Hall of offerings
G. Royal tomb

Figure 3.8 Plan of the Royal Tomb of Queen Shubad (Puabi), with arrangement of sacrificed victim, ca. 2400 B.C.

Plate 3.9 Bust of a young woman wearing funerary ornaments. Reconstructed from finds in the Royal Cemetery of Ur, ca. 2685 B.C. (Hirmer Fotoarchiv.)

then embellished with timbering and lined with plaster. The roof vault, most typically a corbeled barrel vault, was supported in a few instances by a genuine keystone, illustrating a knowledge of the true arch millennia before its appearance in the classical world. Draft animals, drivers, soldiers, musicians, and female servants were obliged to follow their sovereign to the future world. Each individual was interred with the impedimenta of his craft or profession: soldiers were clad with armor, musicians carried their intruments, craftsmen were accompanied by the tools of their trade. In addition, they were provided items for their personal needs, such as ceramics which probably contained food.

The wagons which carried the royal Sumerians to the afterworld provide a parallel to the Egyptian boats which were buried with the Egyptian nobility. Though the agents of transportation were different in Egypt, the lavish ceremony which cost the lives of dozens of retainers indicates a common ideology. Despite the similarities in funerary ritual, there is, however, a fundamental difference between the pharaohs of Egypt and the Sumerian kings. The former were considered gods, directly responsible for the inundation of the Nile and its life-giving force. The Sumerian kings were merely nobles whose authority was a gift of the gods. Sumerian nobility derived the right to mortal rule from a pantheon of gods and goddesses.

In addition to the evidence provided by the tombs, excavations of the cities and towns have provided a wealth of information about Sumer. From the size of the sites, we can deduce an increase in population. By 2500 B.C., both Eridu and Uruk exceeded a thousand acres. The number of people living in cities may have been less a factor of increased birthrate than the redistribution of populations through the abandonment of previously inhabited sites such as Jemdet Nasr. Frankfort estimated that the imperial city of Ur would have housed 25,000 people. It is unlikely that any of the third-millennium cities ever exceeded 50,000 inhabitants.

In addition to the demographic information provided by the size of sites, their city plans tell us a good deal about the occupants' daily life. Increasing militarism throughout the third millennium is indicated by the attention given to fortification walls, which surrounded every major city. Within the city an inner wall set apart the temple-palace precinct from the inhabitants of the community. Man-made canals and land routes enabled villagers to bring their produce and manufactured goods safely to the markets of major cities.

With the advent of Sumerian kingship in the Early Dynastic Period, the political structure of the city-state was transformed from a *theocracy* (a government run by temple priests) to a *monarchy,* a government ruled by a king from his palace. This notion is confirmed by the archaeological record. A monumental building at Kish depicted in Figure 3.9, dated to 2800 B.C., was most assuredly the palace of an earthly ruler and not a temple. This palace had hundreds of rooms and was larger than Versailles. It contained the quarters of the king, his family, and his harem; there were industrial areas for craftsmen and scribes and offices for the administrators of the city-state.

Under the king's authority the centralized Sumerian city-state perfected a bureaucratic system which was responsible for the

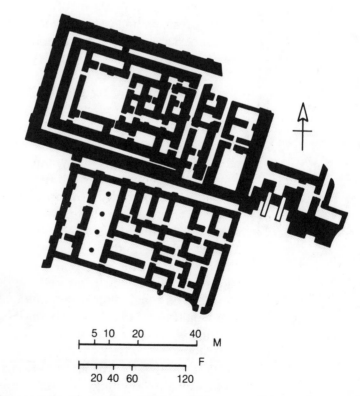

Figure 3.9 Plan of the palace at Kish—one of the earliest royal residences excavated in Sumer.

administration of the economy of Sumer. In order to comprehend Sumerian civilization, it is first necessary to understand the working of this unique system—the temple-palace redistribution system.

TEMPLE AND PALACE

The Sumerian state was fundamentally dependent on the productive force of its principal economic activity: agriculture. Successful agricultural production depended on the development of an irrigation technology, which in turn required a bureaucracy to administer the water rights for the network of canals and the management, distribution, and storage of surplus. A. Leo Oppenheim, the distinguished Assyriologist, has called this bureaucracy the "Great Organization"—the twin pillars (temple and palace) of Sumerian Early Dynastic society.[17]

The Mesopotamian temple-palace dominated the skyline of the Sumerian city. Its construction represented an enormous expenditure of human labor: it is estimated that 1500 laborers working a ten-hour day would have spent five years building one of the temple terraces at Uruk. It is difficult for us to comprehend what motivated citizens to cooperate in the building of monumental temples and palaces. The building of these monumental structures coincident with the beginnings of the state recalls the building of the pyramids in Egypt and Mendelssohn's conception that early state formation was involved with the formation of controlled corporate labor.

These temples were the physical homes of their deities, whom all citizens believed were the presiding spirits, the resident numina, that assured the successful result of human labors. An absolute faith in the omnipotent powers of their deities was surely one factor which inspired the construction of the temples.

All citizens, including slaves, belonged to a particular temple as one would to a household. They were referred to accordingly: at Uruk, we read of "the people of the god E-Anna." The temple community comprised a cross-section of the population: officials, priests, merchants, craftsmen, food-producers, slaves. It also assumed community responsibilities—for example, for the care of orphans, widows, the blind, and indigent citizens unable to care for themselves.

Plate 3.10 Gypsum statuette of a man holding a goblet from the Abu Temple at Eshnunna, ca. 2900 B.C. (height 19⅛ in.). (Hirmer Fotoarchiv.)

Beyond this, the temple also wielded a tremendous administrative responsibility. The activities of the temple coordinated the construction of irrigation canals that often involved the cooperation of several communities. Under the patronage of their deities, an enormous concentration of manpower was harnessed to produce the goods and surplus required by the growing city-state.

The increasing centralization of economic activity demanded the development of a complex recording system. The thousands of account tablets, presumably recording receipts and expenditures, reflect the temple's role as an administrative unit concerned with the management of surplus, collection of taxes, and the procurement of resources through the organization of long-distance trade. Indeed, the presence of professional scribes illustrates the high caliber of individuals maintained by the temple and/or palace. The Great Organization trained and supported craftsmen, and by the end of the Early Dynastic, they monopolized the production of all crafts, including metallurgy, textiles, cylinder seals, and ceramics.

Three specific factors converged in the rise of the temple-palace administrative complex. First was the irrigation system itself. In order to maximize agricultural production, water resources had to be managed. Successfully doing so assured a surplus; it also demanded a great deal of labor. Canals had to be dug far upstream to deliver water to distant fields, and after that, continuous maintenance was necessary to prevent the silting-up of the canals, which were often over 25 miles long. A second factor was the need for a voice whose authority surpassed all of the special-interest groups in the society. The temple-palace played a crucial role in mediating the relationships and disputes between farmers, herdsmen, fishermen, craft specialists, and the state. A third factor in the comparatively rapid growth of the Great Organization may have been the lack of natural resources in the alluvium. Meeting the ever increasing demand for resources was the responsibility of temple agents who acted not only as private merchants but as emissaries representing the city-state.

Using archaeological and textual evidence from the second half of the third millennium, we can summarize a number of simultaneous developments—both pressures and responses—that transformed the Great Organization into a city-state.[18]

First, the temple expanded in all its aspects, including enlargement of its buildings, diversification of activities, and growth of administrative duties and staff, throughout the Early Dynastic. The consolidation of agricultural territories fell increasingly under the control of the temple-palace bureaucracy, as did the training and recruitment of specialists in various crafts. A simultaneous development within the temple-palace complex was the increasing institutionalization of power in the hands of the ruling elite.

Second, there was an increasing differentiation of wealth and status, both within the temple-palace staff and its corps of retainers and between the outside world and the Great Organization. This differentiation may have resulted from an incipient shortage of arable land as population increased. The growth of the temple was possible only through social approval of differential access to the main productive resource: land. Without evidence for the use of force, we must assume that the distribution of wealth was socially sanctioned.

Third, there was an increasing specialization of labor, both within the temple-palace and in response to secular demand. With increasing differentiation of wealth and status, free citizens were more and more controlled by the society's powerful participants. As military crises became more frequent during the Early Dynastic Period, sovereignty of the assembly (the elected members of the nobility from different communities) might have passed de facto to the leaders without a sense of loss or even change.

Another key factor in the transformation of the temple-palace into a city-state was the growing development of a market economy. Differentially increased wealth within the community is based primarily on the evidence of an increasing number and value of objects held in the hands of different classes. We can safely link this trend with the concurrent expansion of the crafts. A supplementary mode of production in the form of a market became increasingly important.

The market created direct relations between craftsmen independent of the temple. Additionally, expansion of the crafts intensified social differences by providing alternatives to the agricultural means of production and new avenues to status and wealth. By increasing the community's dependence on scarce and expensive imports, it also created new tensions for supply and

Plate 3.11 Limestone statue of a worshipper in the Abu Temple at Eshnunna, ca. 2900 B.C. (height 11⅜ in.). (Hirmer Fotoarchiv.)

Plate 3.12 Limestone statuette of a praying woman from Khafaje, ca. 2900 B.C. (height 14½ in.). (Hirmer Fotoarchiv.)

demand. These tensions may have also created serious motivations for warfare: increasing militarism is well documented throughout the third millennium. This may well in turn be related to the development of crafts since militarism supported smiths, carpenters, and so forth by increasing the demand for weapons. Sanctions for war could therefore be found in the need for raw material.[19]

Analysis of late-third-millennium texts indicates the existence of privately owned lands, private production of crafts, and private merchant corporations not aligned with the temple organization. The division into royal or temple lands and privately owned community lands is analogous, in fact, to the division between the state sector versus the private sector in modern times.[20] In Sumer (and not unheard of in modern times), the state sector became increasingly inflated at the private sector's expense.

This aggrandizement of the nobility to the detriment of the rest of the population represents a fifth crucial development solidifying the city-state structure. It seems clear that the hereditary possessions of patriarchal families were increasingly purchased by the nobility and temple. Analysis of the deeds of sale indicates that the families were unable to compete with the increasingly larger estates of the nobility. When large tracts of land were sold, the approval of the entire family acting as witnesses (thus preventing their later protestation) and the approval of the entire assembly were required. Diakonoff views the early bureaucratic dealings of the assembly and extended families over land as the primary cell for the creation of the state.[21]

The Sumerian population consisted of four distinct social classes. First, the nobility (administrators, merchants, and priests) owned land privately and administered temple lands using client and slave labor on both types of land. Second were common members of the community, who worked plots of family-held lands. Third were well-to-do clients of the temples. This group consisted mostly of artisans who temporarily received small plots of temple lands in return for rations of wool, food, and the like. The fourth class consisted of slaves.

The lines of separation between the four classes were often far from clear. This resulted, in effect, in a two-tiered social hierarchy composed of the nobility on the one hand and everyone else on the other. The development of the Sumerian economy occurred through a cumulative increase in the powers and wealth of the nobility and the concomitant reduction of other classes to a client relationship. The need for credit evidenced in the later records gave rise to the rapid increase in usurious rates of interest which allowed only those with very large estates to survive. Large debts led to bond slavery, an increase in the number of individuals involved in communal labor service, and increasing numbers of fugitive outlaws who looted at the edges of the large cities.

The exploitation of debtors and the employment of slave labor grew as capital fell into the hands of the larger estates. Labor services to the large estates were paid by rations in kind or by service land allotments. The growth in personnel who controlled and supervised these estates increased throughout the Early Dynastic, and it would appear that the production of consumable commodities, handiwork, and international trade were entirely in the hands of the state sector by Ur III times (2113–2006 B.C.). The private estates simply could not compete with the state in handicraft production, which formed the principal export commodity.

This trade economy formed an important basis for the Sumerian state. Raw materials were brought into the city and manufactured by the temple, then used by the nobility in their homes and also in their graves. (Private graves throughout the Early Dynastic attest to little accumulation of wealth in the private sector, in sharp contrast to the rich nobles' graves seen at Kish and Ur.) Surplus grain production was necessary in order to secure the needed imports of industrial raw materials. The trade and export of finished goods apparently took place mainly between competing Sumerian city-states: remarkably little of the finished handiwork of Sumerian shops has been found on contemporary sites outside of Sumer.

Thorkild Jacobsen has argued that Sumerian myths describe the political system prior to the rise of kingship and depict a form of "primitive democracy."[22] Suggesting that the anthropomorphic world of gods described in the myths reflects earlier political institutions, Jacobsen offers the following reconstruction for the rise of Sumerian kingship. Political authority originally rested in an assembly of free adult males. In times of stress, the assembly elected a temporary war leader, who, returning from military campaigns, refused to relinquish authority to the assembly.

Kingship evolved as the result of his retaining absolute power. Such a view, though speculative, can be supported by Sumerian texts. Jacobsen's hypothetical reconstruction for the rise of kingship continues to hold a powerful influence on our understanding of early Sumerian political formation.

SUMER: AN OVERVIEW

In the first half of the third millennium the palace was a parallel organization to the temple, owning large estates, employing labor reserves, supporting an army, collecting, storing, taxing, and redistributing goods. Labor conscripted by the palace was far less voluntary than that undertaken for the temple. In the Epic of Gilgamesh, workers complain bitterly about the state forcing them to labor for the construction of the walls around the city of Uruk. Sumerian kings set up business in palaces in direct competition with the temples. They were quick to claim divine support and imitate the organizational structure of the earlier temple. Throughout the third millennium, the palace grew in power and wealth, and there is little doubt that it did so at the expense of the temples.

It is not our purpose here to review the full achievements in technology, crafts, law, education, religion, literature, music, the arts, and architecture of the Sumerian world. To do that would require a separate book for each topic. The educational system is well indicated by the innumerable "textbooks" found in ancient schools and libraries; the technology and crafts by the production of cire-perdue objects of copper, gold, and silver; and the legal code by the presence of tablets. The laws were liberal at first (money fines for crimes of violence at 2100 B.C.) but became more severe. Eventually the "eye for eye, tooth for tooth" principle was adopted, a code familiar to us from the Old Testament. The sound and scales of their music are unknown to us but not the shape of their instruments, as the spectacular lyres recovered from the Royal Cemetery attest.

The gods and goddesses were recognized beyond the lands of Sumer in antiquity, and they are known to us today from tablets recovered in their temples and palaces. Beyond that, many of their myths are commonly told today, albeit under a different name. The texts reveal epic tales of a universal flood, the creation of man from clay and woman from man's rib, and others, all clear prototypes of the Old Testament.

From ancient texts, too, we learn that the functioning of the universe was governed by divine laws. Over a hundred of these laws, called *měs,* are known. To the Sumerian, these laws defined the only reality—the universe and everything in it, including the activities and institutions of human society. All was immutable, established by law, never subject to change. The *měs* were originally given by Enki (the god of water) to the city of Eridu. E-Anna stole them and gave their knowledge away to others, the *měs* concludes, "since which time nothing else has been invented." This statement, referring to the earliest memory of Sumerian history, summarizes that culture's view of the unchanging nature of the universe.

It was an increasing awareness of foreign cultures and with it increased militarism that must have challenged the static Sumerian view of world order. This increasing interaction throughout the third millennium turns us once again to the area of the Iranian Plateau.

THE SUMERIAN MARKET NETWORK

By developing new productive forces and corresponding relations of production, man develops an historical nature which determines for him the character of living nature and the spiritual as well as the political character of society.[23]

In Marshall Sahlins' view, production represents a dialectic between self and others. In the process of satisfying their own needs, people produce new needs; this has the effect of altering the structure of social relations.

This view may seem abstract and philosophical, but it finds concrete representation in the production and trade relationships that developed during the third millennium between Mesopotamia and the Iranian Plateau. The development of the Sumerian temple-palace represents a particular form of organizing production; alternative forms existed in the specialized craft production that developed within the various communities on the Iranian Plateau. Between the two, a dialectic emerged that influenced the historical, social, and religious organization of both societies.

Plate 3.13 Sandstone "Victory Stele" of Naram-Sin, King of the Akkadians and grandson (?) of Sargon (height 6 ft 6¾ in.). It was found at Susa ça. 2380 to 2353 B.C. The stele depicts Naram-Sin standing over conquered foreigners. (Hirmer Fotoarchiv.)

At the heart of this dialectic was the different character of each area. The historian Ferdinand Braudel has hypothesized that areas of geographical uniformity (for instance, alluvial plains) lead to centralization and population clustering, while areas of geographical diversity (such as mountain regions) tend to remain decentralized.[24] His hypothesis receives confirmation in the scattered settlement distribution of the Iranian Plateau compared to the dense settlement of Mesopotamia around 2600 B.C.*

As was mentioned earlier in this chapter, the Proto-Elamite state had colonized sites on the Iranian Plateau like Tepe Yahya and Sialk by around 3000 B.C. This period of colonization was not long-lived. The sites having a strong Proto-Elamite presence at 3000 B.C. were no longer under their influence by 2800 B.C.; even literacy was abandoned. By the mid-third millennium, cultural regionalization was increasingly marked. No longer integrated under the Elamite state, particular geographical areas became consolidated into distinct culture areas. These separate communities maintained relations individually with the Sumerian state.

Relations between Mesopotamia and the Iranian Plateau were characterized by the same sharp dichotomy outlined by Braudel. The urban lowland centers, situated in the alluvial plains, depended on irrigation agriculture to produce surplus foodstuffs; they established settlements along major waterways and canals with nucleated centers and centrally organized authority. In contrast to this, the highland communities existed in areas of dry farming with a lower agricultural productivity, less nucleated areas of settlement, a lower population density, and relative autonomy and isolation from neighboring areas.

This dichotomy served as the basis for an important trade network. The needs of one area suited the needs of the other: what brought them into a dialectical relationship was their complementarity. The highland communities were rich in resources: a list of their products includes copper, turquoise,

---

*As we will see in Chapter 4, however, some exceptions seem to exist. Data from Mesoamerica are not as supportive: the Central Mexican highlands, for instance, show very dense occupation in Precolumbian times.

carnelian, lapis, chlorite, wood, and animals, especially horses. In return for these resources, the tablets of lowland centers inform us that perishable food commodities and manufactured goods like textiles were exported to the highlands.

Sumerian texts referring to long-distance trade in the Early Dynastic Period indicate that the temple-palace played a dominant role in directing traffic in finished objects and natural resources between the communities of the Iranian Plateau and Sumer. The pursuit of private gain (or, as Adam Smith called it, man's inherent motivation to "truck and barter") was combined with the state directive to stimulate expansion of long-distance trade. Particularly instructive in relation to long-distance trade is the Sumerian epic "Enmerkar and the Lord of Aratta."[25]

Enmerkar, king of Uruk (2800 B.C.), in his drive to embellish the temple of his patron deity E-Anna, dispatched a messenger to the lord of Aratta. The city of Aratta, undiscovered by archaeologists, is reported to be east of Sumer across "seven mountain ranges" and rich in mineral resources, particularly lapis lazuli. Enmerkar's emissary was sent to Aratta to purchase the "stones from the mountains" in return for Sumerian grain. The lord of Aratta did not need grain, and so he rejected the offer. Soon after, his lands suffered from a severe drought, apparently inflicted by E-Anna. After an exchange of threats the lord of Aratta capitulated, the drought broke, and the "stones of the mountain" were shipped to Sumer in return for grain to produce such works as depicted in Plate 3.14. It is significant that despite the different cultural settings of Sumer and the Iranian highlands, the might of E-Anna was both recognized and feared. The shared religious ideology of Enmerkar and the lord of Aratta had facilitated trade and the veiled threat of E-Anna's might substituted for open warfare.

Two communities, excavated within the past ten years, best illustrate the interaction between Mesopotamia and the Iranian Plateau. These are Tepe Yahya, mentioned earlier in the text, and Shahr-i Sokhta, located in Seistan, eastern Iran. At 2600 B.C. the sites of Yahya and Shahr-i Sokhta were involved in the production and transshipment of specialized resources to fill the demand of Mesopotamian centers. Their resources were different, as were the production technologies. Tepe Yahya manufactured highly elaborate chlorite bowls from a local resource and exported the

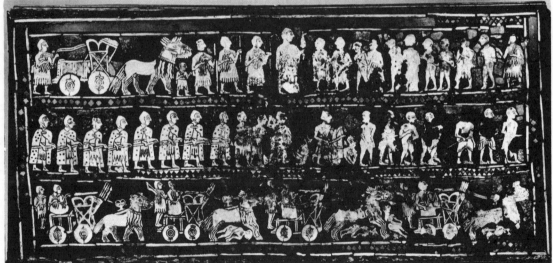

Plate 3.14   The so-called "Standard of Ur" from the Royal Cemetery of Ur, ca. 2685 B.C.: a mosaic of shell, lapis lazuli, and carnelian, resources which had to be imported into Mesopotamia (height 8 in.). The inlay is on both sides of a rectangular box. The top view is thought to depict the "peace side" and the bottom view the "war side." (Hirmer Fotoarchiv.)

finished products to the west. Shahr-i Sokhta imported lapis lazuli from the east, worked it locally, then transshipped it further west.

The chlorite bowls from Yahya have complex motifs and are identical to those found in virtually every Sumerian temple and palace, as well as in the Royal Cemetery of Ur. Analyses by neutron activation have shown that the chlorite mines, 25 kilometers from Yahya, were the source utilized for production of these bowls. Furthermore, analyses have shown that the products manufactured at Yahya were exported as far as Mari in northern Syria.[26] At Shahr-i Sokhta, a number of lapis lazuli workshops have been excavated, replete with stone tools for manufacture and large quantities of lapis flakes.

While the workshops of Yahya and Shahr-i Sokhta are essentially contemporary, there is virtually no lapis at Yahya or carved chlorite bowls at Shahr-i Sokhta. This differential distribution of manufactured products suggests that there was little demand for each other's product on the Iranian Plateau. Instead, these communities were producing a supply for the specific demands of the Mesopotamian market.

Besides telling us about the economic network between Sumer and communities of the Iranian Plateau, findings of the local products also give us some idea of shared cultural traits. The elaborate motifs carved on chlorite bowls at Yahya, assuredly representing complex religious beliefs, corroborated the existence of common ideologies between the Sumerian lowlands and the Iranian highlands (as was also indicated by the "Enmerkar and the Lord of Aratta" epic). This is further confirmed by the style of cylinder seals at Yahya. Though the style is distinctive, several of the religious motifs—winged goddesses sitting in chairs, males with vegetation protruding from their bodies—also appear on Mesopotamian cylinder seals. While there is little evidence in the material culture at Yahya and Shahr-i Sokhta to indicate contact or even knowledge of Sumer, these manufactured products clearly attest to an established relationship between the two areas.

The production of chlorite bowls at Yahya and of lapis lazuli at Shahr-i Sokhta indicates craft specialization. How the work was directed and organized, however, cannot be determined from the excavated evidence. At Yahya, the workshops appear to be in open areas. In over 600 square meters of excavation, not a single substantial domestic or administrative structure has been uncovered. Domestic buildings have been identified at Shahr-i Sokhta. But here, too, there is no evidence for an administrative structure. The presence at each site of an indigenous material culture that lacks parallels not only with the lowlands but also between each other suggests that work was controlled by local authorities on a scale far less centralized than the Mesopotamian temple-palace complex. Just as economic subsistence patterns differed sharply between the lowlands and the highland communities, so the level of social integration differed between the dense populations of the lowland urban states and the sparsely populated highland towns organized by tribal confederations.

By contrasting the features of the Mesopotamian lowlands and the Iranian highlands, we can reach some understanding of the basic market network that united the two areas. The process by which the relationship grew was almost spiral in nature.

As the highland colonies became independent, there was a need to establish indigenous administrative hierarchies to fill the vacuum left by the Proto-Elamite retreat. The relationship with Sumer added to this need: the highland communities' production

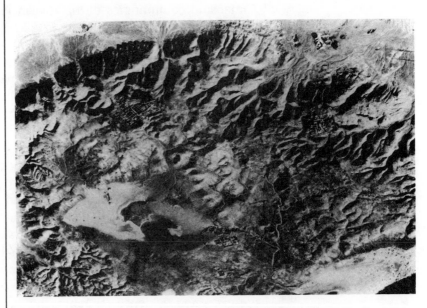

Plate 3.15   Aerial photograph of the mound and excavations at Shahr-i Sokhta. (Courtesy of ISMEO.)

why was it necessary to get rid of it, why didn't they just throw it out?

and export of resources had become institutionalized for lowland demand centers, establishing craft specialization and increasing needs for a division of labor and for stronger leaders to organize production and redistribute essential lowland imports like textiles and subsistence produce.

In the lowlands, the importation of desirable raw materials, together with the influx of metals, ores, and elaborately manufactured luxury goods from the highlands, was also affecting the social order, underscoring already developing social inequality. At the same time, the Sumerians were effecting a change in their own internal economy by importing highland commodities. Just as highland economies became more specialized and more dependent on lowland export to feed their labor forces, the greater became Mesopotamia's need to ensure a market for its continuing surplus production. In sum, Mesopotamia's economy required the constant importation of new raw materials and luxury goods in order to rid itself of its agricultural surpluses. Seen in this light, the conspicuous consumption of the Royal Cemetery at Ur seems comprehensible: in removing "capital" from circulation by burying it, the elite of the community permitted their successors to build up their own "portfolio" through further import and export.

In the market relationship between the highland communities and Sumer, an essential feature stands out: its basic inequality.

Plate 3.16 View of the mound and excavations at Tepe Yahya, southeastern Iran. (Courtesy of Peabody Museum, Harvard University.)

186

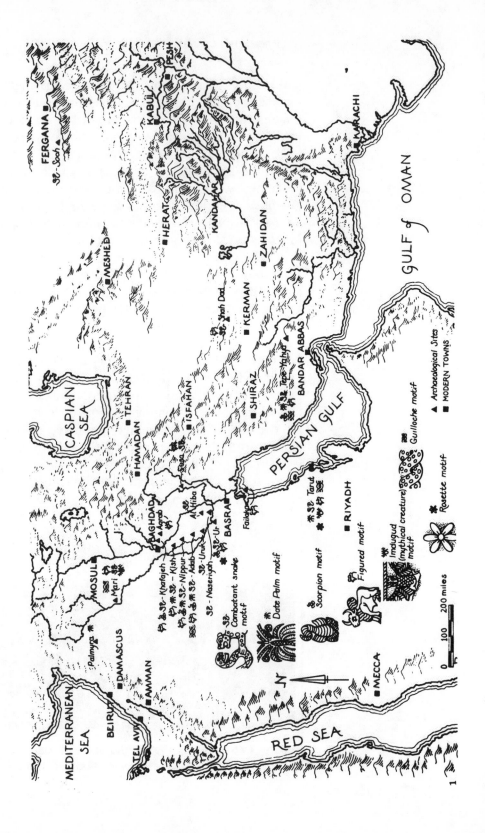

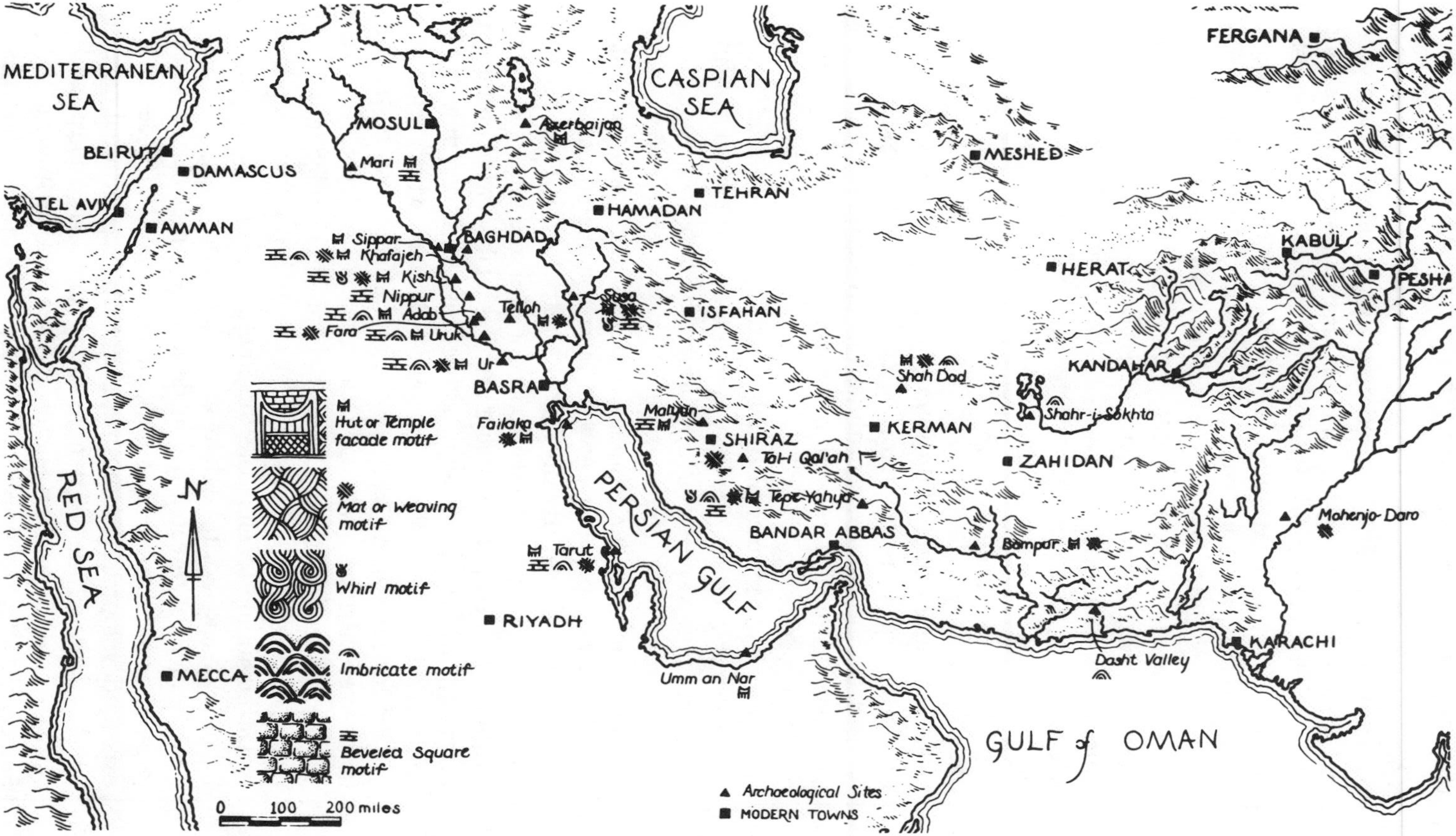

Map 3.4 Distribution of carved chlorite bowls in the third millennium showing widespread identity in similar motifs carved on the bowls. (Map by Romayne Timms.)

Lowland urban centers required highland resources to legitimize class differences through an unequal distribution of wealth. But while the lowlands needed highland resources, they were not dependent on a single source or commodity. Several suppliers were available, and they were able to manipulate multiple sources. This clearly gave the urban centers of Mesopotamia the upper hand. If the trading partner refused to cooperate, they could literally starve their partner to submission or find an alternative supplier (the underlying theme of "Enmerkar and the Lord of Aratta"). Long-distance trade affected the highland communities by promoting an internal division of labor; the long-term effect was to make them more dependent on Sumer for subsistence trade.

This model of interaction uniting Mesopotamia and the Iranian Plateau is a new theory. It challenges the concept which necessitates the "pristine" evolution of civilizations through their own "genius" unrelated to events and historical processes in contiguous areas.

This new model may also help shed light on another unanswered question. We have mentioned that Mesopotamian-Egyptian interaction is elusive. Though the two great civilizations were aware of each other's existence from at least 3000 B.C., they charted their individual courses of development with seemingly far less contact than that between Mesopotamia and smaller communities on the Iranian Plateau. Just why this is so remains unclear. Perhaps the Egyptian concept of a god-king was such anathema to Mesopotamia that it acted as a taboo which reinforced conscious avoidance between both civilizations. Certainly, it could not have been the geographical distance which acted as a barrier, for lapis lazuli came to the Sumerian city-states from a far greater distance. Archaeological research in Egypt, like that in Sumer, has tended to emphasize the "pristine" indigenous nature of those civilizations. Recent research on Pharaonic Egypt is just beginning to elucidate the interaction between Dynastic Egypt and neighboring cultures such as Nubia.

Archeological research has made it increasingly clear that a very large geographical expanse must be considered in order to explain developments within parts of it. The interactional patterns which integrated the third-millennium relations of Egypt and Nubia, Sumer and Egypt, Sumer and the Iranian Plateau, and Sumer and the Indus region remain poorly understood. It is increasingly obvious from the archaeological record that the urban process within one area cannot be understood without considering contiguous areas.

In the middle of the third millennium, at the time in which the Sumerian world was responsive to the highlands of the Iranian Plateau, there appeared, further east, along the banks of the Indus River, the Indus or Harappan civilization. The formation, distribution, relationship, and dissolution of this largest of geographically distributed Old World civilizations has been a major research interest of Asian archaeologists for four decades.

The Indus Civilization

The civilizations of the ancient Near East, however dimly perceived, have always been part of our general knowledge from Biblical accounts. But the equally ancient civilization along the Indus was completely unknown until the 1920s. Hints of its existence appear in the sacred literature of India, just as references to Mesopotamian civilization exist in the Bible, but they had been discounted by scholars. In 1921, Sir John Marshall excavated the major metropolises of the pre-Aryan Indus civilization—Harappa and Mohenjo-Daro (both located in the valleys of the Indus River)—and provided the world with the first view of the most extensive of all preclassical cultures of the Old World: the Indus civilization.

The origin and formation of the Indus civilization have been the source of great speculation but limited evidence. For decades, it was commonplace to maintain that the Indus civilization appeared suddenly, in a mature form, around 2400 B.C., the result of diffusion from Mesopotamia. This view can no longer be maintained. Recent excavations on the Iranian Plateau at Tepe Yahya and Shahr-i Sokhta confound any simple diffusionary mechanism for the rise of the Indus, for there is little doubt that both these non-Sumerian sites had contact with sites of the Indus civilization. (These smaller cultures cannot be seen as the generators of the Indus any more than can the Mesopotamian city-states.)

We still know very little about settlements in Pakistan and northwestern India prior to the Indus civilization. Few excavations have examined such settlements—not because pre-Indus levels do not exist, but simply because so few have been dug. The limited evidence at hand, nevertheless, does not

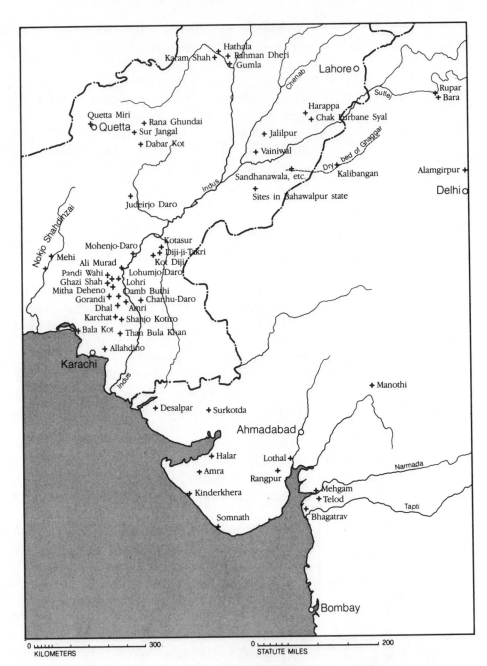

Map 3.5 Distribution of the Indus civilization, ca. 2000 B.C. (Redrawn from David and Ruth Whitehouse, *Archaeological Atlas of the World*. 1975. London: Thames and Hudson Ltd. © 1975 Thames and Hudson Ltd.)

support the contention that the Indus civilization developed suddenly or was the result of diffusion from the west.

Only six Indus sites have been excavated which reveal pre-Indus settlement. These are Mohenjo-Daro, Harappa, Kalibangan, Kot Diji, Amri, and the ongoing excavations at Rahman Dheri (see map). In general, the early pre-Indus materials on these sites differ from the typical Harappan or Indus repertoire. There are, however, certain pottery and metal types which suggest that the settlements underlying the Harappan may have formed its ancestry.

Other clues come from the northwest highlands. Many sites in the hills of northern and eastern Baluchistan (in modern Pakistan), dated to the first half of the third millennium, have materials prototypical to those of later Indus sites. It is entirely possible that these towns formed the background for the evolution of the cities along the Indus. The site of Mohenjo-Daro, illustrated in Plate 3.17, has approximately 12 meters of unexcavated occupational debris beneath the excavated city. We do not know if these underlying levels belong to the Indus civilization or not. Furthermore, the ongoing excavations at Margarh, in east-central Pakistan, have revealed 10 meters of aceramic Neolithic, surely

Plate 3.17   View of the mound of Mohenjo-Daro. (Courtesy of George Dales.)

dating back to the sixth millennium, which promise to shed new light on the formation of the Indus civilization. It is clear that we are just beginning to understand the prehistoric background to the formation of the Indus civilization. There can be little doubt that when sufficient excavation is undertaken we will comprehend more fully the independent genesis of the Harappan civilization—as independent a creation as that of Egypt and Mesopotamia. Though all three civilizations were contemporary, they were entirely distinctive in their forms.

INDUS SETTLEMENT PATTERNS

To date there has been no systematic research on the settlement or subsistence patterns of the Indus civilization. We remain almost entirely uninformed, therefore, about the hierarchy of settlement size within particular geographical areas. Of the more than one hundred Harappan settlements known, two stand out: Mohenjo-Daro in present-day Sind in the Indus lowland and Harappa in the highlands of the Punjab. With the exception of these two sites, most settlements were small: it is the extraordinary Indus settlement (as it is in Mesopotamia and Egypt) that exceeds 15 acres. Both Harappa and Mohenjo-Daro occupy more than 330 acres.

The site of Mohenjo-Daro is of comparable size to the city of Uruk in Mesopotamia, while both Uruk and Mohenjo-Daro are larger than the third-millennium settlements of Egypt.

More than the size of Harappa and Mohenjo-Daro is exceptional. Though the sites of these two major cities are more than 600 kilometers apart, they are culturally indistinguishable. It has been suggested by Stuart Piggott that these two sites were the principal capitals of the Indus civilization—indicating a duality of control.[27] Such a duality is quite plausible on geographical grounds: Mohenjo-Daro could have been the capital of the lowland Indus alluvium, and Harappa the highland capital in the Punjab. This kind of bipartite control has, in fact, characterized the political organization of northern India at various times in the historical period. Professor S. R. Rao has made an alternative suggestion: the Indus civilization was an "empire" centrally unified by Mohenjo-Daro through various provincial and secondary capitals.[28] Whatever explanation applies, it seems clear that the political organization of the Indus differs from that of Mesopotamia where the individual city-states were usually autonomous. In the Indus the picture which emerges is one of unity, with both greater centralization and larger geographic tracts.

Not only Mohenjo-Daro and Harappa but the excavated Indus towns and cities in general share a far greater number of features than do the communities of Mesopotamia. Regardless of size, all Indus communities were laid out on a grid. This is apparent not only at Mohenjo-Daro but also in the excavations of the village (estimated population less than 5000) of Allahdino. These settlements represent the first concerted efforts we know of for town planning, and they provide a ready contrast to the random growth of the Mesopotamian settlements. The formalization of town planning on Indus sites, compared to the random growth of Mesopotamian settlements, may indicate a more rigorous central control within the community than existed in Mesopotamian communities.

The Indus communities were not all fortified, though some, like Mohenjo-Daro, surely were. The sites of Harappa and Kalibangan were walled communities before the rise of the Indus civilization. Communities throughout the area made similar use of baked brick (compared to the sun-dried brick of Mesopotamia) and highly organized drainage and sewage systems, surely the earliest and most elaborate in the ancient world.

The extent of town planning is best attested at the site of Mohenjo-Daro. Mohenjo-Daro is typical of other Indus sites in its separation of the city into two parts: a citadel, consisting of monumental public buildings, and a lower town where the citizens lived. Systematic fortifications with massive, solid, baked brick towers have been uncovered at several points around the citadel. The principal public buildings on the citadel are the Great Bath, the Granary, and a large area incorporating the College and Assembly Hall. The Great Bath, perhaps the most unusual of the buildings, illustrated in Plate 3.18, represents a considerable accomplishment in water engineering. A community swimming pool perhaps restricted to the elite, it was 12 meters long, 7 meters wide, and almost 3 meters deep. One side had an enclosed portico, behind which were rows of small rooms. The other side had eight small, private bathrooms, separated by a passage with a drain running down the center. The

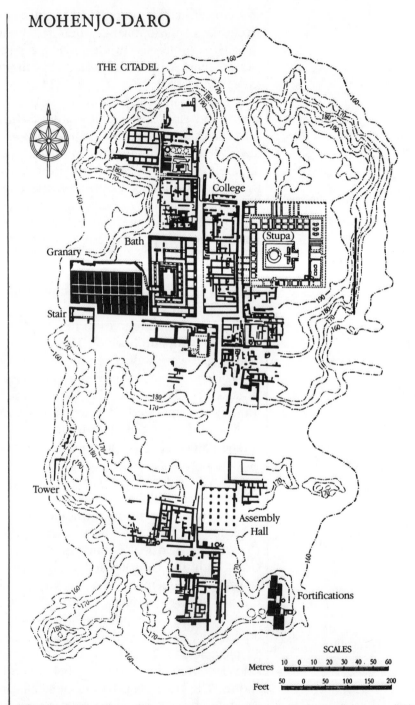

Figure 3.10 Plan of the principal structure at Mohenjo-Daro, ca. 2000 B.C. (Cambridge University Press.)

Plate 3.18 The Great Bath of Mohenjo-Daro. (Courtesy of George Dales.)

apparent concern for ritual ablutions and cleanliness suggests the function of this complex may have been connected with the religious life of the city.

To the west of the Great Bath, the Granary towered above the city. This massive structure illustrated in Plate 3.19, covering an area in excess of a thousand square meters, consisted of solid blocks of brickwork separated by narrow passages. Above this platform a multistoried timber superstructure was built with windows for ventilation. The construction of this monumental building represented an enormous expenditure of human labor. It, and a similar one on the citadel of Harappa, must have been a communal granary: a storehouse for the collective produce of the community's agricultural products. In the absence of money, the state-controlled granary would have functioned as the state treasury, providing subsistence for both full-time workers and those who administered the affairs of the city. In Mesopotamia, documents of the Third Dynasty of Ur inform us of the existence of state granaries, though their remains have eluded the spade of the archaeologist. In the Indus, state control over the productivity of the agricultural fields is inferred from the archaeological evidence but the textual confirmation is lacking.

The College was located to the northeast of the Great Bath. Sir John Marshall, who excavated the building, believed it to be either the residence of a high official or perhaps a college for the training of the priests who officiated in the ceremonies conducted in the Great Bath. The Assembly Hall in the northern sector of the citadel consisted of a large hall 28 meters square. It was divided into five aisles by rows of brick piers. The function of large buildings like this and the Granary remains elusive; their public orientation is suggested by their size alone.

Excavations of the lower town area have produced intelligible plans of rectangular city blocks about 250 by 370 meters. Main streets were as much as 10 meters in width, intersected by smaller streets and alleys as narrow as 1.5 meters. The unpaved streets still bear the grooved scars from the passing of heavy carts. Small posts at intersections protected buildings from these carts, which turned corners without benefit of rotating axles. Major streets were equipped with brick drains and manholes for the regular clearing of waste. The city wells were dug through more than 10 meters of earlier habitation. Both in private houses

Plate 3.19 View of Mohenjo-Daro with the granary in foreground and later Buddhist stupa in background. (Courtesy of George Dales.)

and in public courtyards, the wells adjoined latrines that articulated with the street drains.

Houses of the citizenry were commodious two-story buildings with a central courtyard. Excavations in this area attest to a prosperous middle class, a specialization of labor, and the existence of productive technologies comparable to those of Mesopotamia. A number of buildings in the lower town have been identified as places for industrial production of beads, textiles, and metals. Small temples or shrines have also been located here, as well as other buildings with a barrackslike atmosphere that may have housed slaves or indentured servants.

TRADE AND INTERNATIONAL CONTACT

Prior to the 1950s, the presence of the Indus civilization in the area of Gujarat, south of the Rann of Kutch, was wholly unsuspected. The site of Lothal, in Kathiawad, has documented the existence of the Indus civilization in this region of India and

Plate 3.20 View of the buildings at Mohenjo-Daro with sanitation canals in foreground and round wells in upper right (DK area). (Courtesy of George Dales.)

provides the first picture of an Indus port city. The importance of this finding is clear: the Indus civilization depended on trade. The town of Lothal, which dates from 2100 to 1900 B.C., covers an area of 12 hectares. It is surrounded by a defensive wall and has all the characteristics of an Indus settlement: town planning, a citadel, elaborate drainage systems, and an identified granary. Of greatest interest is a large rectangular enclosure, measuring 225 by 37 meters, faced with baked brick set in waterproofing bitumen. This construction technique was similar to that used in the Great Bath of Mohenjo-Daro. The structure, with a sluice gate at one end, is thought by the excavator to have been a dock for harboring ships at low tide.[29] If this interpretation is correct (and it has been challenged by several archaeologists), it represents the first port installation discovered in the Indus civilization or, for that matter, anywhere else. The presence of this port focuses attention on the importance of trade within the Indus civilization.

The absence of readable texts within the Indus hampers our understanding of its civilization compared to Mesopotamia. The Indus had greater proximity to natural resources than Mesopotamia, and it was less dependent on long-distance trade. Nevertheless, there is more than adequate evidence to support the existence of a well-organized and far-ranging trading system. Lapis lazuli came from the same sources in Afghanistan that the Sumerians used; prized shank shells came from southern India; turquoise from northeastern Iran; carved chlorite bowls from the Iranian Plateau; and jade from central Asia, Burma, or more distant China. Metal ores (including copper, lead, and silver) were all available either within or close to the territory of the Indus civilization. Tin was widely used in the Indus, and also in Mesopotamia and Egypt, by the end of the third millennium yet its source has vexed archaeologists working in the Near East and the Indus.

The facts concerning tin are clear, their meaning opaque. At Mohenjo-Daro, approximately 25% of all bronzes were alloyed with tin; in Mesopotamia, 10 to 15% of the bronzes were manufactured with tin. That both cultures, as well as Egypt, utilized tin for alloying is incontestable—as incontestable as the absence of tin sources in the Near East: there is not a single unequivocal source of tin between the Indus and Mediterranean. A possible source exists in the eastern desert of Egypt; known sources (exploited in the third millennium) exist in Spain, the Scilly

Plate 3.21 Indus stamp seal from Nippur in Mesopotamia depicting humped bull beneath Indus script. Note its close similarity to the seal from Mohenjo-Daro. (Courtesy of MacGuire Gibson.)

Plate 3.22 Stone stamp seal from Mohenjo-Daro with Indus sign above humped bull, ca. 2000 B.C. (Courtesy of George Dales.)

Isles of Britain, Kazakstan in central Asia, and perhaps Bohemia in central Europe. It is also possible that the recently discovered Indus sites on the Oxus River in northern Afghanistan produced tin. Slag and crucibles litter the surface of these sites, which must have been involved in metal ore extraction and transshipment (perhaps of tin) to the centers of the Indus civilization. The absence of tin sources for use by Egyptian, Mesopotamian, and Indus smiths within the confines of their own civilization underscores the wide-ranging trade that brought distant areas into a pattern of economic interaction.

We know from Mesopotamian texts that Sumer was actively involved in trade with the Indus. On several Sumerian sites, archaeologists have uncovered the products of Indus craftsmen in the form of etched carnelian beads, characteristic stamp seals with Indus inscriptions, bone inlay, dice, and possibly statuary. These objects all appear on Sumerian sites between 2400 and 1900 B.C. What is puzzling is that this evidence of exchange seems to be in one direction. Indus objects have been found on Sumerian sites, but not a single Mesopotamian artifact has been recovered from an Indus settlement (though occasional stamp seals reflect motifs reminiscent of Sumerian origin). As with the evidence on the Iranian Plateau, where Mesopotamian artifacts are present but rare, we are left to assume that Mesopotamia exported only perishables: barley, fruits, vegetables, oils, textiles. The presence of Indus artifacts in Sumer and the absence of Sumerian products in the Indus rules out the possibility of Sumerian trading colonies in the Indus—while suggesting that Indus colonies were present in Sumer.

It is likely that two major trade routes connected the two cultures. Although conjectural, it seems probable that some overland trade took place between Sumer and the Indus, handled by middlemen from the Iranian Plateau. That Mesopotamia and the Indus civilization engaged in maritime trade is certain. Seafaring enterprises along the coast of the Indian Ocean and up the Persian Gulf are documented by both archaeological and textual evidence.

Mesopotamian tablets highlight three foreign commercial centers at the end of the third millennium: Dilmun, Magan, and Meluhha. Dilmun has been identified as the modern island of Bahrein in the Persian Gulf. Magan refers to settlements on the Arabian and Persian shores of the gulf, and Meluhha is believed to be the Indus civilization. Mesopotamian texts refer to ships sailing from Dilmun, Magan, and Meluhha with merchandise for Sumerian markets. Texts record the imports and exports and provide evidence for the staggering extent of this trade: in one case (ca. 2100 B.C.) 30 tons of copper were sent in a single shipment from Magan via Dilmun to Mesopotamia.

The clearest evidence for this maritime trade comes from the Danish excavations on Bahrein under the direction of Geoffrey Bibby.[30] Excavations at Bahrein, and on the small island of Failaka off the coast of Kuwait, provide a framework for our understanding of a late-third-millennium culture, referred to as Dilmun, contemporary with the flourishing of the Indus civilization and Akkadian Mesopotamia.

Evidence from the excavations on Bahrein and Failaka attests to the presence of a distinctive regional culture. The ashlar masonry of its architecture, best seen in the excavations of a temple on Bahrein, contrasts with the brick construction of Mesopotamia and the Indus. Equally distinctive are the round "Persian Gulf seals" and ceramic products. Though related to the Indus stylistically, the Persian Gulf seals are best interpreted as indigenous products. These seals have been found in a wide range of locations: at Lothal in the Indus, at Tepe Yahya on the Iranian Plateau, and on a number of Sumerian sites.

Seals from the Indus culture also attest to wide-ranging trade. A single inscribed seal of Indus type was found at Failaka in the Persian Gulf; other Indus-type seals have been found in Mesopotamia at Nippur, Ur, and Tell Jokha. Among these findings and others, the only tangible evidence for the overland trade which surely existed between the Indus and Susa comes from Tepe Yahya in the form of a potsherd bearing a seal impression with unmistakable Indus script.

The absence of Mesopotamian exports on the islands of Bahrein and Failaka is difficult to explain. Both the islands are small and neither possesses resources; nor is there evidence of large-scale manufacture. The islands functioned as "ports of trade" dealing with natural resources as well as manufactured products. They acted both as intermediaries uniting the Indus and Mesopotamia in trade and as transshippers of goods for third parties (the Arabian ports of Magan) between the major Mesopotamian and Indus centers. Cuneiform script and the Akkadian language were in use on the islands of Failaka and Bahrein, but it is unlikely that this was the native language of the Dilmun civilization.

If we consolidate the evidence from Mesopotamian documents with the archaeological evidence derived from Dilmun, the Indus civilization, and sites along the Iranian shores of the Persian Gulf, a coherent picture begins to emerge. The islands of Bahrein and Failaka, and perhaps towns along the eastern shores of Arabia, were involved in maritime trade between the Indus civilization and Sumer. The absence, however, of appreciable quantities of imports in the three distinct centers of Mesopotamia, the Indus, and Dilmun suggests that trade was in unfinished raw resources and perishable commodities. The site of Tepe Yahya is alone on the Iranian Plateau in having objects of all three centers represented: Persian Gulf seals, Indus sealings, and Mesopotamian ceramics. This slim evidence, however, surely masks the true extent of trade in perishables and natural resources.

Plate 3.23 View of the terrace wall from the last phases of construction of the temple at Dilmun, ca. 1900 B.C. (Courtesy of Peder Mortensen.)

A similar argument can be put forth for understanding trade between the Indus and Mesopotamia. Sumerian cities imported raw resources, metal ores, timber, and precious and semiprecious stones; they exported perishable commodities and manufactured goods. Dilmun acted as an entrepôt, principally serving as the middleman in transshipping but also engaged in the export of dates and "fisheyes" (pearls). It seems likely that the growth of towns on the islands of the Persian Gulf paralleled those on the Iranian Plateau; both areas were involved in supplying Mesopotamian markets and both received surplus Mesopotamian produce in return.

SOCIAL STRUCTURE AND CULTURAL ACHIEVEMENTS

Unfortunately, our understanding of the Indus social organization which structured this international trade is far less complete than our knowledge of Sumerian society. One reason for this is the absence of deciphered written documents. Inscriptions exist from about 2400 B.C., but to date, all attempts to "crack" the

Plate 3.24 Five stamp seals from Bahrein, ancient Dilmun, found in the temple complex of Barbar, ca. 1900 B.C. (Courtesy of Peder Mortensen.)

language have been unsuccessful. The script, unrelated to any other, contains at least 396 distinctive symbols, an apparently unchanging hieroglyphic system. Inscriptions have been found on small copper tablets and as incised graffiti or stamped messages on potsherds. Most frequently they appear on square seals as seen in Plate 3.25, are short, rarely exceeding ten signs with a maximum of seventeen. Recent work by Finnish and Soviet scholars using similar computer methods suggests that the structure of the Indus language is akin to the Dravidian family of languages.[31] Though potentially helpful in permitting philologists to decipher the language, this analysis does not allow us to read the script. We do know that the texts clearly differ from the accounting tablets of Mesopotamia, for they contain no mathematical system. Records and accounts of production, trade, and land ownership must have been registered on more perishable materials. The purpose for which the written language of the Indus civilization was used is unknown.

In the absence of deciphered written documents, we have little but the archaeological record to guide our reconstruction of Indus society. Since recoveries of Indus sites have been far less complete than those of Sumer (or even Egypt), much of our reconstruction must be inferential.

The archaeological evidence does support a view of an authoritarian, hierarchical social and political system: the extraordinary cultural unity maintained over that vast geographical expanse could not have been possible without a high degree of centralized authority. The large granaries, efficient drainage system, and planned settlements required central control. Whether this control was democratic, despotic, royal, or priestly we do not know. Was it a system led by secular kings as in Mesopotamia, god-kings as in Pharaonic Egypt, or priests deputized by the gods to rule as in predynastic Sumer? To date, not a single temple or palace has been uncovered, not a single royal tomb excavated, not a single artifact found which can be identified as the trappings of royal privilege or rule. We remain uninformed not only of the personal names but also of the collective name of the Indus people. Our ability to answer many questions—the extent to which the state-controlled economy competed with the private sector; the existence of an aristocracy as well as the existence and powers of ruling kings or priests; the status of merchants, craftsmen, and the military that manned the defenses—must wait for future excavations that address these subjects.

We are somewhat more informed about the Indus subsistence economy. As in Mesopotamia, the Indus people depended on surplus production of cereal agriculture achieved through irrigation. In the Indus, however, the evidence for canals, dikes, and irrigation networks is buried under modern alluvial deposits. There is evidence that cereals, barley, and wheat were exploited in the Indus and that rice was cultivated at Lothal. Cotton cloth from Mohenjo-Daro and Lothal provide the earliest evidence for the cultivation of cotton. Village farmers had domestic cattle, as well as camels, horses, pigs, sheep, dogs, and cats. The elephant

Plate 3.25   Indus seal with four signs of Indus script above bull, ca. 2000 B.C. (Courtesy of George Dales.)

appears in association with man-made objects on several stamp seals, and it may have been domesticated.

These seals, like their Mesopotamian counterparts, are "little masterpieces of controlled realism." Besides elephants, they also depict human and semihuman forms, an oxlike creature with one horn (dubbed the "unicorn"), buffalo, rhinoceroses, tigers, crocodiles, and antelope. In addition to these works, there are a large number of more mundane artifacts: terra-cotta figurines of humans; models of carts; frequently found polished stones clearly representing phalli; and tiny faience figurines of sheep, dogs, squirrels, and monkeys. Naturalistic figures of stone and bronze have also been found. Among them, the famous bust of the "priest-king" and the small bronze "dancing girl," both from Mohenjo-Daro and dated about 2000 B.C., are remarkable not only for their quality but also for their rarity.

Radiocarbon dates for the presence of the mature Indus civilization provide a range from 2400 to 1800 B.C. If archaeologists do not yet fully understand the formation of this civilization, we have been even more puzzled by its apparently rapid and nearly total collapse. It is uncertain whether the dissolution was sudden or if it took place gradually with regional variation. Present evidence supports the latter theory. Settlements to the east of the Indus River system, in northwest India, are later and may represent migration from a declining "heartland." But why?

What happened is clear; why it happened is not. The cities of the Indus civilization were abandoned, perhaps to be taken over by nonurban "squatter" occupation. Reasons advanced for the decline of the Indus civilization fall into two categories: destruction through warlike invaders or collapse resulting from environmental factors.

The earliest theory advanced, and still tenacious in the literature, holds that the Indus cities were destroyed by an invading population—often identified as the Vedic Aryans. The *Rig Veda,* a sacred book of the Hindus, describes the arrival of the Vedic Aryans in the Indus Valley, the large, walled cities occupied by "dark-skinned" peoples, and the destruction the Aryans caused. The only Indus city which offers any evidence for this theory is Mohenjo-Daro. Broken skeletons of men, women, and children were discovered in several areas of the city, showing indisputable evidence of having been ruthlessly butchered. This may be interpreted as a massacre of an indigenous population by invading Vedic Aryans. While this theory certainly seems plausible, it raises some questions that have yet to be answered, especially since only the evidence from Mohenjo-Daro supports it. Why would a civilization, occupying a million square kilometers, fall apart with the destruction of one of its capitals? Why were the northern cities, which would have been encountered on the way to the southern capital of Mohenjo-Daro, left untouched by the invaders?

The second explanation for the demise of the Indus civilization has more geological and archaeological support, but it too leaves questions unanswered. It has long been recognized that there were environmental pressures on the Indus cities. The stamp seals at Mohenjo-Daro indicate conditions which do not exist now, for animals (such as tigers, rhinoceroses, crocodiles, and elephants) depicted on the seals are no longer indigenous to the area. Humans themselves undoubtedly altered the environment through overgrazing, overcultivation, and deforestation. These factors may have led to a gradual decrease in agricultural production, a breakup of central control, and eventual pressure to locate in new and more suitable areas.

Beyond this, there may also have been environmental changes of a more drastic nature. Geomorphologists and hydrologists have argued recently that the cities along the Indus River in the province of Sind, Mohenjo-Daro included, were inundated by prolonged flooding in the first half of the second millennium, requiring the construction of large-scale retaining walls to hold back the encroaching waters. This convincing theory receives support from archaeologists who see progressive deterioration in the quality of building and city planning at Mohenjo-Daro. Nevertheless, we are left with the same skepticism that the Aryan invasion hypothesis raised: why should the destruction of a limited number of cities in Sind cause an entire civilization to collapse?

Whatever the answer may prove to be, it is clear that a single factor is not sufficient for an explanation. Both of the preceding hypotheses may be correct, probably in combination with other factors. Only further excavation, surveys, radiocarbon dating, and environmental evidence can answer the many questions that remain about both the nature and the downfall of the Indus civilization.

Summary | In explaining the rise of civilization, scholars today no longer concentrate on single factors, such as the practice of irrigation leading to surplus agriculture and a bureaucratic state. Instead, they describe the rise of civilization as the result of the interaction of several different factors: environment and subsistence economy, population increase and demographic stress, the growth of trade, changing economic and social organization, and technological developments. In our discussion of Egypt, Mesopotamia, and the Indus civilization, it seems clear that in each separate case no single cause can be isolated as the reason civilization developed: these same combinations of factors were of importance to all, as recently emphasized by Dr. Ruth Whitehouse.[32]

ENVIRONMENT AND SUBSISTENCE

The environmental setting plays a fundamental role in the development of any civilization, for it sets the conditions for the subsistence economy. It is no coincidence that the great civilizations of the Old World—Egypt, Mesopotamia, the Indus, and Shang China, as well—were located in alluvial plains. Irrigation permitted either the original settlement of these riverine valleys or the expansion of early settlement; with irrigation, they produced a surplus of agricultural crops which differed in each respective environment but had the same effect in all three areas. The crop surplus allowed for higher population densities.

Other effects followed, including social differentiation and craft specialization. Irrigation produces higher yields than dry farming—an increase of up to 50% in modern times. This in turn enhances the value of land, for irrigated land offers a far higher yield than soil dependent on rainfall. Differences in the value of land lead to a competition for land ownership, differential wealth from the surplus production, and a concomitant specialization of labor and social stratification.

It is probably quite true that civilization would not have emerged in Mesopotamia, Egypt, or the Indus without irrigation. But it is quite another thing to say that irrigation was the primary cause of that civilization: too many other factors were also involved. It can hardly be doubted that we must comprehend environmental conditions before we can appreciate the evolution of a civilization. But though this is a necessary condition, it is not entirely sufficient. Other aspects are also of great importance in explaining the evolution of urban civilization.

POPULATION

The archaeological record confirms dramatically that the food-producing revolution resulted in a clear increase in population. Earlier populations, dependent on food production, appear to have maintained an equilibrium between population and resources, whereas following the development of agriculture there was a consistent increase in population. This fact, documented in the archaeological record, seems to involve population pressure as a prime cause in the development of prehistoric societies. As the permanent villages of the eighth through sixth millennia are larger in size than the earlier hunting and gathering sites, so the towns of the fifth and fourth millennia in the Old World are larger than the earlier agricultural villages.

It appears certain that populations were increasing in Europe, Asia, and Africa, as well as in the New World, before the Urban Revolution. Population expansion may result in either of two responses: the establishment of new communities or the growth of existing communities. The first mechanism, the establishment of "daughter" communities, explains the geographical expansion of early farming villages, and it appears to have continued until Ubaid times in Mesopotamia (around 4000 B.C.). After this time, the second mechanism seems to have grown in importance. Population increases were contained within restricted zones: one sees the gradual increase of settlement in Egypt and Mesopotamia so that by 3000 B.C. there are major centers of large towns and cities.

What caused the new response to increasing population? Some scholars favor the direct demographic explanation of an increase in birthrate. Others prefer to consider a combination of factors: increasing population, increasing efficiency in the subsistence economy, sedentism of nomadic peoples, and a social organization directed toward the concentration of populations. In reviewing the evidence as understood from Egypt, Mesopotamia, and the Indus Valley, it seems clear that population increase—within a geographically circumscribed area which was agriculturally productive when irrigated—played a fundamental role in the development of civilization. An expanding population in turn was related to an increasing economic specialization and social stratification within the civilizations of Mesopotamia, Egypt, and the Indus Valley.

TRADE

In recent years, trade has been seen as a primary factor in the development of complex societies. The excavation of such sites as Tepe Yahya on the Iranian Plateau and the recovery of the Dilmun civilization in the Persian Gulf have underscored the importance of economic interaction in the Near East. The alluvial plains of Mesopotamia, and to a lesser degree those of Egypt and the Indus, lacked mineral materials—copper, gold, lapis lazuli, turquoise, carnelian—even building timber. Essential as well as luxury materials had to be imported, often from very considerable distances, into the cities of these civilizations. Merchants involved in this trade operated not only as full-time traders but as foreign emissaries to distant city-states.

Trade within the literate urban centers of Egypt, Sumer, and the Indus must have been organized in a different manner than the trade which distributed obsidian throughout the Neolithic communities. Neolithic communities could survive without obsidian, but the Sumerian city-state depended on the uninterrupted supply of essential raw materials. Particular mechanisms were established to assure a constant flow of resources. The mechanism established by the Sumerians as well as in Pharaonic Egypt was to place the control of trade in the hands of the temple and palaces—thus institutionalizing trade within the hands of the state, assuring its efficient continuity, and speeding the development and centralization of economic affairs. The extent of the state control in the Indus remains less clear, chiefly due to our inability to read the texts. The procurement of rare resources from distant areas, the evidence of surplus production, and the existence of large administrative structures in Indus cities compare with those of Egypt and Mesopotamia and suggest a comparable state control.

SOCIAL ORGANIZATION

Each of the civilizations dealt with had a distinctive social organization. In Egypt, the entirety of the country was unified under one political leader, the god-king pharaoh; in Mesopotamia, each city-state was led by a king. The social organization of the Indus civilization is little understood, but it may have been like that of Mesopotamia—organized into independent city-states.

Despite differences, though, the three civilizations shared common features of social order. The social and economic factors for the rise of cities are fundamentally dependent on the integration of a centralized economic and political power, social stratification, and economic specialization. These three factors contributed to the development of the Urban Revolution, and in each of the areas where they interacted they led to the development of a complex society. Economic specialization, a stratified society, and the centralization of power depend on the development of a surplus production of subsistence goods to support those engaged in trade, administration, and the crafts. Social differentiation in turn depends not only on surplus production but on the uneven distribution of this surplus—the development of a class-structured society. The individuals able to appropriate the greater surplus assumed greater power, not only economic but political. The development of a central authority became essential in the control of long-distance trade, warfare, the management of storage, and the redistribution of food, raw resources, and manufactured commodities. The complex social order resulting from an increasing economic specialization, social stratification, and centralization of authority initiated a process which once set in motion was irreversible.

TECHNOLOGY

That technology would have an impact on the development of civilization seems obvious. The discovery of new subsistence systems through domestication; the increase in population resulting from irrigation; the invention of metallurgy, the wheel, and seafaring ships—all are major technological innovations which preceded or accompanied the urban revolution. Recognizing this fact, one may ask two questions: Could civilization have developed without these technologies? And what effect did these inventions have on the societies which developed them?

In general, the answer to these questions involves three different, though related, considerations. First; technological inventions encourage the rate of economic specialization. Second, technological inventions increase the efficiency of production. And third, technological inventions allow for the further elaboration of new activities (military, ceremonial, recreational).

A single example, the development of metallurgy, will suffice to illustrate our meaning. Processes involved in metallurgical production were far more complex than those used in making stone tools. The production of metals involved smelting, casting, and ore extraction. The smiths that mastered these techniques were almost certainly full-time specialists removed from processing their own food supply. Such specialization encouraged other specialization, for smiths had to be supported by the surplus foods produced by farmers engaged exclusively in agricultural production. The development of metallurgy increased not only specialization but also the efficiency of production. Compared to stone, a metal tool holds its edge longer, is far easier to sharpen, and in its greater durability has the added advantage that one can melt it down and recast it as a new tool. Lastly, it is all too obvious that the invention of metals has led to the elaboration of new activities even today in practical, military, and recreational activities.

The factors mentioned above are not the only conditions which led to the rise of complex societies. In recent years, they are thought to have been the principal forces behind the urban revolution. But there are also other factors, such as military activity and warfare, which influenced the development of a central authority and the expansion of states. Further archaeological work will assign different emphasis to the causes discussed here. It is clear that no factor can be discounted; yet no factor is of such overriding importance as to be the sole cause for the rise of complex societies. It is in the interrelatedness of these conditions that the evolution of civilization is to be understood.

Notes

1. Emery (1961:30–37).
2. Butzer (1976:109–110).
3. Kraeling and Adams (1960:124–136).
4. Helck (1975).
5. Kemp (1977:185–199).
6. Ibid.
7. Adams (1972).
8. Childe (1950:123–145).
9. Adams (1966; 1972).
10. Schmandt-Besserat (1978:50–59).
11. Masson and Sarianidi (1972:128–136).
12. Vidali and Lamberg-Karlovsky (1976:237–250).
13. Merriggi (n.d.).
14. Frankfort (1951:90–102).
15. Mallowan (1949:48–87).
16. Matthiae (1977:244–253).
17. Oppenheim (1977:95ff.).
18. Adams (1966); Diakonoff (1969); Oppenheim (1977); Gelb (1952).
19. Adams (1966).
20. Lamberg-Karlovsky (1976:64–73).
21. Diakonoff (1969).
22. Jacobsen (1943).
23. Sahlins (1976:133).
24. Braudel (1972:vol. 1, pp. 355–460).
25. Kramer (1963:269–272).
26. Kohl (1978).
27. Piggott (1950:135–216).
28. Rao (1973:117–119).
29. Rao (1973:50–79).
30. Bibby (1969).
31. Zide and Zvlebil (1976).
32. Whitehouse (1977).

4. Ancient Mesoamerican Civilization

213

Mesoamerica, or Middle America, is a term used by archaeologists to designate a geographic area within whose borders a distinct cultural system flourished in Precolumbian times. Such well-known cultures as the Olmec, Classic Maya, Toltec, and Aztec rose, prospered, and collapsed in this archaeologically famous area. In this chapter, we look at the rise and development of complex societies in this culture area. Readers should keep in mind as they mentally compare the developments of Mesoamerica with those of the Near East that Mesoamerica covers a much smaller area. It also seems to have displayed more cultural unity over a 3000-year period than did the region from Anatolia to the Indus. Despite these basic differences, though, some strikingly similar developmental patterns characterized the beginnings of agriculture and the later rise of civilizations in both the Old and New World localities.

Ancient civilization first arose in Mesoamerica about 1200 B.C. among the Olmecs on the Gulf Coast of the modern-day Mexican states of Veracruz and Tabasco. As we discuss below, the Olmecs soon began to spread their influence to other parts of Mexico, into Guatemala, Honduras, and Salvador, even as far south as Costa Rica. It is about this time period, certainly by 1000 B.C., that we can say the Mesoamerican culture area (or better yet, the Mesoamerican civilizational system) comes into being.

Geography and Climate

Mesoamerica was first defined as a culture area by the anthropologist Paul Kirchoff in 1943. Although its geographic borders shifted as different groups expanded and cultures changed, basically the boundaries of Mesoamerica stretch from the Rio Sota de la Marina and the Rio Sinaloa in the north of Mexico to Honduras, Salvador, and the Nicoya Peninsula in the south (see Map 4.1). The area thus includes much of Mexico and all of Guatemala and Belize.

The environment of Mesoamerica contains tremendous variety. Topographically, the area is dominated by great north-south mountain ranges such as the Sierra Madre Oriental and Sierra Madre Occidental in Mexico. These ranges include many active volcanos, particularly in Central Mexico and throughout Guatemala and Salvador. These highland areas of Mesoamerica are also dissected by numerous rivers flowing toward either the Atlantic or Pacific oceans. Some of the largest highland valleys and basins, such as the Valley of Mexico and the Valley of Oaxaca, were

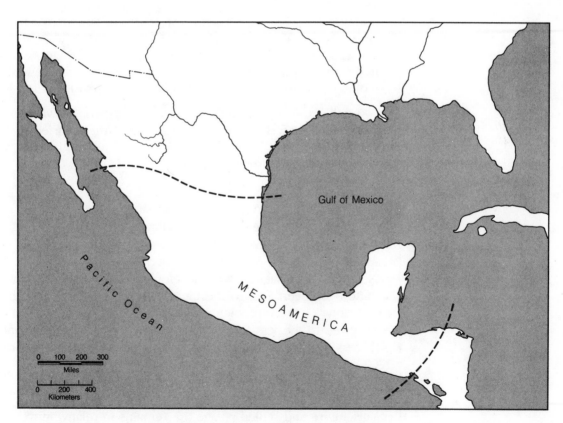

Map 4.1 The boundaries of Mesoamerica.

centers of complex prehistoric cultural developments for several thousand years.

In discussing Mesoamerica, the geographer Robert West has remarked that "few parts of the earth of similar size have such a varied and complex surface configuration and geology."[1] The extremes of the Mesoamerican environment can be seen by contrasting the semiarid highland valleys, such as the Valley of Teotihuacán where the magnificent city of Teotihuacán arose, with the dense tropical lowland rain forests which supported cities such as the great Classic Maya center of Tikal. As archaeologist Muriel Porter Weaver has noted in her general text on Mesoamerican prehistory:

> When man settled in Mesoamerica, he could live at an elevation of 8000 feet, at sea level, or at intermediate points. He had a wide choice of dwelling sites: alluvial plains, terraces, caves, valleys, inland basins. He could choose to live near a lake, spring, or river in areas with abundant rainfall, or he could choose a dry, semi-desert climate. Lush tropical forests, savannas, deciduous forests, and barren desert-like terrain offered very different opportunities for exploitation.[2]

As we will see in the ensuing discussion, the peoples who inhabited Mesoamerica took full advantage of these varied environments and often exploited both their living and nonliving resources with great sophistication.

The Rise of Agriculture

Through the years, the sites of the Olmec, Maya, Teotihuacán, Toltec, and Aztec civilizations have attracted the attention of many archaeologists. As a result, our archaeological knowledge of Mesoamerica is relatively well developed. Unfortunately, most attention has been paid to the highly visible remains of the great civilizations of Precolumbian Mesoamerica. Little attention has been given to the less spectacular remains of early hunters and gatherers or settled villagers who lived in the same area prior to 1200 B.C. and provided the cultural foundation for the later developments. Thus, in contrast to the well-publicized civilizations of the Maya or the Aztec, our knowledge of the rise of agriculture and settled village life remains in relative poverty. However, recent work in the Tehuacán Valley of Puebla, Mexico, which has largely been published, and the Valley of Oaxaca, Mexico, which is just beginning to be published, has added considerably to our knowledge of the cultural foundation upon which the ancient civilizations of Mesoamerica were built.

A limited number of archaeological discoveries have been made in Mesoamerica which pertain to the last part of the Pleistocene ice age or "Early Man" or "Big Game Hunting" periods before 8000 B.C. Evidence indicates that the hunting of now-extinct large mammals was not of great importance in Mesoamerica, certainly not south of the Valley of Mexico. Big game probably formed only a minor part of people's diets in comparison to gathering of plants and fruits and hunting of small animals, even in northern Mesoamerica.

With the end of the Pleistocene and the concomitant climatic changes around 8000 or 7000 B.C., small game hunting and gathering became the rule. Our only archaeological evidence for human activities at this time and for the next several thousand years comes from the highlands of Mexico and Guatemala. In particular, archaeologists have uncovered many data which pertain to this time period from the semiarid uplands of Mexico. There is no archaeological evidence for occupation of the lowlands of Mesoamerica until as late as the third millennium B.C.

To gain some understanding of the processes which led to the growth of complex societies in Mesoamerica, it is necessary to consider the beginings of both agriculture and settled village life. Unlike the Old World, animal domestication never played a crucial role in Precolumbian Mesoamerica.

In contrast to the situation in the Near East, our data on the rise of agriculture and settled village life in Mesoamerica are relatively meager and not nearly so well synthesized. Whereas the richness of archaeological materials on the Neolithic period of the Near East obliged us to devote a full chapter to our discussions of these data, there is very little published information on the comparable time period in Mesoamerica—a situation which forces us to include our examination of early agriculture as a background section to this chapter's discussion: the rise of civilization in Mesoamerica. Fortunately, however, the published data for one particular area in Mexico, the Tehuacán Valley of southern Puebla (see Map 4.2), are as strong as any comparable site or area in the Near East. From an examination of the developments that took place in that highland valley, we can draw some inferences about this period in other areas of Mesoamerica.

THE TEHUACÁN VALLEY

Archaeological investigations have revealed that plants were first domesticated in Mesoamerica at a much later date than in the Old World. In the Tehuacán Valley, the process seems to have begun in the seventh millennium B.C. but did not really become established until the second millennium B.C. (Plate 4.1).

 As archaeologist Kent Flannery has noted, the people of Tehuacán and other inhabitants of Mexico

survived on the basis of a collecting strategy with many alternate moves and alternate food sources, depending on whether the rains

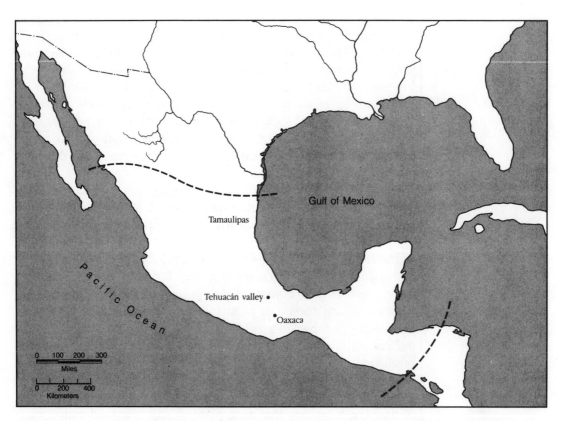

Map 4.2 Regions of early agricultural development.

came too soon or too late, the spring was too cool or too hot, the deer were in the valleys or up in the forest, the pinyon nut crop was heavy or meager. Finally, by 5000 B.C. one of their ultimate strategies became the artificial increase of certain edible plants by selection and planting. Beans, squashes, pumpkins, amaranths, chiles, tomatoes, avocados (and perhaps even prickly pear, maguey, and a whole series of semi-tropical fruits for which we have only Indian names) came under cultivation not long after this date. But the most important of these was maize or Indian corn.[3]

Within that valley, an intensive interdisciplinary research project directed by the archaeologist Richard S. MacNeish (Plate 4.2) has uncovered our best information to date about the rise of agriculture in Mesoamerica. MacNeish's archaeological excavations have been concentrated in a relatively small area (about 70 miles long by 20 miles wide). Although the area is not large, the findings have been unusually rich. The dryness of the Tehuacán Valley has preserved a wide variety of normally perishable materials in the valley cave sites, so excavations have provided a wealth of information about the beginnings of food production and settled life in this area. From twelve stratified

Plate 4.1 General view of the Tehuacán Valley. (Courtesy of R. S. Peabody Foundation.)

sites (454 sites in all), "10,000 artifacts, 500,000 sherds and 50,000 ecofacts (remnants of the environment)" were discovered.[4] Those data enabled the excavators to define a long cultural sequence that began in roughly 10,000 B.C. and continued until the Spanish Conquest in A.D. 1521.

The Tehuacán Cultural Sequence

Within this sequence, MacNeish has distinguished nine cultural phases; the first six (from about 10,000 B.C. to 850 B.C.) are especially relevant to our own inquiry about the rise of agriculture and village life. The earliest cultural phase in the valley has been called the *Ajuereado;* it lasted from 10,000 to 7000 B.C. The population consisted of small nomadic microbands.

On the basis of the sizes of the sites (either small camps in open areas or cave occupations) and number of fireplaces, it has been estimated that these microbands consisted of two or three nuclear families. Throughout the period, there may have been from one to five of these groups in the valley. On the basis of the animal and plant remains found in Ajuereado sites, scientists have been able to show that inhabitants occupied a site for only

Plate 4.2   Richard "Scotty" MacNeish (in white sweater) at a cave excavation. (Courtesy of R. S. Peabody Foundation.)

one season at a time and then moved on to another. Such determinations are possible because plants and seeds are available only in a certain season, and also because the kind of animal, its age, and characteristics of its bones can give strong clues as to the season in which it was killed. If all the plant and animal remains in a single occupation level of a camp or a cave indicate they were collected or killed in only one season, then the archaeologist can infer that the people living there moved on to another site after the end of the season. If several seasons are represented in a single level, more permanent habitation can be inferred. The excellent preservation of perishable materials such as plant remains in the dry climate of the Tehuacán Valley has obviously aided the archaeologists in their reconstructions.

The Ajuereado peoples subsisted on the hunting of small animals and the gathering of plants and seeds. They used chipped stone projectile points, which they sometimes made into a laurel leaf shape, for hunting. They also used chipped stone knives, scrapers, choppers, and gravers for other activities.

The second cultural phase, the *El Riego,* lasted from about 7000 to 5000 B.C. During this time, the archaeological evidence

Plate 4.3 Excavations at Coxcatlan Cave in the Tehuacán Valley. (Courtesy of R. S. Peabody Foundation.)

indicates that in the summer months the microbands joined together to take advantage of the rich vegetable resources. For the first time, there are indications of agriculture: MacNeish estimates that up to 6% of the people's diet came from agricultural produce. Population clearly was increasing. Again, on the basis of the number of sites or levels at sites found, their size, and their length of occupation, MacNeish estimates that by the end of this period, there might have been at least a hundred people living in the valley. "Macroband" camps are identified on the basis of size (they average about 7000 square meters in extent) and by the presence of three or more hearths. The areas occupied for all of the El Riego Phase are about twenty-five times greater than for the Ajuereado Phase.

Findings from the El Riego period include many distinctive projectile points, including dart points, scrapers, and choppers. For the first time, people were using ground and pecked stone mortars, pestles, and milling stones for grinding plant remains. Evidence for weaving and woodworking was also found in archaeological levels dating to this period. Due to the dry climate of the valley, pieces of nets, blankets, baskets, and traps were preserved. Finally, burials with bodies wrapped in blankets were discovered, indicating some degree of simple ceremonialism in the treatment of the dead. MacNeish and his colleagues query: "Is it not possible that the ceremonialism which is so characteristic of the later Mexican periods began at this time?"[5]

The trends of the El Riego Phase continued into the *Coxcatlan* Phase (5000–3400 B.C.). During this period, agricultural produce formed 14% of the diet. Of great importance, there is initial evidence for the cultivation of domesticated maize or corn. There also is evidence for the cultivation of beans, squashes, and gourds. MacNeish believes that some of these latter domesticates may have been brought into the valley from regions outside, although it is uncertain how they might have been brought in or in which particular highland valley or region they could have originated.

More macroband encampments were found from this phase, indicating that the population may have increased to several hundred people (Figure 4.1). There is even some evidence that the different bands in the valley had separate territories. For the first time, true ground stone *manos* and *metates* were used for grinding plants. (Similar "rollers" and shallow "grinding bowls"

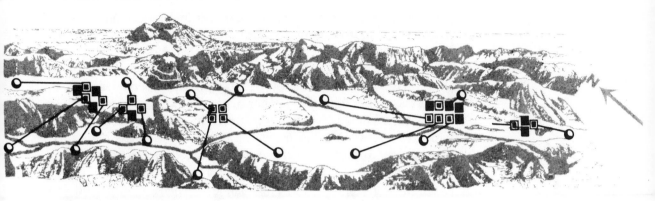

Figure 4.1 Coxcatlan and early Abejas settlements in the Tehuacán Valley. At this time (5000 to 3000 B.C.), semi-sedentary macrobands had wet-season fall camps or annual camps but often separated into dry-season micro-band camps. (From R. S. MacNeish, "Ancient Mesoamerican Civilization," *Science,* vol. 143, copyright by the American Association for the Advancement of Science.)

are used today in Mexico for grinding maize.) Although there was a general continuity in stone tools, some new types of projectile points came into use, and, by the end of the period, fine chipped blades were being made.

By *Abejas* times in the Tehuacán Valley (3400–2300 B.C.), an important change in settlement patterns apparently had taken place, and we finally see one of the consequences of the slow but growing utilization of domesticated crops. During this time period, MacNeish found the first evidence for centrally based bands with permanent camps or hamlets. These hamlets average 15,000 square meters in overall extent and contain the earliest definite residential structures in the Tehuacán Valley. Throughout the valley, MacNeish found four oval pit (or partially subterranean) houses dating to the Abejas Phase. There are no indications, however, of public buildings or centralized authority at this time. The hamlets probably were lived in nearly all year round, but they also served as central bases for hunting and gathering forays at some distance from the hamlets.

In the succeeding *Purron* Phase (2300–1500 B.C.), the first examples of the manufacture and use of pottery were discovered. Two types of crude pottery ("Purron Coarse" and "Purron Plain") were uncovered. Neither showed any decoration, and they were shaped in both bowl and jar forms. The Tehuacán pottery is very similar to pottery from roughly the same date discovered on the Pacific Coast of the Mexican state of Guerrero. The nature of possible contacts between Tehuacán and the coastal lowlands at this time is unknown. Moreover, whether the Tehuacán pottery was a local invention or whether the idea for ceramic manufacturing was imported from, say, Panama or South America, where even earlier pottery has been found, remains an open question. Other than the pottery found in Purron levels of sites in the Tehuacán Valley, little is known about this phase. It remains one of the most poorly understood of all the periods in the Tehuacán sequence.

More is known about the *Ajalpan* Phase, which lasted from 1500 to 850 B.C. MacNeish has located twelve hamlets dating to this phase. Almost all of these were situated next to one of the rivers which flow through the valley—a characteristic which has earned them the title "waterway hamlets." The Ajalpan period was a time of impressive change. By its end, villages with houses and public architecture had arisen. By this time, however, the complex society of the Olmecs had already evolved in the Gulf Coast lowlands.

During the Ajalpan Phase, agriculture formed 40% of the inhabitants' diet and was sufficiently developed to support year-round habitation. As MacNeish states, the Ajalpan people "were growing sufficient food in only one season to last all the year and for this reason I refer to this system as subsistence agriculture rather than effective food production."[6] Houses during Ajalpan times were either oval or rectangular in shape with wattle and daub walls. The first painted pottery dates to this time and ceramic figurines became plentiful. Large solid female figurines are a particular time marker for the Ajalpan Phase. Population, which continued to grow throughout the Tehuacán archaeological sequence, probably exceeded a thousand people in this period. Succeeding phases from 850 B.C. up until the time of the Spanish Conquest saw the slow growth of increasingly larger villages and eventually city-states in the Tehuacán Valley.

Agriculture and Sedentism: An Overview

MacNeish has proposed a simple but convincing model to explain the slow transition to settled village life based on agricultural production. He believes that over a long period of time, the nomadic hunter-gatherers of the Tehuacán Valley gained intimate knowledge of the seasonal changes in all the different microenvironments of the valley. They learned to schedule their seasonal movements to take maximum advantage of particular seasons in particular microenvironments. They returned year after year to those microenvironments which had most to offer in the way of hunting and collecting. One result of the oft-used camps and consistent clearing of their surrounding areas was the growth of genetic mutations of some of the plants and fruits the nomads relied on. Slowly, and probably accidentally at first, the Tehuacán peoples began to practice horticulture and eventually agriculture.

These changes allowed the inhabitants to start to build up small food surpluses and permitted them to stay in one camp for a longer time, perhaps for two seasons instead of just one. These trends resulted in an ever-increasing manipulation of aspects of the environment. The growing control reached a culmination in the second millennium B.C., when the inhabitants of the Tehuacán Valley were able to live in villages all year round.

There is evidence that the same sort of spiral trend was taking place in other highland regions of southern Mexico. In the Valley of Oaxaca, about 100 miles to the south and east, Kent Flannery's studies indicate a similar chain of developments. He carries MacNeish's interpretation one step further to suggest that village life may not just have been "allowed" by the growing productivity of agricultural practices; it may actually have been required, as macrobands became committed to stay in one area to plant and harvest subsistence foods.[7] In other words, increasing dependence on domesticated plants eventually forced the inhabitants of highland valleys like Tehuacán and Oaxaca to remain in villages year round.

How did this cumulative dependence on agriculture and sedentism develop? In Flannery's view, the changes can be seen as an example of positive feedback that might never have taken the turn it did except for the accident of genetic mutations which tilted the equilibrium of the early prehistoric cultures and their ecosystems:

> Such "insignificant or accidental initial kicks" were a series of genetic changes which took place in one or two species of Mesoamerican plants which were of use to man. The exploitation of these plants had been a relatively minor procurement system compared with that of maguey, cactus, fruits, deer, or tree legumes, but positive feedback following these initial genetic changes caused one minor system to grow all out of proportion to the others, and eventually to change the whole ecosystem of the Southern Mexican Highlands....
>
> Starting with what may have been (initially) accidental deviations in the system, a positive feedback network was established which eventu-

ally made maize cultivation the most profitable single subsistence activity in Mesoamerica. The more widespread maize cultivation, the more opportunities for favorable crosses and back-crosses; the more favorable genetic changes, the greater the yield, the greater the yield, the higher the population, and hence the more intensive cultivation.[8]

The models proposed by MacNeish and Flannery provide important leads to the general processes in the rise of agriculture and the beginnings of settled village life. Even though specific ecological conditions differed in the Old World and the New World, MacNeish himself has suggested that it is more than likely that the increasing need to stay near planting areas was basic to the development of permanent villages in Sumer, Egypt, and the Indus region as well as Mexico. Of course, important differences existed between the two cultural spheres. As we have seen, Mesoamerica had none of the animal domesticates that provided both protein and services (like transportation and plowing) for the people of the Near East. Climate differed, and so did crops: while grains like wheat and barley formed an important part of the subsistence base in the Old World, the mainstay of the ancient Mexicans was maize. We turn now to an examination of the "food-producing revolution" in Mesoamerica, specifically to explanations of the developing dependence upon maize.

The Domestication of Maize

Maize, or corn, was one of the basic crops, perhaps the most important crop, which the ancient inhabitants of Mesoamerica domesticated. It did not occur in nature during the earliest phases of the human occupation of Mexico: only through a series of genetic changes did it develop into the basic crop of Mesoamerica. How did those changes take place, and what ancestral wild plant did maize develop from? Scientists have studied this plant for years and still are not in complete agreement about the botanical nature of its domestication from a wild plant to the domesticated corn we know today.   One of the leading experts on the domestication of maize, Paul Mangelsdorf, has hypothesized that through a series of genetic changes and cross-fertilizations, a wild, now extinct ancestor of maize was transformed into domesticated maize. He believes that the earliest corncobs, discovered by MacNeish in the

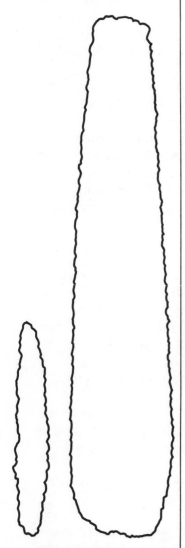

Figure 4.2 Comparison in size between early cultivated maize (from the Abejas Phase) and maize from about the time of the Spanish Conquest. (After Byers and MacNeish 1967– 1976: Vol. 1.)

Tehuacán Valley, are examples of this extinct ancestor. These cobs, dating to at least 5000 B.C., are quite small, measuring less than 75 millimeters in length (see Figure 4.2).

In recent years, Mangelsdorf's views have been challenged by other plant geneticists and botanists, principally George Beadle, former president of the University of Chicago. Beadle believes that the ancestor of maize was *teosinte*, a wild grass found in many parts of highland Mexico. Through simple genetic mutations, *teosinte* could have been transformed into maize. A majority of archaeologists have come to favor this simple but elegant hypothesis, which parallels some explanations for plant domestication in the Old World. Flannery has pointed out that the *teosinte* hypothesis and its explanation of the genetic changes are very similar to the hypothesis for the rise of domesticated wheat in the Near East proposed by Hans Helbaek.

The question of exactly how and why this change took place remains an open one, of course. In Coxcatlan times, *teosinte* and subsequently early maize would have been low in eating preference among the inhabitants of the Tehuacán and other highland Mexican valleys (a third-class crop, according to Flannery). The transformation from *teosinte* to productive domesticated maize may have taken several thousand years and much experimentation and labor on the part of these early farmers. Why the early inhabitants of the Mexican highlands would have attempted to cultivate *teosinte* at all, in fact, is a question Flannery raises in a more recent publication. He notes that hunters and gatherers did not often eat *teosinte*. (Nor, for that matter, did hunters and gatherers in other parts of the world eat the ancestors of other major seed crops such as wheat in the Near East.) He analyzes both the disadvantages and the advantages:

> But the ancestors of these seed crops had a number of characteristics which most of the "first-choice" foods of the Pleistocene hunter did not have. They are mostly annual; they yield a high return (200–800 kg per hectare) [1 hectare=2.2 acres]; they tolerate a wide range of disturbed habitats; they store easily; and they are genetically plastic. Thus, they could be used to replace the "native" vegetation with a plant that in less than a year after planting would cover a disturbed patch with a dense growth of storable food. And as time went on, they responded with favorable genetic changes which made them either more productive, easier to harvest, easier to prepare, or all three. If what you want is a plant which will increase the carrying capacity of

each hectare, and which can be stored to last out the year, they are your obvious choices. The disadvantages are that (a) farming may be more work than hunting, judging by the available ethnographic data, and (b) an unstable man-modified ecosystem with a low diversity index results. Since early farming represents a decision to work harder and to eat more "third-choice" food, I suspect that people did it because they felt they had to, not because they wanted to. Why they felt they had to we may never know, in spite of the fact that their decision reshaped all the rest of human history.[9]

Population Pressure and Plant Domestication

Some scholars have not been as hesitant as Flannery to point to a reason why hunters and gatherers in Mesoamerica and elsewhere "had to" turn to farming after the end of the Pleistocene. These writers have argued that population pressure may well have been the major factor behind the rise of agriculture. Building on the pioneering suggestions of Ester Boserup in her book, *The Conditions of Agricultural Growth* (1965), Mark Cohen has recently argued that "population growth and pressure are contributing factors in the origins and growth of an agricultural economy worldwide."[10]

The argument that population pressure was critical in the rise of agriculture is an appealing one. But it is not totally convincing when we look at its application to Mesoamerica in general and the Tehuacán Valley in particular.

The work of MacNeish, Flannery, and others clearly shows a steady trend of population growth from the end of the Pleistocene to the second millennium B.C. During this long time span, domestication of various plants was accomplished. While the rise of agriculture was a slow process, the rise of settled villages was slower still: plant domestication did not lead immediately to settled village life. Rather, as it became possible to increase the yields of certain plants and to store them, people in highland valleys such as Tehuacán began to be able to live in one locale for more than one season. In Tehuacán, it was not until Ajalpan times (1500–850 B.C.) that people began living in permanent year-round settlements with relatively large populations, and not until the end of this phase did agricultural produce form more than 50% of the Tehuacános' diets.

But does the trend of population growth indicate the presence of population stress or pressure? Certainly the evidence for large, permanent villages comes several millennia after the rise of agriculture. Cohen, however, argues that the only reason people would have experimented with low-priority seeds such as maize over several thousand years was the stress of population pressure. Population density appears to be relatively low in highland Mexico during the period when plants were first domesticated, but this evidence is not conclusive. We simply do not know what densities would have caused stress given the available resources and technologies.

While Cohen's argument as applied to Mesoamerica is a plausible one, so is Flannery's feedback model based on the genetic flexibility of *teosinte* and maize. Until we have detailed, published data on more than just the Tehuacán valley, and until we have better quantitative data on carrying capacities and population densities from several different highland regions in Mesoamerica, it is difficult at best to evaluate the suggestion that population pressure led to the use of agriculture in Mesoamerica and throughout the world.

OTHER REGIONS, OTHER CROPS

To avoid leaving a false impression, we should make it clear that Tehuacán was not the only valley where early domestication took place and maize was not the only important crop. We do have archaeological data about other significant cultigens in the Tehuacán Valley and other parts of ancient Mexico.

Richard MacNeish's archaeological research in the late 1940s and early 1950s in the caves of Tamaulipas (see Plate 4.4), to the south of the Rio Sota de la Marina on the Gulf Coast side of Mexico, has revealed important data about the early domestication of plants such as beans and squashes as well as maize. Moreover, recent surveys and excavations by Flannery and his colleagues in the Oaxaca Valley also promise to make very significant contributions to our knowledge of the rise of agriculture in Mesoamerica.

MacNeish's excavations in the late 1940s at La Perra Cave in the Canyon Diablo in Tamaulipas revealed an early, primitive maize, radiocarbon dated to about 2500 B.C. (Moreover, he began his important and productive collaboration with Paul Mangelsdorf in search of the origins of domesticated maize.)

Plate 4.4   General view of the Tamaulipas environment. (Courtesy of R. S. Peabody Foundation.)

Due to his initial successes in Tamaulipas, MacNeish decided to continue his research there. He returned in 1953–1954 to undertake new excavations, this time in the southwest portion of the region. In the Canyon Infiernillo, he dug several caves which yielded excellent stratigraphy and evidence of long occupation. One of these caves, Romero's Cave, revealed seventeen distinct stratigraphic levels. No very early maize was found here, but other domesticates, from levels earlier than those in the Canyon Diablo, were discovered. On the basis of these findings, MacNeish was able to conclude that Mesoamerican agriculture had multiple origins, with food production happening at a number of different times in a number of different places.[11]

While maize did not appear in the Tamaulipas region until nearly two thousand years after it had been domesticated in Tehuacán, at least one species of squash shows up in the archaeological record in Tamaulipas by 7000 B.C., and it probably was domesticated at that time. That particular species of squash does not appear in Tehuacán until two thousand years later. In Oaxaca, Flannery's recent work shows that this squash appeared there even before it did in Tamaulipas. On the other hand, a different species of squash appears a thousand years earlier in Tehuacán than in Tamaulipas.

Wild beans have been discovered in Oaxaca as early as 8700 B.C. and slightly later in Tamaulipas. The exact time when beans were domesticated, however, remains unclear. It should also be noted that *teosinte* seeds have been found as early as 7000 B.C. in Oaxaca, but it is not yet known where in highland Mexico, or when, the transition to domesticated maize was accomplished.

The widely differing dates for the first appearances of cultigens like squash, beans, and maize as well as many other edible plants, and the general similarities in subsistence, settlement patterns, and tool use in different parts of early Mesoamerica, have led scholars such as Mark Cohen to believe that sequences like those of Tehuacán, Tamaulipas, and Oaxaca are the result of "parallel economic adaptation rather than diffusion of crops."[12] Nevertheless, as we can see by the close similarities in many stone tools such as projectile points, knives, and scrapers over much of highland Mexico, there must have been regular contact among various valleys and regions. And certainly some knowledge about domestication—if not the domesticates themselves—must have diffused from place to place.

The nature of these contacts is unknown at this time, as is the impact of contacts among different groups in Mesoamerica. As we will see, trade becomes a crucial factor in civilizational development later on in Mesoamerican history, as it was in ancient Near Eastern developments. Until further archaeological research is undertaken, however, it is difficult even to speculate about the role of trade prior to the growth of complex societies in Mesoamerica.

While evidence indicates that a process of independent adaptation probably played some part in the appearance of agriculture in several areas of Mesoamerica, the process of cultural diffusion was important in the spread of agriculture from Mesoamerica (and, in the case of manioc, *to* Mesoamerica). It seems clear that a number of agricultural practices diffused from Mesoamerica to the American Southwest many thousands of years after the process of domestication had first begun in Mexico.

The best evidence of Mesoamerican maize, beans, and squash comes from the Mogollon area of the southern half of New Mexico and southeastern Arizona. At the site of Bat Cave in New Mexico, archaeologists led by Herbert Dick found a very early form of maize, dated from 3000 to 2000 B.C., which definitely appears to have come from Mesoamerica. Moreover, through later levels at Bat Cave, investigators have been able to trace the evolution of a more modern form of maize, apparently derived from repeated crossings between local maize and new imports from Mesoamerica.

Maize pollen dating after 2000 B.C., as well as other examples of maize dating to the centuries before the Christian era, have also been discovered in the Mogollon area. As archaeologists have pointed out, all these early finds come from an upland part of the Southwest—an area which is environmentally similar to highland areas in Mexico where maize had just been domesticated. In the words of a noted Southwestern archaeologist, Professor Emil Haury: "We are left ... with the inference that the earliest maize, probably a variety adjusted for higher altitudes, spread along the cordilleran spine of the greater Southwest and found lodging in east-central Arizona and west-central New

Mexico."[13] In Haury's view, the Southwestern American people had probably already domesticated some plants (for instance, chenopods and amaranths)—perhaps as early as 4000 B.C. This experience, as well as their possession of tools for processing plant foods, made it relatively easy for them to accept and utilize maize, along with the indigenous plants they had already domesticated.

Like maize, other Mesoamerican domesticates such as squash and beans diffused to the Southwest. At first these infusions had little effect on the overall life-style. Only gradually, more than two thousand years after the introduction of cultigens from the south, did the consequence of this and other cultural changes appear as people of the American Southwest began to live year round in farming villages.

Diffusion of maize and other crops from Mesoamerica influenced developments in other New World areas as well as the American Southwest. Maize has been found in the southeastern United States and also in South America—from as early as 3000 B.C. in the southern highlands of Peru, according to recent research by MacNeish, and from 2500 B.C. in the site of Real Alto in Ecuador.[14]

If one accepts the Beadle hypothesis, all this means that maize must have diffused to South America from Mesoamerica, since *teosinte* is not found in South America—unless South American maize followed a completely different developmental course. In any case, the diffusion of agriculture raises many questions about the nature of contacts between Mesoamerica and South America, and between Mesoamerica and the region that is now the southern United States. We do know that the diffusion of more than agriculture was taking place, for many implements of the same type have been found in distant areas within and beyond Mesoamerica. How much trade and cultural diffusion took place between the different cultural spheres? We can also assume that the movement of cultigens and other materials was not all one-directional, from Mexico to other regions, since manioc from South America was being cultivated in lowland Mesoamerica by 2000 B.C. Whether the contact between Mesoamerica and the American Southwest and between Mesoamerica and South America was regular or intermittent, and whether it was undertaken by traders or by explorers, are still unanswered questions.

THE CONSEQUENCES OF
FOOD PRODUCTION: AN OVERVIEW

As we have seen, the practice of domesticating plants took a long time to take hold in Mesoamerica. The pioneering research of MacNeish and his associates over the past three decades has done much to throw some light on the complex processes of domestication in this area. First in Tamaulipas and subsequently in the Tehuacán Valley, MacNeish's interdisciplinary research programs have been able to show the slow development of agriculture over a period of many thousands of years in ancient Mexico.

These studies have indicated that such important staples as maize, beans, and squash were domesticated in the highlands of Mesoamerica between about 7000 and 3000 B.C. The Tehuacán Valley studies in particular have shown how these crops came to be integrated into the diet of the hunting and gathering peoples of the valley and how reliance on domesticated plants slowly grew through time. One of the principal outgrowths of this slow process, the development of settled villages, took even more time to emerge in the Tehuacán Valley and the highlands, although in the Valley of Oaxaca, which also has revealed a long developmental sequence of plant domestication, settled villages may have emerged at a slightly earlier time than in Tehuacán.

While the pattern of agriculture leading to settled village life seems to have been the rule throughout the highland areas, it does not appear to have been typical for all of Mesoamerica. On the Pacific Coast, villages arose in the third millennium B.C. apparently without the benefit of agriculture. In these coastal areas, many varied and rich food resources could be exploited in one locale without the necessity of moving from one place to another. Some new and exciting research has been carried out or is being undertaken on the crucial 2500–1500 B.C. time period in both the lowlands and the highlands, and publication of these studies will be a great aid to archaeologists in their attempts to understand this transitional period. Some scholars have suggested that the diffusion of domesticated crops such as maize to the lowland coastal areas, sometime in the latter part of the third millennium B.C. or the beginning of the second, could have provided an important stimulus to cultural development which ultimately led, as we will see, to the rise of civilization in Mesoamerica.

Following the rise of domestication in the highlands of Mexico, the use of a variety of domesticated plants spread at varying rates throughout Mesoamerica and also to adjacent areas such as the American Southwest and to more distant areas such as southeastern North America and perhaps South America. It should be stressed that Mesoamerica was not the only center of plant domestication in the New World. A complex developmental sequence for the rise of agriculture has been found in the Andean area of South America centering on modern-day Peru, while the greater Amazonian lowlands also may have been a significant hearth of domestication, particularly as regards the development of manioc, an important root crop.

Given this background, we now turn our attention to one of the major consequences of the growth of agriculture and settled village life in Mesoamerica: the rise of civilization in both the highlands and the lowlands. While the transition from a nomadic hunting and gathering way of life to that of permanent settled villages was a slow one, the transition from a simple village existence to a complex one was relatively rapid. By 1200 B.C., the growth of settled agricultural villages in Mesoamerica was beginning to be accompanied by other cultural developments: increasingly complex sociopolitical organization, expanding population, growing intercommunity exchanges, and rising wealth (along with differential access of people to it). In the following sections, we will explore these trends toward growing complexity and see how they led to the rise of Mesoamerican civilization, first among the Olmecs of the Gulf Coast of Mexico and later among Teotihuacános, the Maya, the Toltecs, and ultimately the Aztecs.

The Cultures of Ancient Mesoamerica

Archaeologists have traditionally viewed the development of complex societies in Mesoamerica in terms of a sequence of discrete civilizations in different regions of the area. In recent years, however, as archaeological knowledge has rapidly increased, scholars have been impressed with the strong continuities in civilizational development from 1200 B.C. to A.D. 1521. They have also been struck by the influence which the different civilizations from the Olmec to the Aztec appear to have had throughout all of Mesoamerica. New information has led some archaeologists to the position that ancient Mesoamerica had one civilization which arose around 1200 B.C. and lasted 2700 years—until the Spanish Conquest in the sixteenth century. They view this great civilization as a system which integrated Mesoamerica economically, politically, and spiritually. As the archaeologist Ignacio Bernal has stated:

> In Mesoamerica there has been but one civilization, although the forms have changed in time and in space. . . . From now on I will not speak of a Maya or Teotihuacán or Aztec civilization. I believe they are all the same. The Maya or the people of Teotihuacán or the Aztecs only represent different cultures within a civilization, just as western Christianity is but one civilization in spite of differences that exist between Spanish, German, or English cultures.[15]

In the remainder of this chapter, we will focus our attention on five of the principal manifestations of Mesoamerican civilization: the Olmecs; the Maya; the city-state of Teotihuacán; the Toltecs; and the Aztecs (Figure 4.3). But while looking at the individual characteristics that distinguished each culture from the others, we will try to point out the interconnections among them and the ways they influenced various parts of Mesoamerica. Particular attention will be paid to the questions of how and why different cultures developed and how they came to control the ancient Mesoamerican civilizational system. Some observations on the differences and similarities between these developments and those of the ancient Near East described in Chapter 3 will be offered in the concluding chapter.

THE OLMECS

By 1200 B.C. the Olmecs had created the first civilization in Mesoamerica. In the Gulf Coast lowlands of Mexico (see Map 4.3), these ancient people built ceremonial centers which featured both monumental architecture and sculpture. They were superb craftsmen who carved objects as small as tiny jade pendants and as large as 20-ton basalt heads in their own distinctive style. Their religious and economic influence spread from southern Mexico south to Costa Rica.

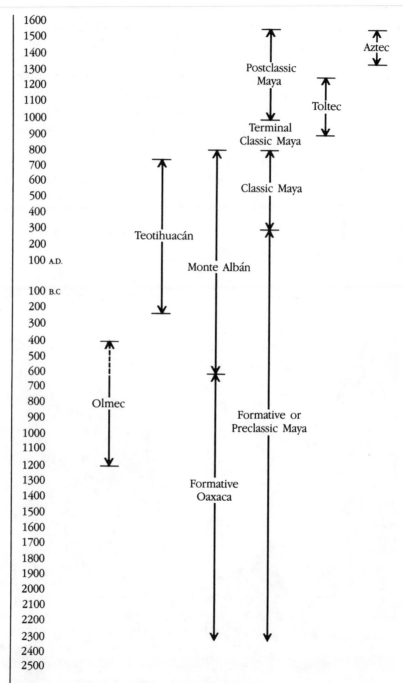

Figure 4.3 Chronology of ancient Mesoamerican civilizations.

In recent years, archaeologists have come to accept the Olmecs as the innovators of many features that were to characterize later Mesoamerican civilizations. This acceptance, however, has not come easily, and the intellectual battles behind it have made the story of the discovery and elucidation of this early civilization a fascinating one. As recently as four decades ago, the Olmecs were virtually unknown to archaeologists. In fact, knowledge of their true antiquity was not revealed until the late 1950s. In many ways, the scientific discovery of the Olmec civilization is as engrossing and exciting as Schliemann's discovery of Troy, although it is not nearly so well known.

One of the scholars who was principally responsible for the uncovering of Olmec civilization was the late Matthew Stirling of

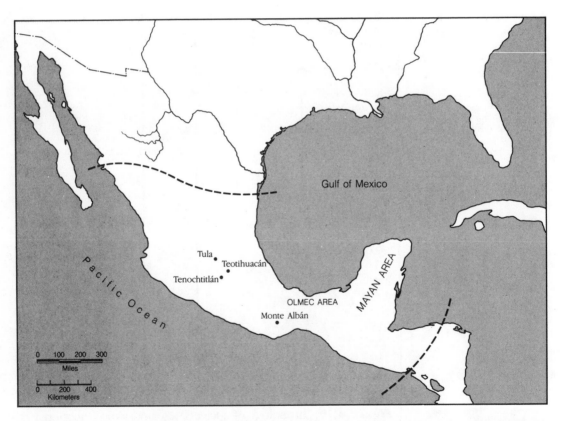

Map 4.3   Principal Mesoamerican sites and areas discussed in the text.

the Smithsonian Institution (Plate 4.5). Although by the late 1930s such great Olmec sites as Tres Zapotes and La Venta had been visited and large sculptures and jade objects in the Olmec style had been found, both the nature of these sites and objects and their dating were still unknown. As the archaeologist Michael Coe has stated: "By about 1938 there were strongly grounded suspicions that an entirely new civilization, somehow related to the Maya, but different from it, and of an unknown age,

Plate 4.5 Matthew Stirling in the field, kneeling next to a huge Olmec stone head. (Courtesy of National Geographic Society.)

was to be discovered in the jungle strongholds of the southern Gulf Coast plain."[16] Stirling was the discoverer.

From 1939 to 1942, Stirling explored and excavated the sites of Tres Zapotes and La Venta. As a result of this work, he was able to begin to construct a picture of Olmec civilization with its monumental art style and its complex religious iconography. His excavations associated the massive basalt sculpture of the Olmec with their fine jade carvings. Moreover, he discovered part of a carved monument (labeled Stela C) at Tres Zapotes which had a fragmentary hieroglyphic inscription. Stirling believed that the glyphic system was the same as the later Maya, and he read the glyphs as a date corresponding to 31 B.C.

To put it mildly, Stirling's interpretations were controversial. In effect, he was arguing that prior to the rise of Classic Maya civilization in the jungle lowlands of Guatemala and Mexico, the Olmec civilization had flourished in the Gulf Coast lowlands. Moreover, he claimed that the Olmecs had invented hieroglyphic writing and had initiated a great art style before the Maya. This

Plate 4.6 Gulf Coast lowland environment. (Courtesy of Peter D. Harrison.)

kind of proposal was tantamount to heresy to the Mayanists of the time. Such redoubtable scholars as J. Eric S. Thompson scathingly criticized Stirling's reading of the inscription at Tres Zapotes and stated that the Olmec monuments dated to Late Classic times at the earliest—the Olmec civilization did not predate the Classic Maya but derived from it. Stirling's only vocal support came from Mexican scholars who also recognized an early dating for the Olmecs and saw them as the "mother culture" for all later civilizational developments in Mexico.

The question of who the Olmecs were remained unresolved for nearly two decades. As other archaeologists uncovered more Olmec materials, it became clear that a new civilization had been discovered; but its dating remained clouded. In the mid-1950s, however, a group of archaeologists led by Phillip Drucker and Robert Heizer returned to La Venta to undertake new excavations. They unearthed a wide variety of Olmec objects and were able to define the Olmec civilization with more precision (see Plates 4.7–4.10). But even more important, these archaeologists were able to obtain organic materials which could be dated by the radiocarbon method. In 1957, the results were published. The dates showed that the Olmecs not only antedated the Classic Maya but had developed their complex culture at least eight centuries before the time of Christ. Stirling had been right.

Before we turn to a consideration of what our present knowledge can tell us about the Olmec civilization and its development, one more event in the ancient civilization's rediscovery should be noted. More than thirty years after Stirling discovered part of Stela C at the Tres Zapotes site, another fragment of the monument was uncovered in a field. This new piece contained the rest of the inscription which Stirling had read as 31 B.C. For Stirling, vindication was complete, since the remainder of the inscription was just as he had predicted!

The story of the discovery of Olmec civilization is a useful one to begin an examination of the growth of complex society in Mesoamerica. Above all, it shows how major new archaeological discoveries can be made even in the mid-twentieth century and how the intellectual perseverance of a minority viewpoint in the archaeological community can lead to eventual acceptance— even after initial rejection.

Plate 4.7 Main north-south trench at La Venta. A massive offering can be seen in the foreground, while a column tomb is visible in the background. (From P. Drucker, R. Heizer, and R. Squier, *Excavations at La Venta, Tabasco, 1955,* by permission of the Smithsonian Institution.)

Plate 4.8 Stela 3 at La Venta. (From P. Drucker, R. Heizer, and R. Squier, *Excavations at La Venta, Tabasco, 1955,* by permission of the Smithsonian Institution.)

The First Mesoamerican Civilization

Since the discoveries of Stirling and his colleagues, further exploration—including recent excavations by M. D. Coe at the important site of San Lorenzo Tenochtitlán and other excavations at Olmec and Olmec-related sites in the Mexican highlands—has greatly expanded our knowledge of the Olmec civilization. From Coe's work at San Lorenzo, located next to a tributary of the Cotzocoalcos River and about 40 miles from the Gulf of Mexico, we have an emerging picture of the physical plan, cultural achievements, and archaeological sequence of this early ceremonial center.

San Lorenzo was first occupied around 1500 B.C. It actually consists of three neighboring sites with San Lorenzo being the largest. The site of San Lorenzo rests upon an immense artificial platform—an architectural feat that attests to the huge amount of human labor the Olmecs must have employed to construct and decorate their ceremonial centers. San Lorenzo itself is not a city,

Plate 4.9 Buried mask mosaic which was uncovered at La Venta. (From P. Drucker, R. Heizer, and R. Squier, *Excavations at La Venta, Tabasco, 1955,* by permission of the Smithsonian Institution.)

nor is there any evidence of any true cities during Olmec times. Like La Venta and Tres Zapotes, it was a ceremonial center that had none of the wide differentiation nor the great population of the early Near Eastern cities or later Mesoamerican cities. San Lorenzo's ceremonial center apparently housed only a limited number of residents; the bulk of the population that supported the center (peasants who produced crops to sustain themselves and the rulers who lived in the center) lived in the surrounding area. The total population of San Lorenzo Tenochtitlán and its sustaining area at about 1000 B.C. probably did not exceed several thousand. Besides raising agricultural crops, the support population of peasants also provided the seasonal labor which helped build its center and transport the stones for the monuments erected there. The priestly rulers who supervised these activities lived in the centers, along with their families and acolytes and a small number of artisans.

It is commonly assumed by archaeologists that the Olmec civilization was a theocracy: peasants supported the rulers with their agricultural surplus and their labor in return for assurance

Plate 4.10 Offering of figurines and celts from La Venta. (From P. Drucker, R. Heizer, and R. Squier, *Excavations at La Venta, Tabasco, 1955,* by permission of the Smithsonian Institution.)

that the rituals carried out by the priests in the centers would help bring some degree of security to their lives and agricultural livelihood. The Olmec priests evolved a religion and a complex iconography which centered on a number of gods, most notably a jaguar god who is depicted throughout Olmec art.

The best-known attribute of the Olmec civilization, the colossal stone heads found at San Lorenzo, La Venta, and Tres Zapotes, attests to the craftsmanship of the Olmecs (Plate 4.11). These heads were carved from basalt which originated in the Tuxtla Mountains, as much as a hundred miles from the sites where they were found. Blocks of basalt weighing many tons had to be brought from their source to the Olmec sites, a feat requiring not only tremendous physical labor but also leadership that was equal to the task of orchestrating it. While the Olmec civilization was not an urban state, its priestly rulers wielded a great amount of power.

Plate 4.11 Huge Olmec stone head from the site of San Lorenzo. (Courtesy of Michael D. Coe.)

Explaining the Olmec Civilization

The ceramics of this initial occupation at San Lorenzo are very similar to those found at the same time period in agricultural villages on the Pacific coast and in parts of the highlands. During this period San Lorenzo probably functioned as a farming community much like communities in the highlands and on the Pacific coast. Yet within three hundred years, a fundamental change had taken place. The attributes of Olmec civilization, including massive construction and the carving of large sculptures in typical Olmec style (Plate 4.12), had all appeared, first at San Lorenzo and soon after at other sites as well. This seemingly sudden growth of a complex society on the Gulf Coast has led to much speculation, as we will see, about the reasons for the rise of the Olmecs.

Plate 4.12   Olmec stone sculpture from San Lorenzo. Note that the body originally had movable arms. Professor Michael Coe believes that the figure probably represents a ball player. (Courtesy of Michael D. Coe.)

Perhaps it is easiest to look at the rise and development of Olmec civilization in terms of four general questions. First, what (or where) were the origins of the Olmec civilization? Second, how did the culture become a major civilization? Third, what was the nature of the society, and by what means did it expand its influence to cover such a large geographical area between 1200 and 600 B.C.? And, finally, what kind of relationship did the Olmecs have with the existing highland cultures—cultures that would later give rise to the greatest urban states?

Origins of the Olmec   One of the questions which has always dominated archaeology is that of origin. Who invented something? Where did it begin? Although this kind of question is still of major concern to archaeologists, its focus has shifted from the days when V. G. Childe's followers searched for the center where the Neolithic Revolution began. Today archaeologists are not interested merely in discovering where or when an object, style, or idea first came into being; they also want to know how that invention became integrated into a particular culture. Regardless of where something was invented, why did it become accepted and by what process? Both the question of origin and the question of process are open to considerable speculation in the case of the Olmec; we will look first at attempts to answer the former.

From an archaeological point of view, the Olmec civilization suddenly appeared in a relatively well-developed form around 1200 B.C. As we have seen, its antecedents were few. There seems to have been no long, slow sequence of local growth in the Gulf Coast lowlands prior to the rise of the Olmecs. If the Olmecs did not evolve in the same area where they later flourished, where did they arise? Were the elements of Olmec civilization developed elsewhere and imported to Mexico? While we can dismiss the idea that the civilization originated in such places as Atlantis or outer space as totally without support or merit, other hypotheses involving diffusion of ideas, art styles, and people from areas like the Far East cannot be rejected out of hand. There are some resemblances between Olmec and Chinese art. But there is nothing further to back the contentions of actual connections. Thus, for the moment at least, ideas of diffusion from overseas cultures must be viewed as conjecture.

Stronger arguments have been made linking the Olmec with civilizations to the south. One possible candidate that has been mentioned is the Chavin civilization of the Peruvian highlands. This civilization was roughly contemporaneous to the Olmec, and it shared an emphasis on a feline figure similar to the Olmec jaguar in its art. But beyond this, there is little evidence to link the two civilizations directly. In very recent years, however, a refinement of this hypothesis has been advanced by Professor Donald Lathrap, who sees both Chavin and Olmec having a common ancestor in the lowlands of South America. As mentioned above, increasing archaeological evidence indicates that there was a spread of manioc users from northern South America into Mesoamerica during the second millennium B.C. just prior to the rise of the Olmec; this development lends some credence to Lathrap's hypothesis. Nevertheless, the notion needs more refinement and testing before it can be given much weight.

Thus, although there are suggestions that Olmec civilization might have originated outside the Gulf Coast lowlands of Mexico, the most reasonable position for the moment seems to be "wait and see." Without convincing evidence to the contrary, it seems best to assume that Olmec civilization evolved locally, within Mexico. The assumption of local development, however, still does not answer the basic question regarding Olmec origins. Did the civilization evolve in the Mexican lowlands or in the Mexican highlands? This question has split the ranks of Mesoamerican archaeologists and reflects deep theoretical biases.

The "highland school" claims that such major cultural developments as the rise of agriculture, the beginnings of settled village life, and the origins of complex societies all emanated from the highlands. One of its most vocal proponents in recent years has been the archaeologist William T. Sanders. In a series of publications, he and colleagues such as Barbara Price have argued that the semiarid, highly differentiated highland valleys provided the proper environment and stimulus for all the cultural developments which ultimately led to the rise of urban civilization in Mesoamerica.[17]

The core of the highland viewpoint can be seen as far back as the beginning of the century in the writings of Herbert Spinden, who believed that the relatively harsh environment of the Mesoamerican highlands forced people to look for new means to support themselves and provided the initial stimulus for the rise of agriculture and, later, civilization. Conditions in the highlands forced people to build public works such as irrigation systems in order to make the semiarid valleys productive; they also demanded a political organization to exploit local resources and exchange them with neighboring valleys for other necessary materials. In sum, the highland environment itself required people to develop elements of a complex society in order to support their growing numbers.

Supporters of the "highland" point of view have looked to valleys such as Tehuacán and Oaxaca for the origins of the Olmecs, and not without some encouragement. Data indicate that the origins of agriculture and the beginnings of settled village life lie in the highlands, with the appearance of irrigation systems by 1000 B.C. In addition, the continuing discovery of a wide variety of Olmec objects, carvings, and Olmec-related sites in the highlands have lent some credence to the highland argument. To date, however, these objects or sites have proved to be either later than the beginnings of Olmec civilization in the Gulf Coast lowlands or totally undatable. The important work of Kent Flannery and his associates in the Valley of Oaxaca, which is just being published, should shed important light on the viability of the highland hypotheses.

The recent publications of this project indicate that the first public architecture in Oaxaca, a sizable platform, dates as early as 1350 B.C.[18] From this we can infer that sociopolitical organization in Oaxaca began to grow in complexity prior to the rise of the Olmecs. It was not until the period between 1150 and 850 B.C., however, particularly at the site of San José Mogote, that there is good evidence for a rapid takeoff in number and scale of public projects and widespread trade and accumulation of exotic materials. This increased growth may well have been stimulated by contacts with the even more rapidly rising Olmec system of the Gulf Coast.

A second "highland" hypothesis sees the home of the Olmecs in the nearby Tuxtla Mountains along the Gulf Coast. This argument has three points in its favor. First and foremost, scientific analyses have shown that ·the basalt rock used for the great stone heads and other Olmec monuments came from the

Tuxtla Mountains. Second, the mountains are quite close to the Olmec heartland, within 100 miles of the ceremonial centers. And third, it is claimed that the main pyramid at La Venta is fluted and appears to look like a mountain. A few scholars have speculated that the temple might be replicating a mountain homeland of the Olmecs. Unfortunately, volcanic conditions in the Tuxtlas have made archaeological exploration very difficult, so that little is known of these mountains' Precolumbian past. Thus the Tuxtla hypothesis must be put to the side for the time being.

While the highland hypotheses are persuasive, there is also a case to be made for the lowland school. The main argument here is that while advances toward civilization were made in the highlands, there is no evidence that the initial consequences of these advances were first realized in any place but the lowlands. The lowland school has been associated with the late Carl Sauer, a geographer from the University of California, Berkeley; it has been supported by Coe and other archaeologists on the basis of their research in the lowland areas of the Pacific and Gulf Coasts.

The basic tenet of the school is that in the lush tropical lowland regions it is relatively simple to obtain all the food a group needs in a fairly small area. This situation makes life easier and leaves time for other pursuits and experimentation with the environment. In effect, the environment would enable more complex social forms to evolve over many years.

Although agriculture was practiced in the highlands for many thousands of years prior to the beginnings of Olmec civilization around 1200 B.C., and settled villages, too, had slowly emerged by the third millennium B.C., there seem to have been few major advances toward the growth of complex societies in the highlands between about 2500 and 1500 B.C. Societal conditions in the lowlands do not seem to have changed radically during this period of time either. People probably lived in settled villages. Pottery, often seen as a symbol of sedentary groups, was in use in the Pacific Coast lowlands of Mexico as early as 2300 B.C. It is a crude pottery, quite like the earliest pottery in the Tehuacán Valley, which has a similar date. It is possible that due to a spread of peoples and ideas from lowland South and Central America, manioc became a major staple of these Pacific Coast peoples after 2000 B.C. While this marked a change in the subsistence economy, it does not seem to have affected the social structure in any major way. That impetus seems to have come from the highlands.

The spread of maize from the highlands to the lowlands around the beginning of the second millennium B.C. appears to have been the trigger for the lowland advances which ultimately led by 1200 B.C. to the rise of Olmec civilization. Within the new environmental conditions of the lowlands, the highland maize apparently underwent a series of genetic mutations which led to a greatly increased size of cob. In turn, this important new food source offered sufficient food to allow for the growth of a more complex society in the lowlands.

The lowland explanation seems plausible; but, unfortunately, the archaeological picture is not sufficiently clear to link the developments on the Pacific Coast directly with the rise of Olmec civilization on the Gulf Coast. No Olmec remains lie directly above the early agricultural villages on the Pacific Coast, nor have deep early village deposits been found stratigraphically below Olmec remains on the Gulf Coast. Nevertheless, given our present state of knowledge, it is reasonable (if not totally satisfactory) to assume that the developments on the Pacific Coast provided the basis for the eventual rise of Olmec civilization on the Gulf Coast. The 300-year period from 1500 to 1200 B.C. was sufficient time for the various aspects of Olmec civilization to evolve.

Development of the Civilization   If hypotheses concerning the locale for the origins of the Olmecs are tentative and confusing, the reasons for the civilization's development are even murkier. Regardless of the question of where, how did the civilization evolve? There are three principal schools of thought.

One hypothesis sees trade as a major factor in the development of Olmec civilization. Professor William Rathje, one of the leading exponents of this viewpoint, has stated that the need to obtain certain raw materials perceived as essential led to the rise of complex societies.[19] The Gulf Coast was lacking in salt, obsidian, and hard stone in general—materials that were all present in the adjacent highlands. Moreover, a number of other materials which the Olmec relied on—such as basalt, jade, and ilmenite—were available in more mountainous regions. Clearly, the Olmec were deeply involved with the procurement of many important trade goods, and trade played a major role in the life of

Mesoamerica's first civilization. As Rathje suggests, it also played a basic role in the development of that civilization. The need for raw materials provided the impetus for the growth of a local elite group which organized the trading expeditions and controlled the traded goods and their distribution. The control of trade led in turn to an unequal distribution of wealth and the rise of stratified society.

A few archaeologists have advanced a more traditional hypothesis than Rathje's. Noting that the rivers in the Olmec area, such as the Cotzocoalcos near San Lorenzo, periodically overflow their banks, Coe and other archaeologists envision the rich levee lands bordering these rivers as capable of providing surplus agricultural products. Comparing the Olmec situation to Egypt's reliance on the Nile floodplains, they hypothesize that these surplus products could have provided the foundation for the development of Olmec civilization. As in the areas of the Near East discussed in Chapter 3, the ownership or control of these highly productive lands was likely an important basis for the class differentiation that marked the developed civilization. The individuals who controlled the levee lands could have used their position to gain more wealth than their fellow farmers. These people could have used their riches to accumulate goods or organize trading expeditions which could in turn have provided a base for their emergence as an elite with wealth and power.

A third explanation for the rise of the Olmec civilization centers on the role of religious ideology, unquestionably a profound force within the culture. Professor Gordon Willey, for instance, believes that the characteristic Olmec art style symbolized in material form a dominant religious belief system which helped unify the diverse peoples of the Olmec area. He notes that "in a way similar to that of the interchange of objects, plants, and techniques which had previously prepared the village agriculture threshold, the sharing of common ideologies led to the threshold of civilization by enlarging the effective social field."[20] This enlargement must have formed the common basis which joined individuals, social segments, and finally local societies together to combine and coordinate on a larger scale than ever before.

Other scholars have built upon Willey's view. Professor Robert Drennan, for example, has argued that the rise of settled village life was linked to ideological factors, as were the numerous social changes that followed. He believes that the acceptance of new social conventions and authorities was made possible by an increasing emphasis on rituals of "sanctification" which helped legitimize newly emerging schemes of sociopolitical organization. The large-scale trade in exotic materials, immense building projects, and complex iconography among the Olmec were all part of the ritual sanctification of the new Olmec social order, according to Drennan's model.

Michael Coe, too, believes that the agricultural surplus and ideological views are not incompatible and can be combined in attempting to understand the rise of the Olmec. He queries:

> What if some pre–San Lorenzo chief had decided that he wanted monuments carved in basalt to glorify himself and his distinguished ancestors? What if he felt that these monuments should rest on a specially constructed, hill-like plateau that could be seen for miles? He would have to reach out beyond his own tribal domain, by conquest if necessary, to gain access to the basalt. He would have to organize the people within his new territory to do the work necessary. At hand was enough food with which to feed and pay those working for his embryonic state. As in time his chiefly lineage transformed itself into a dynasty, the social and ceremonial needs of the Olmec power became even more difficult to fulfill on the Gulf Coast, and the conquests of more distant regions began. Again, the army was supported by sufficient quantities of transportable food, exactly as the chinampas made it possible for the much later Aztec armies to subjugate Mexico on full stomachs.[21]

Whether trade, differential land productivity, a broad-based belief system, or other factors entirely were the ultimate causes for the rise of the Olmec civilization still remains unclear. Without a good deal more research, we are unlikely to uncover such causes. It does seem likely that some of the ideas noted above, particularly those concerning the role of long-distance exchange, may pave the way for future advances in this area.

Expansion and Growth   As with the questions about the Olmecs' origins and their evolution, there is no simple explanation of how the Olmec influence spread. We do know that it expanded rapidly. Between about 1000 and 800 B.C., the Olmec influence was apparent in several distant areas: the southern border of Mesoamerica in Salvador, Honduras, and Costa Rica; in the highlands and lowlands of Guatemala; and in the Mexican highlands from the Valley of Mexico to Oaxaca.

There are three principal explanations for the expansion of the Olmec from their Gulf Coast homeland. The first sees the Olmec as a state whose expansion took the form of empire-building. The second sees the Olmec as a stratified society whose elite established and maintained economic ties in the form of trade with a number of locations in the Mesoamerican highlands. The third views the Olmec expansion as essentially religious in emphasis and motivation. Obviously, some scholars would see aspects of all three in the Olmec expansion. The "trade" viewpoint certainly is the dominant one today among Mesoamerican archaeologists, and most of the available data appear to support it.

The view of the Olmec civilization as a state has scant archaeological information to back it up. As we have seen, major Olmec centers are few in number and relatively small in size and complexity. There are no Olmec cities. Nor are there physical indications of a large bureaucratic apparatus which would be necessary to coordinate the functions of a state. In addition, the nature of the Olmec presence outside the Gulf Coast homeland is not indicative of conquest or of tight political or economic control. Indications of contacts with the Olmecs often are revealed instead through the appearance of a limited number of Olmec artifacts such as carved jade pieces, Olmec carvings, or an Olmec-derived (or "Olmecoid") art style or ceramic type. Although captive figures are shown on Olmec monuments, there is little indication of warfare and meager archaeological evidence for an Olmec military apparatus or Olmec military conquests.

The argument that the Olmec expansion was purely religious in nature is no stronger than the conquest hypothesis. As we will see, the areas and sites of Olmec influence in the highlands simply do not fit in with a picture of Olmec priests proselytizing the heathen whereas trade and material procurement do. Nevertheless, religion could well have been an important motivating factor in the acceptance of Olmec influence in neighboring areas.

A far stronger case can be made that the procurement of raw materials was of overriding importance in the Olmec expansion. Olmec presence in the form of sculpture, rock carvings, artifacts, or symbols is found at or along routes the Olmecs would have traveled on the way to obtaining materials such as jade, magnetite, obsidian, and salt.

Interaction with the Highlands   If the Olmec expansion out of the Gulf Coast heartland was motivated by the need to procure raw materials, how were they obtaining those materials? Did they send their own people to mine and transport goods, or were they trading with established groups in the highlands? This question leads to another one: what was the nature of the Olmec interaction with the highlands? Was it a relationship between a civilization and an undeveloped area, or were the highlands already culturally developed? Cases of both kinds of interaction can be found. But recent data, particularly from the work of Kent Flannery and his associates in the Valley of Oaxaca and David Grove and his associates from the highland site of Chalcatzingo in Morelos, indicate that the latter interaction was of paramount importance. Their work has also shown that the Olmecs were not procuring raw materials themselves but were engaged in a highly active trade for them.

Flannery has argued that the Oaxaca Valley and other regions in the highlands were developing complex cultures simultaneously with the Gulf Coast lowlands in the mid-second millennium B.C. While these regions may not have grown as quickly as the Olmec, the beginnings of a complex social order had emerged or was emerging by the time of the rise of Olmec civilization. When the Olmec reached Oaxaca, they found a culture which may not have been quite so advanced as the Olmec, but which had a stratified society that was prepared and able to deal with the Olmecs economically and politically.

Without the economic stimulus from the Olmec, the Valley of Oaxaca or other highland areas might have developed a civilization by themselves. As it was, the highlands remained within the sphere of influence of the Olmecs for a short time, although it is clear that the economic needs of the Olmec quickly spurred Oaxaca on to new levels of complexity. Ironically, in the process of obtaining material which led to their growth, the Olmecs were also contributing to their own eclipse. The Oaxacans, with their control of highland raw materials and the potential for intensive agriculture through irrigation, had a much stronger environmental foundation for the growth of complex society than the Gulf Coast lowlands. Once the Oaxacans were stimulated by the Olmecs to further political and economic development, they were able to supersede the latter within a relatively short period of time.

By the middle of the first millennium B.C., the Oaxacans may have been able to assume control of the trade routes created by the Olmecs. Monte Albán, probably the earliest urban center in Mesoamerica, was established by 600 B.C. as the center of an expanding Oaxacan polity. It appears that as the Oaxacans got stronger and assumed more economic power, the Olmecs became weaker. After a relatively brief florescence, their great centers of San Lorenzo, La Venta, and Tres Zapotes declined in power. San Lorenzo was virtually destroyed about 900 B.C., and many of its monuments were mutilated and smashed. Although San Lorenzo continued to be occupied, it clearly had lost its former glory. Construction ceased at La Venta around 600 B.C., and it apparently was abandoned at that time. Although we know less about Tres Zapotes, it appears to have been occupied throughout the first millennium B.C. However, its importance probably was considerably reduced.

By 600 to 400 B.C., the Olmec heyday was over. But brief as their time of ascendancy was, the influence of the Olmec on later Mesoamerican economic, political, religious, and artistic developments was massive. The Olmecs established a cultural pattern which laid the basis for the future growth of Mesoamerican civilization. They also directly influenced and stimulated cultural developments in several different regions of Mesoamerica, including Oaxaca, Central Mexico, Izapa, highland Guatemala, and the Maya lowlands. Although Oaxaca developed chronologically earlier than the other regions, the latter began to grow in complexity at this time, too. We turn now to two of these developments that took place at roughly the same time in different areas of Mesoamerica: the development of the Maya culture in the lowlands and the rise of the great city of Teotihuacán in the Central Mexican highlands.

THE MAYA

By 300 B.C., a great civilization had begun to evolve in an area adjacent to the Olmec lowlands, a region which today includes Mexico, Guatemala, Belize (British Honduras), and Honduras (Map 4.4). Here the Maya built a number of huge ceremonial centers whose distinctive remains have survived the ravages of time and nature. In these centers, archaeologists have uncovered abundant evidence of the artistic and intellectual achievements of the ancient Maya. Visitors to sites such as Tikal or Copán can see clear evidence of their architectural and sculptural skills. Other achievements of the Maya include writing, astronomy, pottery manufacture, and stoneworking, as well as less tangible accomplishments in economic, social, and religious organization.[22]

As with the Olmec, we have many questions about the Maya. What led to the flowering of their civilization in the southern

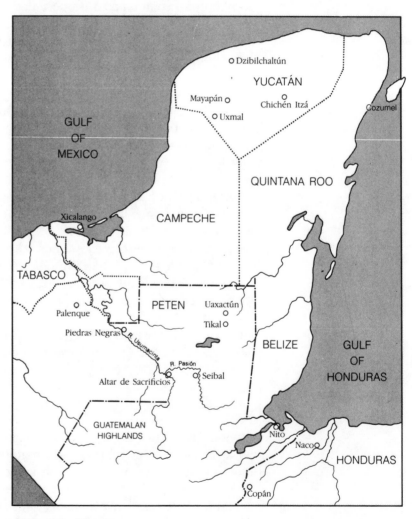

Map 4.4 The Maya area.

lowlands? How did their ceremonial centers function? Why did the Classic Maya civilization of the southern lowlands collapse so suddenly at the end of the eighth century A.D.? And what caused their subsequent revival at Chichén Itzá and later at Mayapán in the northern lowlands? In the following pages, we will briefly examine the answers which archaeologists have proposed.

The Maya lowlands can be divided into two principal environmental and cultural zones (see map). The southern lowlands consist of a tropical rain forest interspersed with large savanna grasslands and swamps. Here the rainfall is relatively high, averaging between 60 and 90 inches a year. The northern lowlands are somewhat drier with a lower and more scrubby forest cover.

The ancestors of the people who developed Maya civilization first occupied the lowlands as early as 2000 B.C.[23] However, our first clear knowledge of the early inhabitants of the lowlands dates to about 800 B.C., during a period known to archaeologists as the Middle Preclassic (see the chronological chart in Figure 4.3). Scholars believe that population increased at this time due to migrations into the lowlands. One ancestral group probably migrated north from the highlands of Guatemala and El Salvador, while another group came from the adjacent Gulf Coast lowlands of Tabasco.

The former group, migrating from Salvador and the Guatemalan highlands, must have received some Olmec influence during the height of Olmec power. They had been situated along important procurement routes for exotic stones and Olmec influence has been noted in their sculpture. While the Salvador migrants exhibited Olmec influence, the Tabasco migrants had probably been part of the original Olmec population.

The reason for the migrations is not yet certain. It is possible that population pressure or political disturbances forced some of the Olmec peasants to move away from their homes. We surmise that these early settlers moved by water, as several of the initial settlements are found along riverbanks. While they had been exposed to Olmec influence themselves, it appears that they brought with them very few artifactual links with Olmec civilization. And so, their influence upon Mayan developments, like their reason for coming, is difficult to interpret.

The early Maya settlements were small villages with populations numbering under a hundred. Over a period of a thousand years, these villages slowly grew in number, size, and complexity as the Maya's agricultural adaptation to the lowland environment enabled them to prosper. One of the first new traits to become visible in the archaeological record was ceremonial architecture. Large platforms which probably had ceremonial functions, as well as small temples, began to appear, indicating that religion was becoming increasingly important in ancient Maya society.

The Rise of Classic Maya Civilization

By the beginning of the Late Preclassic Period in 300 B.C., ceremonial centers of relatively substantial size had appeared. The center was a distinctive feature of Maya culture, acting as focus for the community. Generally speaking, these centers, like the Olmec centers, were not what we would call cities. Although they did consist of a number of large and varied buildings, they did not have a substantial resident population. Some scholars have even labeled these Maya centers "vacant towns." Their permanent population consisted mainly of the priests and their attendants plus a limited number of artisans. The priests lived in big houses or palaces in and around the center. The bulk of the peasant population lived in much more modest wood and thatch homes in the areas surrounding the centers. At certain times of the year, on the occasion of major religious festivals such as the one at the time of the planting of their crops, scholars hypothesize, by analogy to historical and modern practices, that the peasants would flock to the centers to observe and participate in the ceremonies. At other times of the year, some of the peasants would be called into the centers to help in the construction of new temples and palaces dedicated to the glory of the gods and to the comforts of their earthly representatives, the priests. The peasants also would provide the food to help sustain the priests in the centers.

The quid pro quo which the peasants received from the priests was certainly not as tangible as the services they provided. In return for food and labor, the peasants were offered a psychologically and spiritually secure and ordered world. Apparently, this was enough. Agriculture in the tropical Maya lowlands is at best a chancy business: even slight shifts in the onset of the rainy season or the dry season could mean disaster for that year's harvest. The religion of the ancient Maya helped the peasants cope with the precariousness of their lives. If the gods were properly propitiated, the crops would be good—as would life in general.

One archaeologist, Professor William Haviland, argues that it was the centralizing effects of Maya religion that led to the rise of Maya civilization. He believes that the religious centers acted as magnets to peoples living in the surrounding areas. To support the growing populations around the centers, Haviland argues, the agricultural systems became intensified. This led to the evolution of a complex state. As early as 200 B.C. at Tikal, Haviland believes that the "vacant" ceremonial centers had begun transformation toward nucleated urban centers.

While the initial attraction may have been a religious one, economic factors must have been significant, too. Craftsmen were needed by the priests to help build the temples to the gods and to fashion the ornaments which the priests wore at the important festivals. It should be noted, however, that the Maya lowlands lacked many natural resources, including most kinds of hard stone. Materials such as jade or obsidian, which were desired by the priesthood for necklaces, bracelets, earrings, and other ornaments or ceremonial objects, had to be obtained in the adjacent highlands and transported many hundreds of miles to the lowland ceremonial centers. Thus people involved with trade were also attracted to the centers.

How central a role did trade play in the growth of the ceremonial centers? Professor Rathje has extended his Olmec hypothesis to argue that the basic cause for the rise of Maya civilization was the necessity for the Maya to trade for materials such as obsidian, salt, and hard stone for grinding implements. He argues that in order to attract the merchants and their trade from the highlands, lowland sites such as Tikal, which were quite distant from the highland resource areas, concentrated their attention on making their centers bigger and architecturally magnificent. In order to undertake all the building, the priests had to attract more artisans and bring more laborers into the community to do the work. These population increases led in turn to even more building, population growth, greater population density, greater social differentiation, and occupational specialization. The result was civilization as we define it.

Other factors beyond ideology and trade must have been important in the emerging Maya civilization. Cultural diffusion is one influence that seems more and more likely to have played an important role. Recent archaeological explorations have lent substance to long-held suspicions that there were renewed contacts between the Guatemalan highlands and lowlands just prior to the emergence of Classic Maya civilization.[24] These contacts may have brought hieroglyphic writing, which had developed earlier in the highlands, and a new art style into the lowlands. The exact role these contacts had in the rise of Classic Maya civilization and what they consisted of is still far from clear, but they may well be related to the active highland-lowland trade connections of the time. Mayan growth did not occur in isolation. Developments in the Guatemalan highlands and the

a   b

Plate 4.13   The lowland Maya often made sharp blades from the obsidian which they obtained from the highlands. The blades (a) were struck from prepared cores (b). The core is about 7 cm long.

Mexican highlands—particularly, as we will see below, the rise of the Teotihuacán state—had many effects on the rise of Classic Maya civilization.

Cultural Achievements

Whatever the ultimate factors, and they were certainly multiple, Classic Maya civilization had crystalized in the southern lowlands by A.D. 300. In addition to the growth in size and complexity of the ceremonial centers, several other factors add to its status as a civilization. First, there is hieroglyphic writing. Although it was probably first developed by the ancient Oaxacans, the Maya were the ones to refine it to new levels of sophistication.

Figure 4.4 Maya hieroglyphic writing: the day name "Ix."

The Maya erected sculptured monuments (or stelae) with hieroglyphic inscriptions at their ceremonial centers (Plate 4.14). The hieroglyphic texts usually concerned a ruler-priest who also was depicted on the monument. The text might describe some historical event or recount the lineage of the individual who was being commemorated. The dates of the person's death or ascension to power were also often given, accompanied by a rendering of the individual in full ceremonial regalia (including earplugs, noseplug, bracelets, necklace, feather headdress, and the ceremonial staff of authority).

Another major area of Maya achievement lay in their understanding of planetary movements and astronomy. The Maya had a 365-day calendar that was as accurate as those of the Western world prior to the relatively recent advances in astronomical hardware. They had knowledge of the zero, and they developed an arithmetical system (based on twenty rather than ten as ours is). They charted the movements of the sun, the moon, Venus, and other heavenly bodies and were able to make highly accurate predictions of eclipses of the sun and the moon. It is probable that these remarkable achievements followed from the initial need to be able to predict at what time of year to burn, plant, and harvest the agricultural fields.

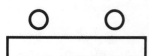

Figure 4.5 Maya hieroglyphic writing: the number "seven." The bar equals five, while the dots equal one each.

Unfortunately, scholars have been unable to decode the Maya hieroglyphic writing system completely. In contrast to the case of ancient Egyptian writing, no Rosetta Stone has been discovered for the Maya. After decades of careful study, those glyphs that relate to numbers, to the calendar, and to most Maya gods have

Plate 4.14   Stela dating to A.D. 849 from the site of Seibal. Note the hieroglyphic inscriptions at the top and the left-hand side. (Photo by T. Maler; courtesy of Gordon R. Willey.)

been deciphered. In addition, certain glyphs which represent specific sites and rulers have been deciphered, along with a relatively small group of glyphs related to certain actions such as birth, death, and marriage. While this represents a sizable body of information, the greater part of the inventory of Maya glyphs remains a tantalizing puzzle to that small handful of dedicated scholars who have devoted their lives to deciphering ancient Maya writing. However, recent breakthroughs in the study of Maya hieroglyphs may revolutionize this realm of research in coming years.

Beyond the achievements of writing, the calendar, and the arithmetical system, the Classic period was also marked by artistic achievement. The Maya developed a great art style which can be seen in such varied media as huge stone monuments, stucco masks on the façades of buildings, wall paintings, pounded bark screens, and small jade ornaments. Designs are so intricate that it often takes a newcomer careful study to be able to pick out the beautifully complex depictions of people, grotesque monsters, or animals on a Maya stela.

The ancient Maya also developed a complementary architectural style which featured the corbeled vault, rather than a true or Roman arch (Plate 4.15). They built large pyramids with small temples on top, as well as long, low, structures with many rooms, which are often called palaces (Plates 4.16 and 4.17). Moreover, they constructed specialized structures such as ball courts, sweat baths, and observatories. The ancient ball game played by the Maya and other Mesoamerican peoples was an event of much religious significance; it was played with a hard rubber ball on specially built courts with parallel sides.

One additional achievement of the Classic Maya is the beautiful painted pottery which the skilled Maya craftsmen produced. Some of these vessels were painted in as many as six colors and depicted scenes of religious or mythological importance. They probably were manufactured in a limited number of centers. The epitome of craftsmanship can be seen in the cylindrical vases, often depicting human figures, that were usually placed in the tombs of the most important rulers (Figure 4.6).

As a final note, it should be stressed that all the technological and architectural skills of the Maya were developed without the aid of metal, which did not become a widespread commodity until after A.D. 900. That is to say, Maya technology was based on

Plate 4.15   Corbelled vaults at Palenque. The front of the temple has
fallen away to reveal the vaults. (Courtesy of Peter D. Harrison.)

Plate 4.16   "Palace" structure at the site of Altar de Sacrificios.
(Courtesy of Peabody Museum, Harvard University.)

stone tools. The achievements of the Maya are particularly remarkable in light of this fact. Imagine, for instance, clearing the jungle away from potential agricultural fields with stone axes or shaping and then carving monumental stelae with stone cutting tools. The complexity and beauty of what the Maya did must be appreciated in the light of what they had to work with.

All the attributes of Maya civilization slowly developed throughout the Late Preclassic Period (300 B.C.–A.D. 300), some invented by the Maya themselves, and others, such as hieroglyphic writing, brought in from neighboring areas where other cultures had developed contemporaneously to the Maya. But even in the latter case, the full development of this achievement was distinctively Maya. By A.D. 300, these attributes had coalesced at sites such as Tikal and Uaxactún into what archaeologists have termed Classic Maya civilization.

Plate 4.17 A burial found inside the structure shown in Plate 4.16. Another burial (a) was discovered near the top of the excavation. (Photo by R. Mata; courtesy of Peabody Museum, Harvard University.)

The Early Classic Period was the heyday of the Maya theocracy, who resided in the ceremonial centers described above. Archaeologists have uncovered dozens of centers which had main ceremonial areas with temples, palaces, large platforms, carved monuments, and big open plazas. The priestly elite and bureaucrats lived in or near the centers, as did a limited number of acolytes and craft specialists who carved the monuments, manufactured the jade jewelry, and produced the many artifacts associated with the Maya elite. The population of most of these sites, with the certain exception of Tikal, which already had exceeded other sites in size and population, probably was not more than several thousand, including the peasants who lived around the centers and provided agricultural support and physical labor to maintain and enlarge the centers. The priests and the bureaucrats who ran the centers were closely intertwined, but it is unclear as to how much overlap in roles existed.

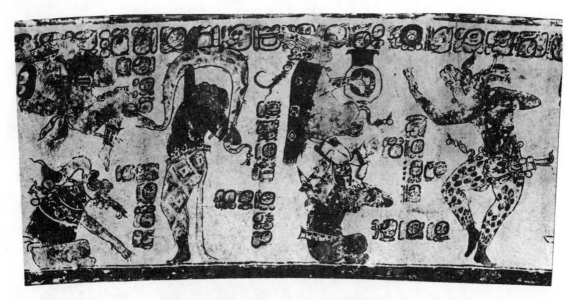

Figure 4.6 Roll-out photograph of a beautiful Classic Maya polychrome vase (the "Altar Vase") found in the upper burial noted in Plate 4.17. Careful research by the archaeologist Richard E. W. Adams has shown that such vases were probably brought by elite personages to the funerals and burials of their peers at other important Classic Maya sites. (Photo by Ian Graham; courtesy of Gordon R. Willey.)

Certainly these people had greater wealth than the peasants, judging by their larger living quarters, wider array of artifacts associated with the houses, richer burials, and greater access to goods for which the Maya traded with peoples in adjacent regions.

The Collapse of Classic Maya Civilization

By the beginning of the Late Classic Period, several trends had appeared which were to drastically change the picture of Maya society outlined above. Certainly, one of the factors which led to the initiation of the new trends was the withdrawal of Teotihuacán's influence on the Maya area by the end of the Early Classic Period. Teotihuacán, the first great city in ancient Mexico, was situated just to the northeast of present-day Mexico City in the highlands. As we will see in more detail below, soon after the time of Christ this urban center spread its political, economic, and religious influence to many parts of Mesoamerica, including the Maya lowlands (see Plate 4.18). The city collapsed in the eighth century A.D.; but its troubles had begun more than a century earlier and it lost its influence in many regions such as the Maya lowlands at that time.

This withdrawal of influence left an economic vacuum which the Classic Maya apparently tried to fill. To take advantage of this vacuum, the Maya elite, it can be hypothesized, attempted to maximize their most marketable skill—that of fine craft production of objects of jade or polychrome pottery, among others. To increase production, the various centers had to attract more artisans. At Tikal, for example, there is evidence for craft workshop areas at this time. To attract artisans and more trade, the elite may have tried to make their particular center larger and more spectacular and hence more attractive. As the number of non-food-producers in a center increased, however, a greater burden was placed on the peasants to produce more food—at the same time that they were being called on to give more of their time and labor to help build new and more spectacular temples and palaces.

In hindsight, it can be hypothesized that the growth of the non-food-producing sector of Classic Maya society in and around the ceremonial centers set in motion a process which within several centuries led to the collapse and disappearance of Classic

Plate 4.18 Stela 31 from the site of Tikal shows Teotihuacán influence in its design. (Courtesy of University Museum, University of Pennsylvania.)

Maya civilization. By using a systems perspective to organize the diverse data about the collapse, archaeologists have been able to see more clearly than before how a variety of interrelated factors reinforced each other and helped bring about the collapse.

In order to see why the growth of population in the ceremonial centers and an increase in the number of non-food-producers could ultimately lead to the collapse of Classic Maya civilization, the nature of the Maya agricultural system must be examined.

In recent years, archaeologists' views on ancient Maya agriculture have been changing rapidly. Traditionally, it was argued that ancient Maya agriculturists utilized a *slash and burn* technique involving shifting cultivation. Fields were cleared by chopping down the large trees with stone axes, and then they were burned. Crops—principally maize, beans, and squash—were planted between the charred tree stumps with a wooden digging stick, and fields were harvested for two years or so. Each field was then allowed to go fallow for at least eight years; then it was cleared by slashing and burning, and the cycle began again. At any one time, a great deal of land would be unused.

This traditional picture was based on both the dispersed settlement pattern of Early Classic sites and analogies to the practices of modern-day Maya peoples living in Yucatán, highland Guatemala, and Chiapas. But new evidence indicates that Classic Maya subsistence activities were much more complex than previously thought. Strong arguments for the use of breadnuts *(ramon)* as a major food staple at Tikal, the presence of ridged fields and terracing in the Maya lowlands, and the possible use of seasonally flooded swamp areas *(bajo),* are among the indications that Maya subsistence was variegated and more intensive than older theories had maintained (Plate 4.19). Yet it is not clear at this time exactly when different crops and intensification techniques were introduced, or how great were regional differences in the lowlands.

The evidence indicates that most ancient Maya sites had a dispersed pattern throughout the Preclassic and Early Classic Periods, with the exception of a few great sites like Tikal. This kind of settlement pattern is often correlated with a slash and burn agricultural system in the Maya lowlands. Such a dispersed settlement pattern with a nearly vacant ceremonial center as the focus for a scattered populace may well have been the normal pattern for the ancient Maya throughout the Preclassic and Early Classic Periods. For some smaller sites, it probably even held true during the Late Classic Period. It has been suggested that the settlement pattern might have followed a central-place, or primate, distribution as discussed in Chapter 3. It has also been hypothesized that there were four regional capitals in the Maya lowlands which had influence over sites of lesser rank in those regions. However, the exact nature of Maya political organization, as inferred from settlement distributions and other data, remains unresolved pending further research.[25]

Due to the factors discussed earlier, the settlement configuration around the larger sites began to change by the start of the Late Classic Period, around A.D. 600. At Tikal, the largest Classic center, this change may even have started much earlier. The new pattern saw many more people living all year round in the center, while the farmers were drawn in close around the center. This trend toward nucleation, which culminated in some sites such as Tikal becoming real urban centers, may have been made possible by

Plate 4.19   A *bajo* in the Maya lowlands. This low-lying area would be flooded during the rainy season. (Courtesy of Peter D. Harrison.)

the introduction of new crops and the use of various techniques such as terracing, which allowed an intensification of the older slash and burn system. Further research is needed to verify that these innovations date to Classic times.

It may well be that even with all the changes in the agricultural system during Classic times—or because of them perhaps—great strains were placed on the agricultural and social systems during the Late Classic period. The organizational capabilities of the elite were probably particularly hard-pressed, and the priestly rulers must have tried to cope with the strain in

Plate 4.20 The huge Temple I at Tikal. (Courtesy of University Museum, University of Pennsylvania.)

various ways. They may have tried to intensify agriculture further. This could have been done by placing greater reliance on crops other than maize, beans, and squash. Breadnut planting, as we have seen, was probably intensified in areas where it could grow. Agriculturists may also have tried to shorten the fallow cycle and plant fields for more than two years using the slash and burn system. While the latter tactic might have increased yields considerably in the short run, the resulting soil depletion would have had disastrous effects in the long run.

In all, the hypothetical picture of events during Late Classic times is one of a vicious circle. As population grew and sites became more nucleated, bureaucratic organization may have become strained, food may have become scarcer, and more work probably was demanded of the peasants—a group that was shrinking in population size relative to other segments of society.

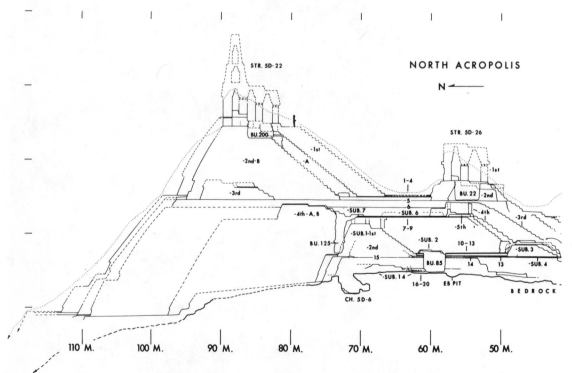

Figure 4.7 Cross-section drawing by William R. Coe showing the major architectural build-up from Preclassic through Classic times at the center of the great Maya site of Tikal. (Courtesy of University Museum, University of Pennsylvania.)

The ancient Maya explanation for such a situation may have been that the gods were displeased: to satisfy the gods, the logical Maya response was to build larger and more magnificent temples and monuments. This kind of thinking would have made eminent sense given the ancient Maya ethos, but the consequences of a new and more ambitious building program would have had an effect diametrically opposed to the one actually desired. More people would have had to be brought into the center to construct the buildings and even greater pressure would have been placed on agricultural and sociopolitical systems. Clearly a number of trends, each reinforcing the other, led to an ever-increasing state of stress in Classic Maya civilization.

At the height of internal instability, toward the end of the eighth century A.D., the Classic Maya had to face heavy external pressures as well. The Putun, a Maya-speaking people from the

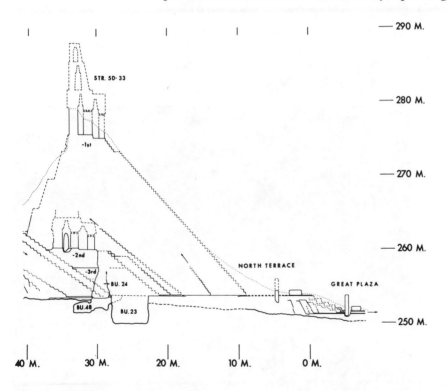

neighboring Gulf Coast lowlands of Tabasco, invaded the western and southern regions of the Maya area. While it is not completely clear whether the invaders were "invited" by the southern lowlands' vulnerability or whether the attack would have happened anyway, the effects are clear. The Putun helped precipitate the total collapse of Classic Maya civilization. By the middle of the ninth century A.D., virtually all major construction had ceased, most ceremonial centers had been abandoned, and the population of the southern lowlands had dropped radically, through both death and out-migration. In less than a hundred years, a civilization which appeared to have been at its height suddenly collapsed; and within a few short years the jungle claimed the plazas and temples where the magnificent religious ceremonies had recently been held.

There is at least one clear lesson which can be learned from the disappearance of Classic Maya civilization. Given a certain level of technology, and sociopolitical organization, the environment poses definite limits on the growth of a culture. These limits can be overcome through technological innovation or sociopolitical

Plate 4.21   Small temple at the site of Seibal built in the early ninth century A.D. (in Terminal Classic times).

Plate 4.22   Stela 13 from Seibal shows evidence of foreign invaders at the site at a time when other Classic sites in the southern lowlands had collapsed. The monument was erected about A.D. 870, according to the archaeologist John A. Graham.

change. If such changes, for whatever cultural reason, are not forthcoming, however, and these limits are broached, great burdens will be placed on the ecological system.

The tropical rain forest of the southern lowlands could support the growth of Classic Maya civilization with the ceremonial centers as long as the population was relatively dispersed. But as the population grew and formed urban concentrations around the centers, huge strains were placed on the environment. Through a series of cultural processes (which made great sense according to the Maya view of the world) short-term strategies may have been devised which alleviated the problems for a limited time but proved disastrous in the long run. If a thriving civilization misuses its environment, it may be sowing the seeds of its own destruction, even at its height, unless proper organizational and technological changes are made. The Classic Maya provide an unfortunate but instructive example.

After the Collapse

Maya civilization did not die out with the collapse. Although Classic civilization in the southern Maya lowlands disappeared and many centers were abandoned, Maya centers to the north in Yucatán began to flourish at this time. The geographic center of Maya civilization shifted, and there were significant changes in economic, political, and religious practices from earlier Classic times. But there also were strong cultural continuities from Classic into Postclassic (A.D. 900–1519) times, as well as significant historical occurrences and growing economic complexity.

With the collapse of Classic Maya civilization in the southern lowlands, the focus of development shifted to the northern lowlands of Yucatán. This shift was not accidental but coincided with major economic changes initiated by the Putun. These Gulf Coast people spoke a Maya language known as Chontal, but had been on the fringes of Classic Maya civilization and not direct participants. They were sea and river traders, principally interested in mercantile profit. They were involved in trading raw materials, finished crafts, and crops: a short list of goods includes cacao beans (which served as money in Precolumbian Mesoamerica), cotton, salt, volcanic stone, and mass-produced pottery. None of these resources could be obtained in the southern Maya lowlands—a lack which was certainly a principal factor in the southern lowlands' total inability to recover after the collapse. There simply was no economic incentive to rebuild Maya civilization here. (In fact, the population in the area has remained at a very low level up to the present day.)

The situation was different in Yucatán, which also was inhabited by Maya peoples. The first region to undergo a florescence was the Puuc region, located in a hilly area to the southwest of modern-day Mérida. Puuc sites such as Uxmal, Kabah, Sayil, Labna, and Xlapak flourished between A.D. 800 and 1000 and were renowned for their distinctive architecture with its ornate and complex stone façades (Plates 4.23 and 4.24). Puuc-decorated pottery became more standardized than earlier ceramics and was traded to distant parts of the Yucatán peninsula. It is highly probable that the florescence in the Puuc region was closely linked with the economic and political expansion of the Putun from the Gulf Coast lowlands.

After two centuries of growth which enabled sites such as Uxmal and Kabah to become as architecturally magnificent as any of the earlier Classic Maya centers of the southern lowlands, they were virtually abandoned. The decline of the Puuc sites was directly linked to another invasion, that of the Toltecs—successors to Teotihuacán and the dominant force in Central Mexico

Plate 4.23 The "Nunnery Quadrangle" at the site of Uxmal in northern Yucatán is an example of Puuc architecture and dates to Terminal Classic times. (Courtesy of Peter D. Harrison.)

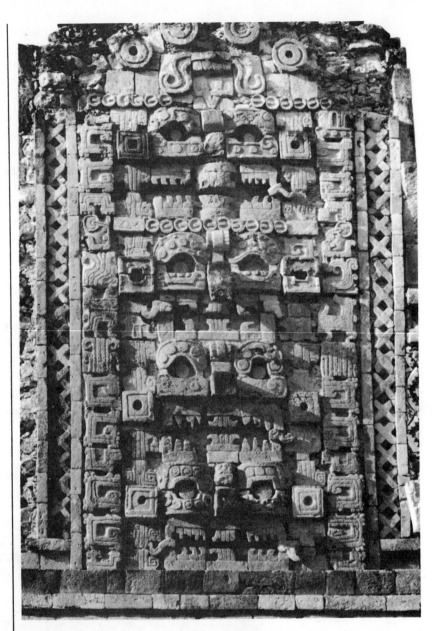

Plate 4.24 Detail from the façade of the "Nunnery." (Courtesy of Peter D. Harrison.)

between A.D. 900 and 1200. In a seeming alliance with the Putun merchants, the Toltecs assumed ascendancy over all the Yucatán lowlands, and Chichén Itzá became the economic and political, as well as the religious, center of the area (Plate 4.25).

The Toltecs' preeminence rapidly faded in the thirteenth century as their capital at Tula was overrun by nomadic invaders and their empire collapsed. Chichén Itzá was virtually abandoned as its political domination over the region was reassumed by the local Maya, perhaps in alliance with the Putun or Chontal Maya. The new, post-Toltec, Maya authority was centered at Mayapán, a walled city which controlled the economic and political life of Yucatán until A.D. 1450. It was during this period of time that the Putun merchants, who had slowly been building their power since the terminal Classic Period, reached the height of their influence. They controlled the sea trade from Tabasco around the peninsula to Honduras. In fact, it probably was a Putun trading canoe which Columbus contacted off the Bay Islands of Honduras during his fourth voyage.

The interior portion of Yucatán's northern lowland, which was controlled by Mayapán (Plate 4.26), formed just one part of a vast trading network of which the Putun dominated a considerable part. The island of Cozumel (Plate 4.27) served as an important way station in the long-distance trading routes of the Putun, while

Plate 4.25 The Castillo at the site of Chichén Itzá. (Courtesy of Peter D. Harrison.)

Plate 4.26   Colonnaded structure at the site of Mayapán. (Courtesy of Peabody Museum, Harvard University.)

Plate 4.27   Small Late Postclassic shrine on Cozumel Island which lies off the east coast of the Yucatán peninsula. (Photo by Loring Hewen; courtesy of Middle American Research Institute, Tulane University.)

Xicalango in Tabasco, Nito in Guatemala, and Naco in Honduras were other major trading ports in the system. The trade goods, as noted earlier, included cacao "money," salt, cotton, honey, and hard stone such as obsidian. The walled center of Tulum on the east coast of the peninsula was another major site of the period (Plate 4.28).

Some archaeologists have viewed the period from the fall of Chichén Itzá (A.D. 1250) to the Spanish Conquest in the early sixteenth century as the Decadent Period. The great architectural and artistic achievements of the Classic Period were gone. In their place were shoddily constructed buildings with heavy coats of plaster covering up the inferior masonry. Mass-produced pottery and artifacts replaced the beautiful craft productions of early centuries. Maya civilization was seemingly decaying.

The apparent artistic decay, however, did not tell the whole story, for it was but one symptom of a broad-scale change in the economic and social order. The influence of the priestly elite had declined rapidly since the end of the Classic Period, while a rising merchant class had gained power. The merchants' values were quite different from those of the priests. With the decentralization of religious authority, huge investments of labor and wealth were no longer put into temples and vast, richly stocked tombs. Thus the so-called Decadent Period in reality saw a growth in economic complexity, the rise of mass

Plate 4.28   The site of Tulum on the east coast of the Yucatán peninsula. (Courtesy of Peter D. Harrison.)

production, the development of more efficient distribution systems, and a general increase in the standard of living among the Maya, along with a decline in the high arts.

These mercantile developments were abruptly ended with the arrival of Cordoba, Grijalva, Cortés, Montejo, and all the Spanish conquistadores in the early sixteenth century. After some difficulties, the Spanish were ultimately able to defeat the Maya and take control of Yucatán. Some of the Maya on the east coast were never entirely subdued, however, and actually led a major rebellion against the Mexican government in Yucatán during the mid-nineteenth century. (The rebellion is known as the "War of the Castes.") Not until the present century were the Maya of the east coast finally pacified by the Mexican army.

TEOTIHUACÁN

As we have noted, the first city in Mesoamerica may well have developed at Monte Albán in the Valley of Oaxaca, sometime between 500 B.C. and the end of the first millennium B.C. The Valley of Oaxaca has received a great deal of attention in recent years, and when the results of the considerable fieldwork are published, our knowledge of the rise of urban civilization in this region will certainly have reached new heights. At the present time, however, the best data about the development of the city in ancient Mesoamerica come not from Monte Albán but from Teotihuacán, which lies about 50 kilometers to the northeast of modern-day Mexico City. Recent surveys and excavations by Professors René Millon, George Cowgill, Bruce Drewitt, and their associates and by the Instituto Nacional de Antropología y Historia have completely changed our conception of this site and have offered new insights into the nature of the rise of preindustrial cities.

Rise of the Urban State

Teotihuacán had begun its growth by 200–100 B.C. Within a few centuries, it had expanded to become a great city: it is the largest Precolumbian urban center visible today in Mesoamerica, perhaps in all the New World. Its gigantic pyramids and overall size make it one of the most impressive archaeological sites in the world (Plate 4.29). Although Tenochtitlán, capital of the Aztecs, may have held more people, most of its remains are hidden underneath modern-day Mexico City. Millon's research has revealed that at its height, between about A.D. 150 and 700, Teotihuacán probably had a population of more than 125,000 people and covered at least 20 square kilometers (8 square miles). It had over two thousand apartment complexes (see Figure 4.8), a great market, a large number of industrial workshops, an administrative center, a number of massive religious edifices, and a regular grid pattern of streets and buildings. Clearly, much planning and central control were involved in the expansion and operation of this great metropolis. Moreover, the city spread its economic and religious influence throughout much of Mesoamerica.

Plate 4.29 General view of Teotihuacán with the Temple of the Moon in the foreground and the Temple of the Sun to the immediate left of the Street of the Dead. (From *Urbanization at Teotihuacán, Mexico,* vol. 1, pt. 1, "The Teotihuacán Map: Text" by René Millon, copyright 1973 by René Millon, by permission of the author.)

How did this tremendous development take place, and why did it happen in the Teotihuacán Valley? As we have begun to see, questions of causation in the development of ancient civilizations are complex at best, intractable at worst. In the case of Teotihuacán, there obviously were a multitude of factors involved in its rise. Of particular interest are Teotihuacán's geographic location on a natural trade route to the south and east of the Valley of Mexico, the obsidian resources in the Teotihuacán Valley itself, and the valley's potential for extensive irrigation. The

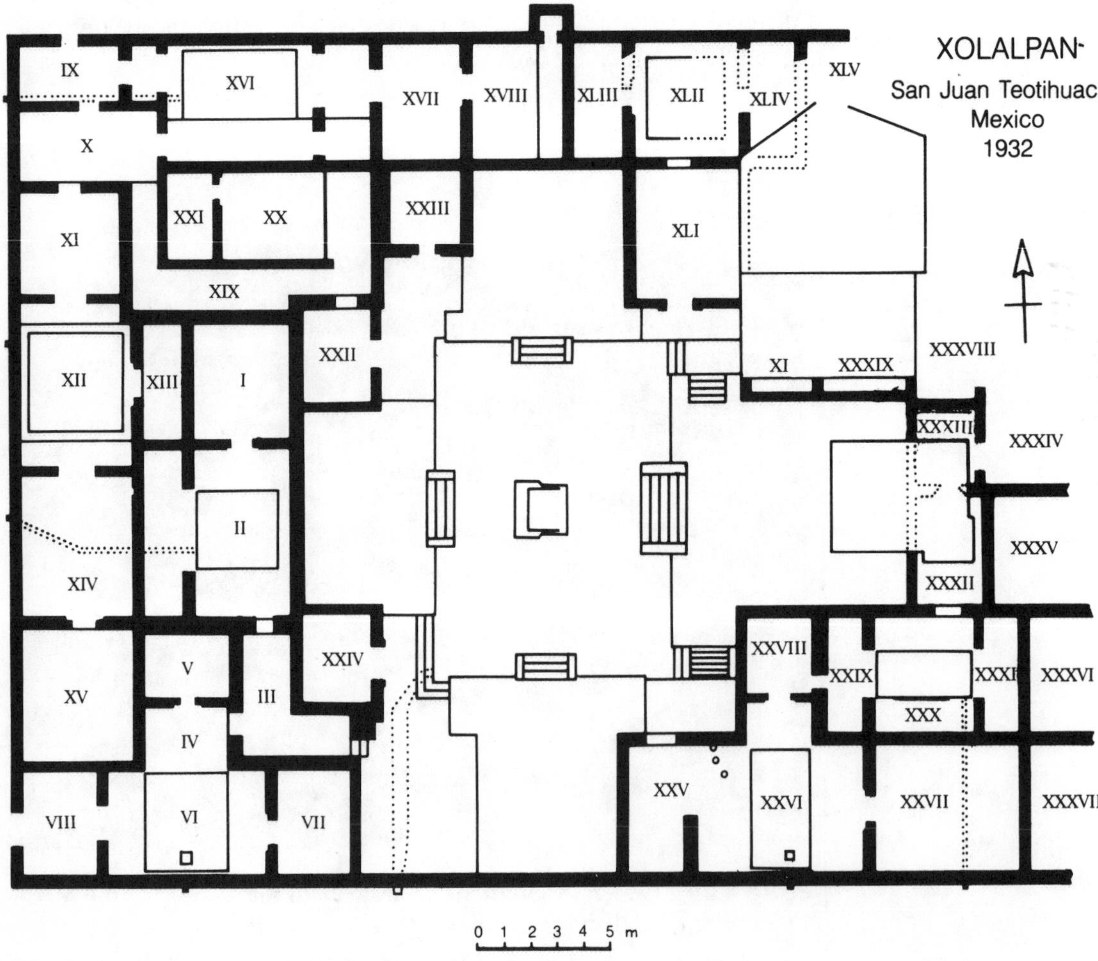

Figure 4.8 S. Linne's 1934 plan of the Xolalpan residential compound at Teotihuacán. (After Linne 1934.)

exact role of other factors is much more difficult for the archaeologist to pinpoint—for instance, Teotihuacán's religious significance as a shrine, the historical situation in and around the Valley of Mexico toward the end of the first millennium B.C., the ingenuity and foresightedness of Teotihuacán's elite, and, finally, the impact of natural disasters, such as the volcanic eruptions of the late first millennium B.C.

This last factor is at least circumstantially implicated in Teotihuacán's rise. Around 200 B.C., a number of relatively small centers coexisted in and near the Valley of Mexico. Just previous to this time, the largest of these centers, Cuicuilco, had been destroyed by a volcanic eruption. With Cuicuilco eliminated as a potential rival, any one of a number of modest centers might have emerged as a leading economic and political power in Central Mexico. The archaeological evidence clearly indicates, though, that Teotihuacán was the center which did arise as the predominant force in the area by the time of Christ. What we do not know is why it, rather than its potential rivals, emerged; why it grew as rapidly and as big as it did; and, finally, what advantage (or adaptive value in ecological terms) its great size gave it, for it certainly thrived at a size that had been beyond the Olmecs' or the Maya's capabilities. Scholars have advanced some intriguing hypotheses in their attempts to answer these questions.

It seems likely that Teotihuacán's natural resources—along with the city elite's ability to recognize their potential—gave the city a competitive edge over its neighbors.[26] The valley, like many other places in Mexican and Guatemalan highlands, was rich in obsidian. The hard volcanic stone was a resource which had been in great demand for many years, at least since the rise of the Olmecs, and it apparently had a secure market. Moreover, recent trace element analysis of obsidian tools found at Olmec sites has shown that some of the obsidian obtained by the Olmecs originated near Teotihuacán. Teotihuacán obsidian must have been recognized as a valuable commodity for many centuries before the great city arose.

Long-distance trade in obsidian probably gave the residents of Teotihuacán access to a wide variety of exotic goods, as well as a relatively prosperous life. Such success may have attracted immigrants to Teotihuacán. In addition, Teotihuacán's elite may have consciously attempted to attract new inhabitants. It also is possible that as early as 200 B.C. Teotihuacán had achieved some religious significance and its shrine (or shrines) may have served as an additional population magnet.

Whatever the initial factor that led to the rapid population increase at Teotihuacán in the second century B.C., it is probable that the feeding of this growing population was accomplished by the increase in the number and size of irrigated fields in the Teotihuacán Valley. As some scholars have argued, such an increase would have given greater power to the elite who managed the irrigated fields and supervised the building of the canals.[27] In addition, more people would be needed to build and maintain the canals.

In sum, the picture of Teotihuacán that emerges is a classic model of positive feedback among obsidian mining and working, trade, population growth, and irrigation. The thriving obsidian operation would necessitate more miners, additional manufacturers of obsidian tools, and additional traders to carry the goods to new markets. All this led to increased wealth, which in turn would attract more immigrants to Teotihuacán. The

Plate 4.30 View of part of the environment of the Teotihuacán Valley showing a cluster of *nopal* cactus. *Nopal* probably was exploited as a food source throughout ancient times. (Courtesy of Peter D. Harrison.)

growing power of the elite, who controlled the economy, would give them the means to physically coerce people to move to Teotihuacán and serve as additions to the labor force. More irrigation works would have to be built to feed the growing population, and this resulted in more power and wealth for the elite. The elite were free to devote more time and wealth to building religious edifices—which in turn could serve as a growing attraction for the new population.

While the model we have just sketched is still speculative, it may give us an insight into some of the trends which could account for the phenomenal increase in size which occurred at Teotihuacán. Professor Millon's research indicates that there might have been conscious planning by the city's elite very early in its occupation, as evidenced by the early grid pattern and layout of the urban center. Discoveries indicate that the building of the huge structures and the growth of the vast population happened relatively early in the city's history and did not take centuries of development. It would appear, for instance, that the grid system upon which the city was organized was established soon after the time of Christ (during the Tzacualli Phase from A.D. 1 to 150). It

Plate 4.31   The Temple of the Sun. (Courtesy of Peter D. Harrison.)

Plate 4.32   One of the many murals preserved on the walls of Teotihuacán's structures. (Courtesy of Peter D. Harrison.)

Plate 4.33   Portion of the sculpted front façade of the Quetzalcoatl pyramid at Teotihuacán. (Courtesy of Peabody Museum, Harvard University.)

is during this phase that the city experienced maximum growth. Millon estimates that it reached its maximum areal size during Tzacualli times, although its population did not peak until succeeding phases.

During the Miccaotli Phase (A.D. 150–200), the great administrative compound known as the Ciudadella (Plate 4.34) was built, the great Pyramid of the Sun was completed, and a number of other major construction projects were undertaken. Teotihuacán's influence also began to spread widely, probably even reaching the Maya area at this time.

Teotihuacán's power and population continued to grow during the Tlamimilolpa (A.D. 200–450) and Xolalpan (A.D. 450–650) Phases, and the role of trade must have been crucial. Even from the beginnings of the rise of Teotihuacán, trade was important for the rising power. Markets were needed for the obsidian tools which Teotihuacán was manufacturing. At first, these markets probably were largely regional, but Teotihuacán soon expanded throughout much of Mesoamerica.

As we have begun to see in examining civilization in Mesoamerica, it is virtually impossible to separate religious motivations from economic or political concerns. Such is definitely the case with Teotihuacán's expansion. The nature of that expansion, which begins certainly by Miccoatli times and

Plate 4.34 View of part of the Ciudadela or central administrative compound at Teotihuacán, looking toward the Pyramid of the Sun. (Courtesy of Peabody Museum, Harvard University.)

climaxes by late Tlamimilolpa to early Xolalpan times, clearly has elements of economic, political, and religious significance. What makes Teotihuacán's expansion especially hard to pinpoint is that in each separate region or site influenced by the great city, the archaeological evidence seems to point to different interactions. The role of Teotihuacán in the life of the Oaxaca Valley (at the site of Monte Albán), in Veracruz (at the site of El Tajin), in the Guatemalan highlands (at the site of Kaminaljuyu), or in the southern Maya lowlands (at the site of Tikal) appears somewhat different in each case. The Teotihuacán presence at Kaminaljuyu, for instance, has most often been interpreted as an example of a complete takeover of the site by some of Teotihuacán's elite, while some archaeologists would see the Teotihuacán influence at Tikal as the result of a Teotihuacán embassy at this Classic Maya city.

At Kaminaljuyu, the presence of Teotihuacán intruders can be seen in the architecture of that culture's Esperanza Phase (A.D. 400–700). The style of these buildings clearly derives from Teotihuacán. Tomb materials, especially ceramics, also show heavy Teotihuacán influence. Archaeologists such as William T. Sanders and Barbara Price believe that Teotihuacán may have seized control of Kaminaljuyu in order to protect the important cacao-producing areas on the Pacific slopes of Guatemala and so ensure continuing trade of this commodity to Central Mexico.

The nature of Teotihuacán influence at Tikal is more enigmatic. However, recent advances in the study of the hieroglyphic inscriptions have revealed that the Teotihuacán presence probably arrived via Kaminaljuyu. While we are unsure of the exact nature of the Teotihuacán influence at Tikal and other Maya sites, it clearly had a profound effect on Classic developments, both economic and political, in the lowlands.

Whatever stimulated the spread of Teotihuacán's power and influence, the economic motivation is certainly present in most cases. Whether to find new markets for its obsidian tools or finely made pottery or to obtain desired raw materials such as cacao, Teotihuacán's expansion certainly enhanced its economic power—just as its growing wealth enhanced its political and religious importance. By Tlamimilolpa times, Teotihuacán's shrines and great market stood out as the most attractive, powerful, and important developments in Classic Mesoamerica. As one archaeologist has succinctly noted: "Teotihuacán rose to a power position never again equaled by a Mesoamerican center."[28]

The huge size of the city obviously enabled it to maximize its economic potential, particularly in respect to the exploitation of obsidian. Even from the all too brief overview of Teotihuacán's development which we have just sketched, the "adaptive value" of Teotihuacán's rapid growth and its achievement of such vast size in population, extent of settlement, and sphere of influence can be seen. The systemically reinforcing nature of the increase in population, procurement of raw material (particularly obsidian), craft production, social stratification, wealth, religious importance, and political power is evident. The growth of the city not only permitted but also stimulated the growth of Teotihuacán's political, economic, and religious power. Moreover, the vast extent of this growth—impossible for the Maya culture—was possible for Teotihuacán because of the ecological makeup of the valley, with its obsidian resources, irrigable lands, and geographic location close to potential trade routes.

Nevertheless, as clear as the systematic relationships appear to be, the question of "prime movers" is cloudy. What led to the initial population surge at Teotihuacán? It appears to have occurred too rapidly to have been the result of internal factors alone. There is no clear evidence that the initial growth of irrigation systems led to early population increases and bureaucratic growth as classic irrigation theory would indicate. Nor do available archaeological data show that exploitation of obsidian was the immediate cause of rapid population increases. Again, there is no concrete evidence to indicate that the religious importance of the site attracted immigrants or that there was a large-scale population movement such as an invasion. Although archaeologists can plausibly argue that certain (and perhaps all) of these factors must have been involved in Teotihuacán's initial growth, it is hard to show the primacy of one over the others.

In fact, the Teotihuacán case may be as good an example as any of the futility of searching for single causes. If archaeologists can come to grips with the relationships of a multiplicity of causal factors in individual cases—as Millon seems on the track of doing at Teotihuacán, or as many archaeologists seem to be doing for the Classic Maya collapse—then it can be hoped that we may eventually be able to perceive regularities in developmental trends among ancient civilizations in general. We will return to this question in the concluding chapter of this book.

Teotihuacán's Fall

As much as we still have to learn about Teotihuacán's rise, there is even more to be discovered about its fall. Given its success throughout the Early Classic Period, why did this great city decline and collapse in the eighth century A.D.? How did its successful adaptation turn sour, especially since most of the great innovations, changes, and expansions which the city and "empire" underwent took place relatively early in its development? It does not appear that some new internal development proved to be immediately destructive. Was the collapse due, therefore, to factors external to Teotihuacán, such as an invasion? If so, why should such a powerful urban center be destroyed? As Millon, certainly one of the leading experts on Teotihuacán, rhetorically asks:

> Was it through Teotihuacán's prosperity and expansionism, its success as a way of life, both within the city and beyond, that its ultimate failure emerged? To resolve predictably increasing contradictions in the dialectic of urban life, were the attractions, the advantages, the positive aspects of urban life negated? To "save" the "Teotihuacán way of life" locally and imperially, was it "necessary" for the Teotihuacán hierarchy and state so to act as to erode it and ultimately to destroy it?[29]

Some data which have been uncovered may eventually help us to answer these questions. First of all, there was a decline in Teotihuacán's population just prior to its collapse, although it does not appear to have been a great decline. Second, there is evidence that Teotihuacán was burned at the time of its downfall. Third, there may well have been a drying up of the climate prior to the collapse. And finally, there appears to have been a contraction of Teotihuacán's sphere of influence in the century preceding the collapse.

Thus there is one indication that Teotihuacán was invaded— the burning. But there are no other archaeological data to back up this explanation. We do know that there were militaristically oriented, seminomadic groups, the same groups from which the Toltecs later came, who lived to the north of the city. More than this, the drying up of the climate might have put strains on the agricultural system, and this in turn could have placed acute pressure on the political conditions of the city. Such a situation, it has been suggested, might have made the city vulnerable to outside attack.

At this point, we can see some possible analogies to the Classic Maya collapse to the south. As Millon suggests, perhaps it was necessary for the elite of Teotihuacán, like the Classic Maya elite, to take steps to salvage a deteriorating situation. Harsher, even more centralized, rule or an increased emphasis on the military in order to combat both external and internal threats might have exacerbated rather than alleviated the strained conditions. These pressures might ultimately have helped speed the deterioration in the city.

Whatever the causes, Teotihuacán's great power had declined by 800 A.D., and for the next two centuries something approaching an interregnum occurred in Mesoamerica. Various sites and regions such as Cholula, El Tajin, Xochicalco, and the Maya lowlands all assumed new significance and influence. Ultimately, two groups emerged by the tenth century A.D. as the new powers in Mesoamerica. These groups were the Toltecs of Central Mexico and their allies the Putun, a Maya-speaking people from the Gulf Coast of Tabasco-Campeche. With their assumption of economic and political power, a new era in ancient Mesoamerican history was born.

THE TOLTECS

With the coming of the Postclassic Period around A.D. 900, significant changes in Mesoamerican civilization can be found. These changes are not sudden introductions, but rather the culmination of trends which began well back in Classic times. Two trends are particularly noteworthy: first, the increasing importance of merchants and long-distance trade, and second, the growing militarism. In many ways, the period between the fall of Teotihuacán and the rise of the Aztecs, by and large the Early Postclassic Period, is one of the most important in the development of Mesoamerican civilization, yet one of the least known. Recent work by Professor Richard Diehl and Professor Eduardo Matos M. at the Toltec capital of Tula (or Tollan) and the ongoing studies of Professor Robert Carmack and his associates in the Guatemalan highlands may throw some additional light on this crucial period.

The Toltecs continued and intensified certain trends which emerged under the Teotihuacán empire, yet they apparently lacked the centralized control and economic influences which were an important characteristic of Teotihuacán's expansion. While Toltec manifestations have a wide geographic spread, they do not often seem to be closely tied in to the Toltec capital. For this reason, in both a developmental and a chronological sense, the Toltecs occupy an intermediary position between Teotihuacán and the Aztecs. The latter group, who combine aspects of both Teotihuacán and Toltec civilizations in the fifteenth and early sixteenth centuries A.D., produced an empire which most closely approximates the empires of the ancient Near East. (The Aztec empire will be discussed in the final section of this chapter.)

As we have noted, after the fall of Teotihuacán there was an interregnum period when a number of sites and regions vied for the political and economic legacy of that great city. By the tenth century A.D., the Toltecs emerged as a dominant force in Mesoamerica. The Toltecs originally were a seminomadic people from northern Mexico who settled at Tula, a site in the highlands which lay to the northwest of Teotihuacán and the Valley of Mexico. It has often been suggested that drought conditions during the late first millennium A.D. (which may also have been a factor in Teotihuacán's demise) caused frontier peoples such as the Toltecs to move south where the climate was better.

The Rise of Tula and the Toltecs

For many years, the exact location of this legendary city of Tula was unknown. Some archaeologists believed that Teotihuacán had actually been the ancient capital of the Toltecs. In the 1940s, however, the work of Mexican scholars located Tula's site in the state of Hidalgo.[30]

Although it is not nearly as large as Teotihuacán, the site of Tula is clearly of urban proportions. It shared other similarities with the earlier highland city. One was the exploitation of obsidian. Tula itself had no indigenous obsidian, but the Toltecs controlled and exploited nearby sources. Obsidian was a major source of wealth for the city, and obsidian workshops have been found there. Like Teotihuacán, too, the Toltec city was an important center of trade. Archaeologists at Tula have found ceramic and artifactual evidence of contacts with all parts of Mesoamerica.

But while the two cities shared many similarities, there were also distinct differences. The exact nature of Teotihuacán's "internationalism" is not always easy to recognize, but the Toltecs' role is more clearly defined. In addition to being a center of trade, Tula was a military power. The city site is replete with symbols indicating the importance of militarism and sacrifice. Friezes of skull racks, warriors with shields and weapons, eagles eating hearts, and prowling jaguars are particularly prominent. The latter two symbolize two major Toltec military orders: the orders of the Jaguars and the Eagles.

Legendary Explanations What were the events that led to the Toltecs' ascendancy? For the first time in trying to reconstruct ancient Mesoamerican sequences and causes, archaeologists enter the difficult realm of what is often called *protohistory*—the times immediately preceding recorded history,

Plate 4.35 The well-known Temple B at the site of Tula.

where a good bit of legend is often mixed with fact. There is a certain amount of information about the Toltecs available in the written record from the time of the Spanish Conquest in 1521 A.D. But given the many centuries which separate the heyday of the Toltecs from the later conquest, history tends to merge into legend, and it may be impossible to disentangle facts from myth.

It is useful, though, to look to Mesoamerican records as a historical source of sorts. In fact, one of the most significant and persistent legends from the Toltec era concerns the probable founding of Tula and the rise of the Toltecs. Meticulous research has shown that these "Quetzalcoatl legends" recorded in the sixteenth century probably had a strong historical component.[31]

The legends describe Topiltzin Quetzalcoatl, his ascendancy to the throne of Tula, and his achievement of semidivine status. Quetzalcoatl subsequently came into conflict with Tezcatlipoca,

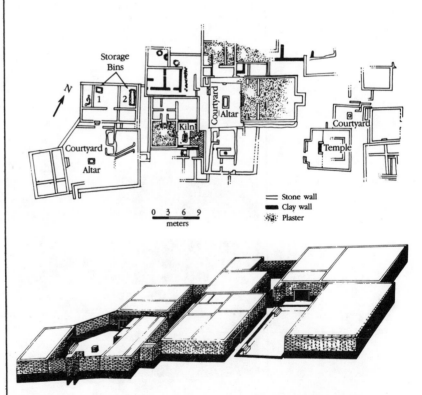

Figure 4.9 House compound at Tula. (From R. Diehl and R. Benfer, "Tollan: The Toltec Capital," *Archaeology,* vol. 28, no. 2, by permission of *Archaeology.*)

another semidivine personage. The former represented the forces of peace and enlightenment; the latter signified warfare, militarism, and sacrifice. After a series of conflicts, Quetzalcoatl lost and was expelled from Tula. He fled toward the east, promising someday to return.

How much fact is included in the Quetzalcoatl legend? As with the earliest entries in the Sumerian King List (discussed in Chapter 3), it is likely that there is a historical basis—although the exact nature of this basis is still a matter of conjecture. In a recent article, Professor Gordon R. Willey of Harvard suggests that Topiltzin Quetzalcoatl was the author of a transcendent philosophy which attempted to bring order to a confused time: the interregnum. Although he failed at Tula, his philosophy apparently did have a lasting effect on the peoples of Postclassic Mesoamerica. And as we will see, his legacy also had a profound effect on the Aztec emperor Moctezuma II at the time of the Spanish Conquest.

Willey further suggests how the social structure of Tula at the time might have provided a very believable framework for the events described in the legend. The new merchant class which was beginning to gain power among the Putun as well as the Toltecs might well have supported a philosophy such as Quetzalcoatl's. In Willey's words:

> As time went on . . . trade appears to have become ever more important, and from what we know of Postclassic society, from documentary sources, the trader or merchant was steadily becoming a more influential figure in this society, pressing, perhaps, upon prerogatives and power formerly held solely by aristocratic and military cadres. In this context, it may not be too much to see the philosophy of Topiltzin Quetzalcoatl as the adaptive and protective ideology of a rising merchant or "middle" class. This by no means ruled out all competition and empire-building, but it was a recognition that some limits were essential.[32]

With the triumph of Tezcatlipoca, who like Topiltzin Quetzalcoatl may originally have been a historical person and an early ruler of Tula who assumed a semidivine status, the ethos of the Toltecs was institutionalized. Militarism and sacrifice became the order of the day.

Archaeological Evidence   At this stage of the Toltecs' story, historical evidence is on more certain footing, for we can infer that by the early tenth century A.D., Tezcatlipoca's philosophy had prevailed. Toltec warriors, as well as Toltec merchants and Toltec influence in general, had spread throughout Mesoamerica. A group of Toltecs conquered Chichén Itzá in Yucatán by the end of the tenth century. From there, aided and abetted by their Putun allies, the Toltecs soon controlled the greater Yucatán peninsula, economically if not politically. At Chichén Itzá, the Toltec presence can be seen in architecture, art style, and artifacts (Plates 4.36–4.38). Toltec control of Chichén Itzá lasted until the mid-thirteenth century A.D.

The Toltecs also had a major effect on the Maya-speaking peoples who lived in the highlands of Guatemala. Important shifts in settlement patterns and political organization of the highland Maya can be seen as coincident with the rise of Toltec power in the Yucatán, even though the Toltecs never controlled the southern regions as they did the northern Yucatán. Instead, highland settlements shifted to defensible locations, and within a short period the invaders were absorbed by local populations. The result of this merger was a Mexicanized Maya culture.

Toltec influence prevailed in other parts of Mesoamerica. Along the Gulf Coast of Mexico, Toltec contacts are evident, while to the north in Zacatecas, the site of La Quemada clearly shows

Plate 4.36 The Temple of the Warriors at the site of Chichén Itzá clearly shows Toltec influences. (Courtesy of Peabody Museum, Harvard University.)

Plate 4.37   Column depicting a Toltec warrior at Chichén Itzá.
(Courtesy of Peabody Museum, Harvard University.)

Toltec influence. Western and northwest Mexico, too, as far north as Sinaloa, probably were actively trading with the Toltecs by about 1000 A.D. This latter occurrence was of great significance. For the first time western Mexico became part of the Mesoamerican cultural system. It has even been conjectured that the Toltecs influenced both the American Southwest and the Southeast between A.D. 1000 and 1200, but many archaeologists discount such a possibility.[33]

Under the Toltec influence, the western Mexican peoples adopted a number of Mesoamerican traits and became involved in active economic exchanges with Central Mexico. The Toltec influence on western Mexico should not be seen, however, as a one-way relationship. Although Toltec economic and political forces influenced life in western Mexico, the latter region also made an important contribution to the mainstream of Mesoamerican civilization. This new contribution was metallurgy, particularly the working of copper.

As a result of western Mexican influence, copper became widespread in Mesoamerica after A.D. 900, as did gold and silver

Plage 4.38 Carved skulls from a small platform at Chichén Itzá are just one indication of the new importance of militarism in Early Postclassic times. (Courtesy of Peter D. Harrison.)

to a more limited extent. In general, these metals were elite items that did not achieve a general utilitarian status: various stone materials remained the principal source for everyday tools. It is not completely clear whether metallurgy was independently invented in Mesoamerica, although there are strong archaeological hints that it was introduced from the south. Panama, Ecuador, or Peru may all have been the source from which metallurgy diffused to western Mexico and then to Mesoamerica as a whole. Metals such as gold were also imported from lower Central America.

The Toltecs in Perspective

In many ways, the Toltec culture can be seen as a bridge between Teotihuacán and the Aztecs, exhibiting less central control than either its successor or its predecessor. Goods and people flowed into the huge cities of Teotihuacán and Tenochtitlán, which acted as major economic, political, and religious centers. But while Tula was both a trading center and a city of great religious significance, it was never as all-important as the others. It seems to have acted not as the only Toltec center, but as one of a number of regional centers in the wide-ranging economic and political system.

Other differences distinguished Tula from the Aztec city and from Teotihuacán. Unlike the other controllers of the Mesoamerican system, the Toltecs did not use any advances in subsistence technology such as irrigation to help them in achieving supremacy.[34] Nevertheless, they made other innovations, namely, new and efficient military arms techniques, to achieve their conquests. And even more significant, they developed a new amalgam of military and economic interests which were the driving force behind the Toltec expansion from Central Mexico. These sectors reinforced each other, backed by the dual ideological philosophies of Tezcatlipoca and Quetzalcoatl.

Indeed, the Toltec period was far from a phase of biding time between two greater empires. On the contrary, it marked not just the continuation of some earlier trends but also some basic changes. As we have seen, the Toltec expansion in the tenth and eleventh centuries A.D. appears to have been more militaristically oriented than Teotihuacán's: the model for the better-known Aztec expansion by conquest and trade in the fifteenth and early sixteenth centuries may well have been forged by the Toltecs. There is no question that the Toltec empire was of major importance. Even at the time of the Spanish Conquest, Tula and the Toltecs still maintained an almost legendary status as the predecessors of the Aztecs.

Tula collapsed in the twelfth century A.D. (Some historical reconstructions place the date exactly in A.D. 1186.) As was the case with Teotihuacán, the causes are uncertain, although they probably were related to the incursions of new groups who, like the Toltecs and the Aztecs, came from the north. With the decline of Toltec strength, regional powers once again emerged in Mesoamerica during the thirteenth and fourteenth centuries A.D. In the fifteenth century, however, a new centralizing power emerged in the Valley of Mexico as the last great Mesoamerican empire. Just prior to the Spanish Conquest, the Aztecs began to spread their economic and political might throughout the Mesoamerican world.

THE AZTECS

Aztec civilization clearly can be seen as the culmination of many long-standing cultural trends in Mesoamerican development. Urbanization, mercantilism, and imperialism, for instance, all reached their Precolumbian heights under the Aztec regime. Since the Aztec civilization was destroyed in the early stages of its growth, it is difficult to predict how complex their cultural system might have become. Still, archaeologists and ethnohistorians know more about the Aztecs than any other Mesoamerican group because of the presence of a host of documentary materials from the time of the Spanish Conquest.

The Rise of the Aztecs

In less than two centuries, the Aztecs evolved from a poor seminomadic group to the rulers of the most powerful empire ever developed in ancient Mesoamerica. From the time they settled in the Valley of Mexico in the mid-fourteenth century, well after the total decline of Toltec dominance, the Aztecs showed themselves to be shrewd politicians and excellent warriors. Through a series of shifting alliances with various political powers in Central Mexico, the Aztecs achieved a preeminent position in the region in less than a century. At first, the Aztecs hired themselves out as mercenaries to the warring city-states in the Valley of Mexico. Through cunning and ruthless military skill, the Aztecs' power and relative condition improved. They subsequently became partners in a military confederation, known as the Triple Alliance, with the cities of Texcoco and Tlacopán. This alliance was able to defeat its main rival, the Tepanecs of Azcapotzalco. Finally, the Aztecs emerged as the superior partner in the alliance and began spreading their control throughout the valley and beyond. By exploiting the agricultural and commercial potential of the region and utilizing their great skills in warfare and politics, the Aztecs rapidly proceeded to extend their domain to the farthest reaches of Mesoamerica. Their new empire was just beginning to take shape when the Spaniards reached the coast of Mexico.

The capital city of Tenochtitlán was founded between A.D. 1325 and 1345. At that time, it consisted of what has been described as a collection of squalid huts on an island in the midst of swamps and reed beds. In the following two centuries, through a conscious policy of land reclamation, the urban concentration that was Tenochtitlán gradually attained its final size (see Map 4.5). In Professor Michael Coe's words:

> It was the cutting of canals and the construction of chinampas [artificial floating gardens built up from water vegetation and lake bottom mud] by the poor and hungry Aztecs who first came here in the 14th century A.D. that filled in the swampy land between the low rocky islands on which they had camped. The work eventually resulted in the coalescence and enlargement of the islands into the marvelous capital city that so impressed the conquistádores.[35]

In 1519, Cortés and his small band of five hundred Spanish soldiers approached the goal of their long march from the Gulf Coast: the capital of Tenochtitlán in the Valley of Mexico. The writings of Bernal Díaz del Castillo, one of Cortés' soldiers whose account has supplied us with much information about the Aztecs at the time of Spanish contact, indicate the Spaniards' reaction:

> With such wonderful sights to gaze on we did not know what to say, or if this was real that we saw before our eyes. On the land side there were great cities, and on the lake many more. The lake was crowded with canoes. At intervals along the causeway there were many bridges, and before us was the great city of Mexico.[36]

Tenochtitlán: The Great City of Mexico

What was the nature of this incredible city of Tenochtitlán, which the Spaniards first saw in 1519 and subsequently conquered in 1521? What agricultural, economic, social, and political subsystems supported the most complex city of ancient Mesoamerica?

Some scholars have estimated that the great capital of the Aztecs had a population of up to 300,000 people at the time of the conquest. Other writers have offered more modest estimates of under 200,000; these are probably closer to reality. Recent research by Professor Edward Calnek, one of the foremost scholars of ancient Tenochtitlán, indicates that the city may have had an

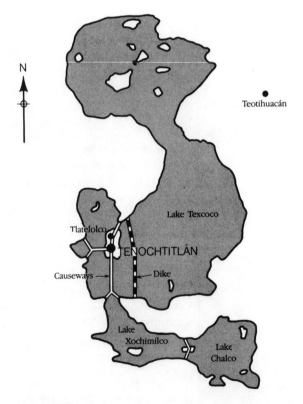

Map 4.5   The Valley of Mexico at the times of the Aztecs. (Adapted from W. Bray, *The Daily Life of the Aztecs.* 1968. London: B. T. Batsford Ltd. © 1968 B. T. Batsford Ltd.)

approximate area as large as 12 square kilometers, close to 5 square miles.

The city actually consisted of two islands in the middle of a saltwater lake, Lake Texcoco, with much artificial landfill. The city was built on a grid pattern with a network of canals and bridges. Two of the major roads were laid out in the shape of a cross with a great precinct at the center of the axis (see Figure 4.10). These roads divided the city into four principal districts, each with its own ceremonial center and market. These districts were further subdivided into twenty wards, which were inhabited by different

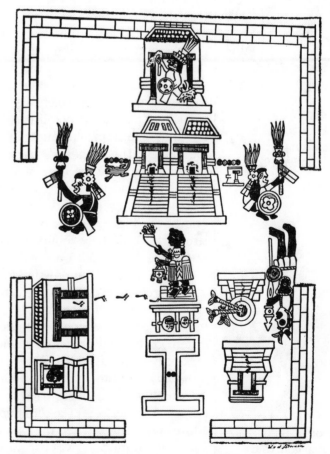

Figure 4.10 Sahagun's plan of the center of Tenochtitlán. (After Seler and Spinden 1928.)

clans or *calpulli*. Each of the twenty *calpulli* also had its own plaza, temple, and market. The great market of the city was located in the neighboring island of Tlatelolco, which had been conquered by Tenochtitlán and incorporated into the city. Three principal causeways connected the islands with the mainland. The city had no major fortifications, since it had the natural protection afforded by the lake.

The sacred precinct was located at the center of the city. Here a large wall decorated with heads of hundreds of plumed serpents enclosed eighteen main structures and groups of buildings, as well as many smaller structures. The most important of these edifices was the Great Temple, or *Teocalli*. This pyramid had twin temples on its summit: one was dedicated to Huitzilopochtli, the god of war (Figure 4.11); the other was devoted to Tlaloc, the god of rain (Figure 4.12).

Other structures in the sacred precinct included a round temple dedicated to Quetzalcoatl, the major Mesoamerican god who was in Aztec times represented as a feathered serpent. In addition, there was a court in which the traditional Mesoamerican ball game was played. As noted earlier, the game had had great religious significance throughout Mesoamerica since the time of the Olmec. The emperor's palace was also housed within the sacred precinct. At the time of Moctezuma II, the last great Aztec ruler, this palace was enlarged to two stories to accommodate the emperor's many retainers. The entire precinct was situated on one of the higher points of land on the island so that the large structures could have foundational support. Substantial buildings elsewhere were built on piles.

Tenochtitlán was impressive in other ways beyond its highly visible architecture: the construction of both a city and its agricultural plots in the middle of a lake represents a masterpiece of not only structural but also hydraulic design. The system of floating gardens or *chinampas* was incredibly productive, and a similar system is still in use today. Each *chinampa* typically measured 100 meters by 5 to 10 meters. The surrounding canals were used as thoroughfares for flat-bottomed canoes. The surface of a *chinampa* plot lay only a few feet above water level. When the plot became too high from renewal with bottom muck, it was excavated back to its original level. In addition, trees were planted to solidify the plot.

Figure 4.11 Huitzilopochtli, the Aztec god of war, taking a captive. (After Spinden 1928.)

Figure 4.12 A representation of Tlaloc, the Aztec rain god. (After Spinden 1928.)

The *chinampa* area required fresh water, and so a dike was built across Lake Texcoco to keep out the lake's salt water. The dike system, complete with a floodgate to regulate the lake levels, was quite impressive. Freshwater springs near Lake Xochimilco fed the *chinampas* and kept water level high within the diked area. There were some springs on the islands, too, but they were not adequate, so aqueducts were built by the Aztecs to bring in fresh water from various mainland springs. As Coe notes: "The entire chinampa zone ... represented a gigantic hydraulic scheme based on land drainage and the manipulation of water resources."[37] The living area, too, required some hydraulic ingenuity. Earthenware water pipes, 5 meters below the surface in some areas, were used for drainage in habitation areas. Still, the problem of sanitation must have been quite serious. To cope with the situation, boats were tied up in the city at strategic points for public use. When they were filled, their contents were sold to fertilize the *chinampas.*

The Aztec Social System

Although they were the instruments of destruction, the observations and writings of the Spanish themselves have given us a clearer picture, not only of the capital city, but also of the entire social system of the Aztecs, than we have for any previous Mesoamerican civilization. A major source of data has been the *General History of the Things of New Spain* (also called the Florentine Codex), which was written by Fray Bernardino de Sahagun between the 1540s and the 1570s.*

From Sahagun's writings, we know that there were four classes of people in the Aztec social system. The first, the *nobles,* received a much fuller education than other persons, could own private land (taken by conquest and expansion), and held

---

*The wealth of documentary materials on the Aztecs, including Sahagun's writings, has allowed scholars such as George Vaillant *(The Aztecs of Mexico),* Jacques Soustelle *(The Daily Life of the Aztecs),* and Warwick Bray *(The Everyday Life of the Aztecs)* to discuss the nature of Aztec life. The descriptions that appear in these pages are drawn largely from these sources.

important government posts. The leading priests belonged to this class, too. The nobility clearly lived well. Warwick Bray, for example, states:

> The house of a rich official, Sahagun informs us, would contain an ante-room, an audience chamber, dining and reception rooms, separate quarters for men and women, store-rooms, kitchen, servants' hall, and even a place of detention! Such a house was usually surrounded by a walled garden. Awnings of cotton cloth shaded the patios, and the doorways were closed by curtains or by hanging mats sewn with gold or copper bells. Locks and wooden doors were unknown.[38]

The emperor, who was viewed as a semidivine personage, had to come from the ranks of the nobility. He was elected to the position by a council of nobles, but most often he was the son, or a relative, of the preceding emperor.

The second social class, the *ordinary citizens,* divided into geographical clans called *calpulli.* They were required to attend school but were not taught reading, writing, astrology, or theology; instead they learned agriculture and warfare. Some citizens became members of artisan or merchant guilds. Social advancement was possible through the military, bureaucracy, or the priesthood. By the time of the conquest, some of the merchants also joined the aristocracy of service (as distinct from the aristocracy of lineage). The *calpulli* owned land in common. These lands were distributed to member families to work, but if cultivation was not continued the plots reverted back to the *calpulli* and were reassigned to other families. Decisions such as those concerning land rights were made by elected officers of the *calpulli.* These officers were often from the same family. It should also be noted that some families within each *calpulli* were ranked higher than others and often held more land. The *calpulli,* in fact, were very much like *conical clans,* which have been described by the anthropologist Eric Wolf as "kinship units which bind their members with common familial ties but which distribute wealth, social standing, and power most unequally among members of the pseudo-family."[39]

The third class, the *serfs,* had none of the privileges of clan (*calpulli*) membership nor use of clan-controlled lands which went with this membership. They lived near the *chinampas* on the outskirts of the city and worked land for the nobility. It has been suggested that many of the serfs may have been relatively recent arrivals in Central Mexico who came from conquered areas. Commoners could also fall to this level if they got into debt or lost their lands. Finally, there was a very limited *slave class* whose ranks were filled mainly by war captives or people from beyond the boundaries of the empire who had been purchased by Aztec merchants. The slaves, both male and female, worked at a variety of tasks including housework and field labor.

In the late part of the nineteenth century and well into the twentieth century there has been a great debate in the literature whether the Aztec social system was a stratified despotism or a clan-based, tribal democracy. It is now generally accepted that the actual situation was not so simple and that there was a great deal of cultural change going on at the time of the Spanish Conquest. The situation probably was closer to stratified despotism than to democracy, however.

In general, as Professor Robert Adams has pointed out in a major comparative work on the evolution of urban society in Mesopotamia and Central Mexico, the trend among the Aztecs was from vertically stratified kin-based social groupings to horizontal classes with strong barriers between the classes. Noting the similarities in trends between the two areas, Adams has stated:

> From the viewpoint of stratification, it is not too much to describe early Mesopotamia and Central Mexico as slightly variant patterns of a single, fundamental course of development in which corporate kin groups, originally preponderating in the control of land, were gradually supplemented by the growth of private estates in the hands of urban elites. And, while such corporate kin groups still remained active and viable in many respects at the termination points in our two sequences, it is only fair to conclude that they had by then become encapsulated in a stratified pattern of social organization that was rigidly divided along class lines.[40]

Adams goes on to conclude that the restructuring of vertical clan groupings along class lines is a process that is clearly, if indirectly, related to the development of the urban state. In both Mesopotamia and Mesoamerica, the same evolution from clan to class structure took place as "older, vertically oriented, solidarist forms of organization were replaced by more functionally specified, authoritarian, and all-encompassing horizontal ones that were better adapted to the administrative requirements of increasingly large and complex societies."[41]

Tribute and Trade

In order to survive as a great urban center, Tenochtitlán depended on tribute and trade; and through the riches so acquired it was able to support a large population occupied exclusively with governmental, religious, cultural, or military pursuits. One instrument which the Aztecs used to help support their capital and expand the borders of the empire was warfare. Aztec soldiers brought new territories such as the cacao-rich Sonconusco region on the Pacific Coast of Guatemala into the empire, and goods from these regions flowed into Tenochtitlán. Warfare also supplied the demands of the war god Huitzilopochtli for sacrificial victims, as war captives were often used for the sacrifices. In fact, one scholar, the late S. F. Cook, has argued that the frequent sacrifices at the great temple in Tenochtitlán may also have served another function: to control population in Central Mexico.

A second instrument of Aztec society to supply Tenochtitlán was the *pochteca*. The *pochteca* represented an institutionalization of mercantilism which saw merchants integrated into the state structure in the service of the nobility. This clearly presented an alternative organizational solution to the control of trade by the state to that noted for the Putun in the Yucatán area where the nobility controlled trade and acted as merchants themselves.

The *pochteca* were extremely effective in extending Aztec influence throughout Mesoamerica and in obtaining needed goods and materials for Tenochtitlán. Warehouses of the *pochteca* have been found as far south as the trading center at Naco in Honduras, and we know that *pochteca* were trading with peoples even farther south in Central America. Occasionally, the *pochteca* also served as spies for the empire, helping to pave the way for eventual military conquests.

Tribute goods as well as items for trade came from all parts of the Aztec empire, which stretched from the Valley of Mexico to Guatemala. The empire itself was principally welded together during the reign of Ahuitzotl (1486–1502). Tribute was substantial. The Aztec lists indicate that each year, 7000 tons of maize; 4000 tons of beans and other foods in like quantity; 2 million cotton cloaks; and large amounts of gold, amber, and quetzal (bird) feathers were brought into Tenochtitlán.[42] All these goods were transported on the backs of men or on boats, since the Aztecs possessed neither wheeled vehicles nor pack animals.

There were numerous centers of trade in Central Mexico. The greatest market was located on the neighboring island of Tlatelolco, where over sixty thousand people traded daily. The markets clearly played a crucial role in the Aztec system. Both luxury and utilitarian goods were exchanged or sold in the markets, with cacao beans serving as monetary units as they had since Olmec and Maya times. Trade was well regulated. A fee for trading was paid to the ruler; in addition, inspectors checked the quality of merchandise and prices. A market court dealt with thieves or sellers of stolen property, and convicted thieves might be beaten to death in the marketplace. Goods could only be sold in the marketplace itself: merchants did not sell their goods on the way to the market for fear of offending the market gods.

The Spanish Conquest

Clearly, Moctezuma's empire was a thriving civilization that in many ways rivaled the achievements of its conquerors. Why was it such apparently easy prey to the Spanish conquistadores? There are at least several reasons—all of which probably reinforced one another.

First of all, it must be remembered that the Aztec empire was still in a state of flux in the early sixteenth century. The great emperor Ahuitzotl had only begun to enlarge the empire significantly between A.D. 1486 and 1502. A second factor is inextricably related to the empire's "unfinished" quality. That is that Aztec rule had only recently been established in many outposts; in other areas, it had not been established at all. And so, the impression which one receives when reading popular books about the Spanish Conquest—that Cortés and his small band of soldiers took on hundreds of thousands of Aztecs and defeated them—simply does not reveal the complete story. Cortés picked up many allies on his march from Veracruz to Tenochtitlán. Various Mexican groups believed they could use Cortés to help bring down the hated power, and so they supported him with men and supplies. It was far more than the five hundred Spanish soldiers who defeated the Aztecs.

Third, the Spaniards had weapons which were superior to those of the Aztecs. In particular, the horse emerged as a potent factor in Aztec-Spanish battles. Its mobility and size overwhelmed the Aztecs. This superiority was reinforced by the advantages which the Spanish gained by their different philosophy of warfare. Whereas the Aztec ethos was to fight to gain captives for sacrifice, the Spanish fought to kill. In Aztec-Spanish combat, these different goals put the latter in an advantageous position, since it is much easier to kill an opponent than to capture him. (Moreover, there is no problem with guarding and feeding captives during and after a battle.)

A fourth factor is one that is hard to assess but which certainly played a key role. This factor involved Moctezuma's state of mind and his impressions of Cortés. We know that Moctezuma had a great interest in history and was very much aware of the Quetzalcoatl legends. At first, Moctezuma apparently thought that Cortés was Quetzalcoatl (or at least a representative) returning from the east. And so, although he presumably could have crushed Cortés when he first arrived in 1519, Moctezuma received the conquistador in a friendly fashion. His indecision about who Cortés was allowed the conquistador to eventually gain the upper hand and destroy both Moctezuma and the Aztec empire by 1521.

Within a relatively short span of time, much of Mesoamerica was under Spanish domination. A combination of diseases such as smallpox, introduced by the conquistadores and against which the native Americans had no natural defense mechanisms, plus Spanish colonial policy, which concentrated the native peoples into towns to be used as labor posts, caused a drastic and tragic population loss. This huge loss, coupled with the attempts to eradicate native ideologies and traditions, virtually finished off indigenous Mesoamerican civilization before the end of the sixteenth century.

Summary

We have looked at the development of Mesoamerican culture and later civilization over a period of eleven thousand years, from hunting and gathering times in the highland valleys, through to the rise of the Olmecs in the lowlands, and finally to the conquest of the Aztecs by invaders from Europe. Our attention has focused on five of the best-known manifestations of Mesoamerican civilization: the Olmecs, the Maya, Teotihuacán, the Toltecs, and the Aztecs.*

While the earliest agricultural practices appear to have evolved in the highland valleys of Puebla and Oaxaca, Mesoamerican civilization first began in the lush lowlands of the Gulf Coast. From this heartland, the Olmec spread their influence into many parts of Mesoamerica for both economic and religious reasons. The many cultural achievements of the Olmecs included a monumental art style rich in iconography, great craft skills, widespread trading routes, and the appearance of a small elite class. The latter lived in and around ceremonial centers and organized the labor necessary to build and maintain them and the trade which provided the basis for their wealth and power.

---

*Readers who are interested in comparing the ancient Mesoamerican experience with another New World civilizational sequence are urged to study the relatively well documented growth of complex societies in the Andean area of South America. The rise and fall of the Chavin, Tiahuanaco and Huari, Chimu, and Inca peoples offer many similarities and contrasts with the rise and fall of the Olmecs, Maya, Teotihuacános, Toltecs, and Aztecs. Edward Lanning's *Peru Before the Incas* (Prentice-Hall, 1967) is one of the most useful introductions to the civilization of the Andean area; Burr Brundage's *Two Earths, Two Heavens* (University of New Mexico Press, 1975) provides a very subjective yet fascinating comparison of Aztec and Inca beliefs just prior to the Spanish Conquest of these two great civilizations.

Readers interested in extending their knowledge of preindustrial urbanism beyond the bounds of Mesoamerica might have found this task exasperating a decade or two ago. On the basis of recent archaeological research, however, it is now possible to compare the research of Millon and his associates at Teotihuacán with the urban developments which have been revealed at sites such as Cahokia (Illinois) in North America and Chan Chan (on the north coast of Peru) in South America. Although the final reports on all these cities have yet to be fully published, readers might turn to Melvin L. Fowler's "A Pre-Columbian Urban Center on the Mississippi" *(Scientific American,* August 1975) or Michael E. Moseley and Carol J. Mackey's "Chan Chan, Peru's Ancient City of Kings" *(National Geographic,* March 1973).

Although the Mexican highlands did not have the lush environment of the Olmec lowlands, they did have a variety of mineral resources lacking in the lowlands, as well as the potential to intensify agricultural yields through irrigation. While Olmec civilization was developing, highland groups in Oaxaca and Central Mexico were also growing in complexity. This growth was accelerated through the stimulus of Olmec trade and contact. By 600 B.C., the highland groups superseded the Olmecs as the economic leaders in Mesoamerica. They not only controlled needed resources, but they had the means to concentrate people to exploit them, and, through intensive agriculture, to support them.

The trend toward intensive agriculture, growing population, developing social stratification, and centralization of economic and political authority in the highlands culminated in the rise of the great urban center of Teotihuacán in Central Mexico. Utilizing the valley's rich obsidian resources and strategic location for trade as well as the agricultural potential through irrigation, the site grew in religious and economic significance so that the elite of Teotihuacán were able to build a huge city that eventually held as many as 150,000 people and was the center of a civilization. Teotihuacán established ancient Mesoamerica's first empire as it brought in the population from surrounding regions to live in the city and spread its influence to the farthest reaches of Mesoamerica.

At about the same time that Teotihuacán was beginning its fantastic growth in Central Mexico, the Maya began to develop their own complex culture in the jungle lowlands of southern Mesoamerica. Building on the heritage of the Olmecs and related groups of highland Guatemala, the Classic Maya developed a civilization whose great artistic and intellectual achievements reached new heights in Mesoamerica. The Classic Maya also developed cities and complex economic relationships with their neighbors, although they never reached the levels of complexity achieved by Teotihuacán.

The fall of Teotihuacán in the eighth century A.D. and the collapse of Classic Maya civilization shortly thereafter left major power vacuums in Central Mexico and southern Mesoamerica. After an interregnum of about two centuries during which a number of centers vied for influence, the Toltecs, a former "barbarian" group from northwest Mexico, emerged as the chief power in Central Mexico. The Toltecs never established a centrally controlled empire of the same order as their predecessors, nor did their capital city of Tula achieve the size or status of Teotihuacán. But the Toltecs did spread their influence to the farthest reaches of Mesoamerica and had a major cultural impact throughout the area. Militarism and mercantilism, which had emerged in Teotihuacán times, reached new heights under the Toltecs.

To the south, the Putun, a Maya-speaking group from the Gulf Coast lowlands, surfaced as a new power in the Maya area with the collapse of the Classic Maya. Political and economic power shifted to northern Yucatán as, both on their own and in alliance with the Toltecs, the Putun established a complex long-distance trade network in and around the Yucatán peninsula. Although the Puuc region, then Chichén Itzá, and finally Mayapán came to dominate the peninsula economically and politically, the new mercantile trends initiated by the Putun remained preeminent.

The fall of the Toltecs in the thirteenth century A.D. led to another period of intense competition which ended with the emergence of the Aztecs as the new controllers of Central Mexico and, ultimately, of a large portion of Mesoamerica.

Like the Toltecs before them, the Aztecs were another "barbarian" people from the north. Establishing a base on the island city of Tenochtitlán, the Aztecs were able to absorb the heritage of both Teotihuacán and Tula from their neighbors as they began to expand their power. The centralized control of Teotihuacán was combined with the militarism and mercantilism of the Toltecs to produce the strongest, most tightly organized empire of Precolumbian Mesoamerica. The Aztecs began to spread their empire by the mid-fifteenth century A.D. and were just starting to consolidate their control when Cortés and his conquistadores arrived in 1519.

Although Aztec civilization was quite different in many ways from that of the Olmecs, it nevertheless reflected many traditions and trends which had been initiated three thousand years earlier. These trends were elaborated by the Maya, Oaxacans, Teotihuacános, and Toltecs, at the same time that new technological and sociopolitical achievements were developing. Aztec civilization was the culmination of the trend toward agricultural intensification, urban development, and economic centralization which had grown over many centuries. The Spanish Conquest ended this development. We will never know what additional achievements the Aztecs might have made if they had had the opportunity.

Throughout our review of the development of complex society in Mesoamerica from Olmec times to the Spanish Conquest, a period of more than twenty-seven centuries, we have seen several important themes appear again and again in our discussions. We have also seen a number of trends which link the Olmecs, Maya, Teotihuacános, Toltecs, and Aztecs and reinforce the perspective noted earlier that sees all these groups as part of one great Mesoamerican civilizational system that thrived for nearly three millennia. Although there are many significant changes through time, each succeeding group seems to have built on the achievements of the earlier ones.

One kind of linkage can be seen in specific cultural traits which are found throughout most of Mesoamerican history. These include the ancient ball game with its courts and associated paraphernalia; stylistic traits in Mesoamerican art; shared deities such as the rain god and the feathered serpent; similar writing and numeration systems; the importance of astronomy; and the use of obsidian implements.

An even more significant linkage, in relation to archaeologists' attempts to grapple with the nature of cultural processes, is evident in the trends in cultural development which can be seen between 1200 B.C. and A.D. 1521 in Mesoamerica. First is the growth of religious centers with small resident populations into large urban centers with populations which, in at least two instances, exceeded 100,000 people. Second is the centralization of power and authority in the growing urban centers. Third is the increasing importance of trade to support these centers, as well as the close linkage between the control and distribution of raw materials and the finished products made from them and the increasing wealth and power of the elite. A fourth trend is the growth of a separate merchant group to handle the increasing volume of trade. Fifth is the growing complexity of social organization, from a simple division between a small elite and peasants to the highly organized class system of the Aztecs. And a final trend is the rise of militarism and warfare to support the

[handwritten margin note: Trade dominates the theory of this book]

expansion of urban states and maintain the trade routes so essential to the existence of the states and their rulers.

Beyond these several threads, two final distinctions may be helpful in establishing a sense of perspective about Mesoamerican civilization and its development. One is that a close relationship existed between the heterogeneous Mesoamerican environment and the several developmental trends that have just been described. Clearly, the rise of the urban state in Mesoamerica depended upon a number of preconditions: the increasing sophistication of agricultural techniques and technology that were necessary to support growing populations; the access to raw materials, as well as the ability to extract them from the earth and distribute them to other areas; and the economic and political ties that formed symbiotic bonds between resource-rich and resource-poor areas and also acted as a stimulant for shifting centers of civilization. The importance of the highland groups after the initial Olmec breakthrough in the lowlands is one illustration of this last relationship.

A second characteristic is the inextricably close linkage that existed between religious beliefs and most aspects of Mesoamerican civilization. Even as Mesoamerican societies grew increasingly complex through time, and as the secular elite grew more and more wealthy and powerful, religion maintained its exceedingly strong hold on the minds and actions of Mesoamerican peoples. Aztec society appears to have been no more secular than Olmec, despite all the changes in technology and economic, social, and political organization.

We now turn to our own thoughts on the significance of the evolutionary trends in Mesoamerican civilization, and how they compare with trends which are visible in the Near Eastern sequences. Such a comparison can help point to directions which archaeologists might take in attempting to understand the reasons for the development of complex societies. Are there regularities in these developments? If so, why? In Chapter 5, we will share some of the insights we have gained in our comparison of the archaeological data from the ancient Near East and Mesoamerica. We will also briefly evaluate some of the recent archaeological thinking on the rise of complex societies in light of the comparative knowledge we have gained both in teaching the archaeology of these two areas and in writing this text.

Notes

1. West (1964:33).
2. Weaver (1972:14).
3. Flannery (1973:287). Quoted, with permission, from the *Annual Review of Anthropology,* Vol. 2. Copyright 1973 by Annual Reviews Inc.
4. MacNeish (1969:307).
5. Byers and MacNeish (1967–1976: Vol. 2, p. 10).
6. MacNeish (1972:80).
7. Flannery (1968a:81).
8. Flannery (1968a:79–80).
9. Flannery (1973:307–308). Quoted with permission, as stated in note 3.
10. Cohen (1977:13–14).
11. MacNeish (1974:218).
12. Cohen (1977:216).
13. Haury (1962:113).
14. Lathrap et al. (1977); Pearsall (1978).
15. Bernal (1969:187–188).
16. Coe (1968:43).
17. Sanders and Price (1968).
18. Flannery (1976); Flannery and Marcus (1976).
19. Rathje (1972).
20. Willey (1962:9–10).
21. Coe (1968:126–127).
22. An earlier version of this section was published by the Carras Company and entitled *The World of the Ancient Maya,* copyright Jeremy A. Sabloff 1975, 1976.
23. Hammond (1977).
24. Graham, Heizer, and Shook (1978); see also Coe (1976), Marcus (1976b), Quirarte (1977).
25. Flannery (1972); Hammond (1974); Marcus (1973; 1976a).
26. Millon et al. (1973).
27. Sanders and Price (1968); Wolf (1976).
28. Diehl, in Wolf (1976:260).
29. Millon et al. (1973:64).
30. Jimenez Moreno (1941; 1966); Acosta (1941; 1956).
31. Nicholson (1957).
32. Willey (1976:212).
33. DiPeso (1974); Kelley (1966); Griffin (1966).
34. Conrad (1974).
35. Coe (1964:97).
36. Diaz (1963:216).
37. Coe (1964:98).
38. Bray (1968:104).
39. Wolf (1959:136), as quoted in Adams (1966:88).
40. Adams (1966:119).
41. Adams (1966:119).
42. Coe (1962:169).

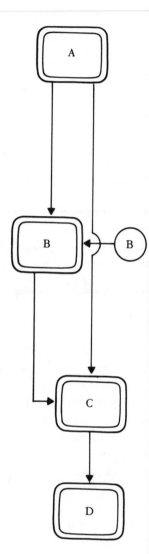

5. *General Considerations and Future Directions*

This final chapter is not a summary of the book, nor does it give a series of path-breaking conclusions concerning the rise and fall of civilizations. Rather, it offers observations on some of the similarities and differences between the civilizational developments noted in previous chapters and points out some ideas worthy of further thought. It ends with suggestions for potential directions that archaeologists might take in the comparative study of ancient civilizations.

It is of interest here to look back briefly at the intellectual history with which we began the book. The reader may recall that much of the earlier discussion centered on theories that argued for either cyclical or linear trajectories in historical growth. These major theories of the past, which have caused so much controversy for so long a time, were barely mentioned in Chapters 2, 3, and 4. The reason for this is the failure of these viewpoints to produce acceptable hypotheses about the general nature of ancient civilizations and their development—a shortcoming that has obviously hastened their demise. Clearly the discipline of anthropological archaeology has moved away from these older positions in recent attempts to utilize a systems framework that is open to several simultaneous causes and processes. Yet modern archaeological thought is far from being totally removed from earlier trends. The evolutionary stance supported by most archaeologists today has, as we have seen, a lengthy tradition in archaeology; so does the general comparative method currently in vogue.

On the whole, though, new archaeological views of ancient civilizations and their development do represent a significant departure from the past. Even though Kroeber held what we would now term a systemic view of civilizations, he had neither a clear vision of how the parts were connected nor an evolutionary view of how they changed through time. Again, V. Gordon Childe certainly maintained an evolutionary view of culture, but his view was not systemic. His classic criteria for defining urban civilization show relatively little coherence: the linkage between new directions in artistic expression and urban populations is never clarified, nor is the necessary relationship between writing and urbanism.

Before discussing the evolutionary systems approach further, it is worthwhile to pause and take stock of the events and processes we have seen in this book. There are both major similarities and major differences in the development of civilizations in the Old and New Worlds. On the one hand, these similarities and differences give us cause for optimism in the search for regularities in the rise and fall of civilizations—on the other hand, they also make this search more complex. How can we evaluate them?

Old World— New World Comparisons

The similarities and differences between developments in the two hemispheres assume particular interest because these developments were essentially unrelated. This is not to say that there were no contacts between the civilizations of the Old and New Worlds in Precolumbian times. There is sufficient evidence, as presented in such recent books on the subject as *Man Across the Sea* (1971), to indicate that some contacts must have taken place. To our mind, however, little data have so far been uncovered to indicate that such contacts had a significant effect on the course of civilizational growth in the Old or New Worlds. As Professor Elman Service, a leading anthropological theorist, has noted:

> The archaic civilizations ancestral to modern civil societies evolved in different times and places. ... This is a most significant fact, for it affects our perspective. Were it one single development that spread to the other areas by conquest, diffusion, emulation, or whatever, then the problem would be "historical"—that is, our concern would be simply, what happened? When? But since it happened several times independently we immediately wonder, even if it only happened twice (in the New World and in the Old World), what *causes* or repetitive *processes* were at work. We want to know, by careful comparison, what were the shared factors: the antecedent conditions; the geographical, technological, economic, social, and ideological settings; the role of warfare and the nature of the surrounding political environment. If civilization had originated only once, it would not even pay to speculate as to whether or not it was an historical accident, with this causal network unanalyzable. But not only did some of the archaic civilizations probably develop independently; they also developed surprisingly similar kinds of new cultural features. ...[1]

As regards the growth of civilization in the Old World itself, there is a consensus that the earliest civilizations were the Sumerian, the Egyptian, and the Indus. How were they related? The chronological priority of Sumerian civilization allows for the interpretation that the Egyptian and Indus civilizations were derived from the Sumerian. Though possible, this is highly unlikely, for it is difficult to exaggerate the *differences* between these three civilizations. The irrigation systems, architecture, and writing systems, as well as the social, political, and religious structures, were entirely distinctive. In Sumer there were at least ten major cities; in the Indus, two; and in Egypt only later times saw the development of major cities. While major settlement in Egypt was restricted in linear fashion to the banks of the Nile, settlements in Sumer dotted the area between the two river systems. In the Indus, people lived in both large and small settlements in the highlands of the Punjab as well as along the Indus alluvium. The form of the cities within the three areas also differed. Sumerian cities grew without direction or design, in contrast to the Indus which had formal "city planning." Finally, writing systems provide the clearest contrast between these civilizations. The earliest writing in all areas was pictographic, but all three were dissimilar. Nor can comparison be made between the more developed forms: the hieroglyphs of Egypt, the cuneiform of Mesopotamia, or the distinctly different hieroglyphs of the Indus.

What kind of evidence is there of relations among these three civilizations? Direct contact between the Egyptians and Sumer appeared primarily in the earliest period: at the height of the Old Kingdom, contact nearly ceased. The contact between Sumer and the Indus is different. Here, contacts appear only during the mature phase of the Indus civilization. This must all be evaluated in light of the formation of these earliest civilizations in the ancient Near East, and our interpretations have changed in the past few decades.

Many years ago Henri Frankfort argued that the primacy of Sumerian civilization acted as a catalyst in "speeding up" Egyptian urbanization and civilization. In looking east of Sumer, Sir Mortimer Wheeler argued a similar case for the formation of the Indus: "But ideas have wings, and in the third millennium the *idea* of civilization was in the air in western Asia. A model of civilization, however abstract, was present to the minds of the Indus founders."[2]

How can we evaluate such an idea which can never be tested? We cannot. The question can be answered only in terms of plausibility and probability. To us, the contention that an abstract *idea* of civilization gives birth to a civilization is entirely improbable. Such a conception can only be argued by modern scholars who attempt to place order where none exists. Cities, writing, monumental architecture, surplus production, and so forth are all parts of this "idea" of civilization. How would the Indus citizen grasp these unseen ideas, and if representatives actually visited Sumer, are we to believe that they abstracted these ideas, returned to the Indus, and translated every one of them into different forms? If they were influenced by the ideas, it seems more likely that they would have made close copies. How is it possible that both the Egyptians and the peoples of the Indus grasped an idea and translated it into something so remarkably distinctive that it bore *no* relationship to the original idea? Again this seems improbable. One may argue that writing is such a complex idea that it could only have been thought of once. We must remember that even in Upper Paleolithic times, humans had a system of notation. With the development of complex social institutions the need for writing emerged independently. It surely did so in the New World, and in these three centers of civilization.

It is our view that the *civilizations* of Sumer, Egypt, and the Indus developed essentially independently of each other. That view does not necessarily extend to the towns of the Persian Gulf, the Iranian Plateau, and Turkmenistan. As this book has suggested, the excavations at Tepe Yahya in Iran show that the town complex arose as a result of demands that developed in Sumer for the natural resources around Yahya, namely the carved chlorite bowls. But while the later development of the highland communities of the plateau was a result of relations with greater civilizations, these towns were not simply derivative. It must be remembered that Yahya was first settled by 5000 B.C.; like other contemporary communities, it had achieved a considerable level of social and economic development before its contact with Sumer and the Indus. The evolving complexity of the social order of Yahya and other plateau communities was brought about through an increasing interaction with foreign peoples.

The civilizations of Mesoamerica provide a picture that contrasts in many ways. These civilizations appear to have built upon one another with much direct interchange and stimulation. In fact, some archaeologists believe that it would be more appropriate to view the Olmec, Maya, Teotihuacán, Toltec, and Aztec civilizations as sequential stages of one great Mesoamerican civilization which began in the mid-second millennium B.C. and lasted approximately three thousand years until the time of the Spanish Conquest.

Only when one sets Mesoamerica in the larger context of the New World as a whole does a situation resembling the Egyptian–Mesopotamian–Indus one described above emerge. The relationships between Mesoamerica and the Andean area of South America and between Mesoamerica and the North American Southeast and Southwest show the same ambiguities which have led to the same plethora of interpretations that characterize the discussions of Egyptian–Mesopotamian–Indus interchanges.

Perhaps the best examples which illustrate the similarities are the possible relationships between early Egypt and early Sumer on the one hand and Olmec and Chavin (in the Andean area of South America) on the other. In both cases there are striking resemblances in art styles and cultural repertoire, as well as close correspondences in chronological placement. Yet at the present time, the arguments which have Chavin influencing the development of Olmec civilization or Sumer stimulating the rise of Egyptian civilization or vice versa are not strongly supported. In the case of the New World, however, there is the additional possibility raised by Donald Lathrap, and briefly noted in Chapter 4, that Olmec and Chavin may have had a common source in the South American lowlands.

Beyond this, there are general geographic resemblances between the areas where civilizations arose in both the Near East and Mesoamerica. The close interaction between highland and lowland regions, between resource-rich and resource-poor areas, or between geographically differentiated and geographically similar locations strengthens the possibility of comparison in the search of processual regularities. On the other hand, the greater length of the chronological scale of civilizational development in the Near East versus that of Mesoamerica allows us to compare different growth rates in similar circumstances.

Given the potential to hold factors like these constant in comparing the Near East and Mesoamerica, the archaeologist has at least the possibility to assess the impact of other factors which are so different in the two areas—for instance, metallurgy, domesticated animals, nomadism, and the scale of urban development. Metals and the technology of their usage played a prominent role in the Near East: they had little impact in Mesoamerica, where metalworking was generally limited to the Postclassic Period. Domesticated animals, too, had a significant impact on the lives of ancient Near Eastern peoples; the few Mesoamerican domesticates had a minor role at best. Again, nomads were an important part of the ancient Near Eastern scene, and their dynamic interaction with settled groups certainly was essential to the development of civilizations. In Mesoamerica, there were no large domesticated animals or beasts of burden, and so herding nomads never became a significant force in the same way they did in the Near East. The Toltecs and Aztecs, however, seminomadic peoples from the north of Central Mexico, did play very important roles in Mesoamerican development. As noted in Chapter 4, these "barbarians" from the north were rapidly "civilized" by the settled peoples in Central Mexico and soon lost their nomadic ways (to the extent that the Aztecs even destroyed the historical records which described their "barbarian" background prior to their settling down in the Valley of Mexico!).

Finally, the scale of such urban centers as Teotihuacán and Tenochtitlán far exceeds comparable urban developments in the Near East and the Indus. Teotihuacán had more than 100,000 inhabitants at its height; Tenochtitlán, perhaps many more. These population concentrations are not rivaled by any Sumerian or Indus city: even very generous population estimates for Mesopotamian centers would not exceed 50,000 people. The question of what factors allowed the larger population growth in the New World and how they might have differed in the Old World is worth pursuing in the future. But even with these major differences in scale, were there other similarities, such as urban plans? It can be suggested that since certain New World and Old World cities, such as Teotihuacán and Mohenjo-Daro, share regular grid layouts, these centers were probably organized in a similar manner. This suggestion can be neither proved nor disproved at the moment, but, hopefully, it will be answerable in the near future.

Several additional similarities on an even more general plane are also worth mentioning at this juncture. First, similar trends can be perceived in the emergence of a class structure in ancient Mesoamerica and Sumer. The emergence of a priestly elite is followed by a gradual secularization of the elite, the growth of a "middle class" of craftsmen and artisans, and the eventual rise of merchants who are either a part of or closely allied to the elite. It should also be noted that the similarities in the growth of elite rulers in both Mesoamerica and the Near East tend to support Elman Service's thesis, which finds the origins of government in "the institutionalization of centralized leadership." This leadership developed into a hereditary aristocracy as it "legitimized itself in its role of maintaining the whole society." In Service's words: "The nascent bureaucracy's economic and religious functions developed as the extent of its services, its autonomy, and its size increased. Thus, the earliest government worked to protect, not another class or stratum of the society, but itself."[3]

Another similarity between the ancient Sumerians and the Classic Maya is the apparent lack of planning or awareness of overexploitation of the environment. In both cases, we have noted how growing population size, density of settlement, and intensification of agriculture apparently led to an overuse of the environment. This overuse had dramatic consequences in both areas. In Mesopotamia, it caused a shift in crops from wheat to barley and eventually led to a major population shift northward, where irrigation did not cause the disastrous salinization that it did in southern Mesopotamia. In the southern Maya lowlands, it has been hypothesized that overuse of the soil was one of the factors which led to the collapse of Classic Maya civilization and the shift in political and economic power to the northern lowlands with its better location and richer resources.

In both the Near East – Indus and Mesoamerica we also can see how the relationship between the centers of civilization and their less complexly organized neighbors played a crucial role in the demise of the Sumerians, Teotihuacános, and the Toltecs. Although invasions of these civilizations are not seen anymore by archaeologists as the sole cause in their collapse, the data in Chapters 3 and 4 clearly indicate that warfare played a significant role in the downfall of ancient civilizations (and in their development, as well). It appears, however, that the success of various invasions in Mesoamerica and the Near East was made possible by a variety of internal weaknesses in the established civilizations. Moreover, such weaknesses may well have resulted from agricultural or demographic overdevelopment, as in the case of Maya and some of the city-states of Sumer and the Indus, or from overdependence on a single resource whose exploitation or distribution could be attacked, as might have been the case with Teotihuacán's demise.

Questions concerning such similarities and differences (and many others which the reader might perceive in comparing the data in Chapters 3 and 4) will certainly form one major focus of future comparative studies between Mesoamerica and the Near East–Indus areas.

In sum, current archaeological evidence indicates that we can use the data from several areas in both the Old and New Worlds in comparative searches for regularities in the rise of complex societies. True, there may have been some contacts, if not between the Old and New Worlds, at least among distant civilizations within each hemisphere. But apparently these contacts were not massive enough to bias our own comparisons of the developmental trajectories of the several civilizations.

This conclusion leads to other questions. What procedures and models might best be employed by archaeologists in understanding such comparisons? Of all the factors involved in the rise and fall of civilizations, what focal points are likely to be the most productive in bringing light to bear on possible regularities from one area to another? Let us turn to a consideration of what might be the most fruitful intellectual road for archaeologists to follow in the next few years.

How Civilizations Evolve

In both the Old and New Worlds, archaeologists have argued for years about the reasons for the rise of complex societies. Many factors have been singled out for special attention, and innumerable books and articles have propounded views on why factor X or factor Y was the prime mover in the rise of civilization. In a recent work on *The First Cities,* Ruth Whitehouse notes that among the factors which have received particular support by archaeologists are environment and subsistence economy, population, technology, trade, and social organization.[4] Other scholars point to other factors. Professor Kent Flannery in one of his papers names irrigation, warfare, population growth and social circumscription, trade and symbiosis, cooperation and competition, and the integrative power of great religions and art styles as causes that have been most frequently argued.[5] Obviously, many other similar lists could be (and have been) constructed.

THE SYSTEMS FRAMEWORK

As we have seen in discussions of the ancient civilizations of the Near East and Mesoamerica in this book, no single prime mover can readily explain the rise of complex societies in both areas. In fact, with the development of systems thinking in archaeology, it has become commonplace in the literature for archaeologists to point out that no one factor caused the rise of civilization: a combination of systemically interrelated factors did. However, whether there exists a universal combination which invariably caused the rise of civilization in case after case through time and space, or whether there were varied combinations of factors in different cases is still a matter of much debate among archaeologists. Questions like this are still unanswered. But the systems approach seems to hold out the possibility that some day this question (and others) may be answered. Without denying the great complexity of the various related processes involved in the development of cultural systems, the approach assumes that this complexity is not haphazard. If there is some systematic organization in the framework and processes by which cultures and civilizations evolve (and the systems approach assumes that there is), then these processes are potentially understandable.[6]

There is confidence in the archaeological community that the systems approach will yield general explanations for a variety of processual questions, including the causes for the rise of civilization. Whether or not this confidence is well-placed remains to be seen.

One of the most important assumptions of general system theorists is that all systems, human and nonhuman alike, operate according to a series of universal rules. In a provocative article entitled "The Cultural Evolution of Civilizations" (1972), Flannery follows this assumption in attempting to explain the evolutionary development of civilizations. He notes that "one way of organizing the variables in such an evolutionary theory is to regard human society as one class of living system, and apply to it a general model for such systems."[7]

Flannery believes that the growing complexity of the state system can best be understood in terms of certain universal processes and mechanisms. The universal processes include first, the increasing *specialization* of parts of the system (as we've seen, for instance, in the development of crafts, merchant classes, and social differentiation); and second, the *centralization* of the system as a whole (for instance, in the rise of a ruling class and the developing hierarchy of settlement patterns).

Flannery feels that there are two universal mechanisms by which these processes occur. These evolutionary mechanisms are *promotion* and *linearization*. By promotion, Flannery means that an institution's role may change from a lower-level, specialized one to a higher-level, generalized one. An example of promotion is the rise of military leaders who initially formed an arm of the state but eventually, in times of stress, were able to promote themselves to positions of overall power. In linearization, "lower-order controls are repeatedly or permanently bypassed by higher-order controls."[8] Linearization is one of the ways by which centralization is achieved. An example is the state's assumption of local control over taxing powers or over irrigation facilities and water distribution.

While Flannery's approach identifies a number of universal principles in the rise of civilizations, it names other elements that are not universal. It is these factors which cause each system to evolve in a way that is distinct and individual. Different conditions, or *socioeconomic stresses,* operate in each particular setting. Such factors include population pressure, irrigation, and trade, as well as warfare and symbiosis (for example, the highland-lowland relationships in both the Near East and Mesoamerica, or Mesopotamian relationships between agricultural communities and nomadic groups). While none of these factors is seen as universal, all have acted in different settings to speed up the process of state development, and, as we have seen, each has been mentioned at one time or another as the prime mover in the evolution of statehood.

To Flannery, the ultimate goal is to establish a series of rules that will eventually allow archaeologists to simulate the origins of complex societies. Flannery's article is one of the most stimulating discussions of the growth of civilizations in recent years; since its publication in 1972, relatively few advances have been made beyond his systems analysis. Whether his model will actually allow us to explain the complex evolution of states, though, is another question.

First of all, it is not yet clear whether all systems operate by the same principles as those outlined above. Second, simulation of a system certainly is not tantamount to explanation. At this stage at least, even if we were to succeed in developing a model, it would be far from complete. We need much better and more detailed archaeological data than we now have in order to flesh out Flannery's model. Finally, how do we determine *which* socioenvironmental conditions are crucial in different circumstances, and, just as important, *why* they are crucial? (And *how* do socioenvironmental conditions speed the processes by which states are formed?)

APPLYING THE SYSTEMS APPROACH

Admittedly, the systems approach has some wrinkles that need to be ironed out. But Flannery's formulation is a good starting point. It has the potential to be a productive foundation for future inquiries into the processes that led to the rise of ancient civilizations. How should we proceed from this starting point? Given the current state of archaeological knowledge, perhaps one way would be to try to understand the socioenvironmental conditions of ancient complex systems—how they operate, and why, and also how local they are—always keeping in mind the larger model proposed by Flannery.

The study of trade seems particularly promising in this regard. Certainly one of the most provocative publications in the last decade regarding the role of trade in the rise of complex societies has been William L. Rathje's "The Origin and Development of Lowland Classic Maya Civilization," which we have looked at in Chapter 4 of the text. Although Rathje's ideas have been subject to much criticism, they also have stimulated considerable thought on the subject.

Rathje's specific hypothesis states that a number of existing conditions—environment, lack of indigenous resources, the subsistence base, and technology—predisposed the Mayan lowlands toward the development of a complex society. With these preconditions, "complex sociopolitical organization in the rain forests of Mesoamerica developed originally in response to the need for consistent procurement, importation, and distribution of non-local basic resources useful to every household."[9] The general conclusion follows that complex sociopolitical organization arises out of the need to procure and distribute resources and services—a point made not only by Rathje but by other anthropologists in reference to other areas of the world.

It is interesting to evaluate Rathje's "trade" theory in light of the more eclectic systems framework. As Marcus Winter notes: "Whether or not one agrees with the specifics, [models such as Rathje's] which integrate economic, sociopolitical, and ideological aspects of culture ... can provide direction for theoretical studies as well as yield specific implications that can be tested archaeologically."[10]

Though Rathje's hypothesis seems to stumble when tested against several sets of data, it clearly should not be discarded. His particular formulation may not provide a complete explanation, but he has led archaeologists to a better understanding of the role of trade, and he seems to have put his finger if not on, at least close to, an important insight into the relationship between trade and the rise of complex societies. Perhaps by expanding and rewording Rathje's hypothesis, archaeologists will be able to produce a theory of greater validity and utility.

Rathje's explanation is similar in many respects to one developed for the rise of complex societies in the ancient Near East. One may compare the preceding quotation from Rathje with its counterpart formulated by one of us for the Near East:

> It appears likely that a trade mechanism was established which in recognizing the value of local resources brought the Iranian highlands into a supply-demand relationship with resource-poor Mesopotamia. Mesopotamian demand ... would have provided in part the economic base for the urban development ... of the Iranian highland communities. This relationship as in a feedback mechanism would have in turn aided in bringing about the developing complexity of sociopolitical and economic structures of the ... Mesopotamian city-state.[11]

This hypothesis and that of Rathje focus in a similar manner on the importance of trade in the rise of complex societies in the Old and the New Worlds. Both also recognize the need to integrate economic, sociopolitical, and ideological aspects in a systemic manner in formulating conceptions.

Within Flannery's systems framework, another productive focus is the transmission of information within and between complex societies. Essentially, this carries Rathje's hypothesis one step further by stressing the exchange of nonmaterial ideas and information as well as material goods and resources—even though it is far more difficult for archaeologists to document nonmaterial exchanges than material ones.

The role of information flow in the contact among ancient groups and in the evolution of civilizations has received growing attention by archaeologists in recent years. Flannery states that "evolving systems . . . generate new information autonomously through the interaction between their parts. Thus one of the main trends in the evolution of bands into tribes, chiefdoms, and states must be a gradual increase in capacity for information processing, storage, and analysis."[12]

Professor Robert Adams builds upon Flannery's suggestion, noting that there was not just a "gradual increase in capacity" to process information as complex societies evolved, but also a growing tendency to centralize and stratify collection and dissemination systems. Adams suggests that research should focus not only on the "storage and retrieval" systems but on the data-sifting process that allows pertinent information to reach decision-makers and be acted upon. In other words, says Adams, "more complex systems, as well as more profound or complex environmental stresses, provided a source of selective pressure on behalf of institutions that could channel and utilize information more efficiently."[13]

Related positions have been developed by other scholars and applied to a number of geographic regions. Professor Bruce Trigger, for instance, uses examples from ancient Egypt, Mesopotamia, and other areas. This information-exchange contention may be taken one step further, as one of us has noted elsewhere:

> It would appear . . . that as cultural groups become more complex, the access to economic and political information gained through established exchange systems seems to become increasingly limited. Information about other groups offers the institution processing it the means of gaining or guaranteeing power.[14]

The implications of these statements are clear. Archaeologists may be able to contribute to an understanding of how civilizations arose by studying the processes which led to growing differentiation of access to goods and information in increasingly complex societies, as well as the consequences of such differentiation. While far from new, such a research direction could place several traditional approaches within the systemic, evolutionary model suggested by Flannery; and, potentially, it can give them a more general relevance. Adams himself sees the tendencies toward increasing class differentiation and political centralization as forming the "vital central axis" in the development of states. Given the growing sophistication of archaeological methods and techniques (a sophistication that was unthinkable or unthought of even a few decades ago), we are gaining an increasingly refined understanding of ancient processes and conditions, including stratification, centralization, information flow, and trade. This "vital central axis" might well be within the reach of illumination.

Perhaps by following the theoretical leads of scholars such as Flannery, Rathje, Adams, and others, as well as the numerous cultural historical leads summarized in Chapters 2, 3, and 4, archaeologists will someday be able to fulfill Flannery's dream: "the establishment of a series of rules by which the origin of some complex system could be simulated."[15] And, even more important, we may eventually be able to comprehend the general reasons for the growth of ancient civilizations.

Notes

1. Service (1975:5–7). Quoted, with permission, from *Origins of the State and Civilization, The Process of Cultural Evolution,* by Elman R. Service. Copyright 1975 by W. W. Norton and Company, Inc.
2. Wheeler (1959:104).
3. Service (1975:3, 8). Quoted, with permission, as stated in note 1.
4. Whitehouse (1977).
5. Flannery (1972). Quoted, with permission, from *Annual Review of Ecology and Systematics,* Vol. 3. Copyright 1972 by Annual Reviews, Inc.
6. Redman (1973:16).
7. Flannery (1972:409).
8. Flannery (1972:413). Quoted, with permission, as stated in note 5.
9. Rathje (1971:278).
10. Winter (1977).
11. Lamberg-Karlovsky (1972).
12. Flannery (1972:411). Quoted, with permission, as stated in note 5.
13. Adams (1975:453).
14. Sabloff (1974:581).
15. Flannery (1972:421). Quoted, with permission, as stated in note 5.

Selected References

Chapter 1

Aristotle. *Politics.* Translated by Benjamin Jowett. Oxford: Clarendon Press, 1923.

Augustine, Saint. *The City of God.* Translated by Marcus Dods. New York: Random House, 1950.

Binford, L. R. 1972. *An Archaeological Perspective.* New York: Seminar Press.

Breasted, J. H. 1926. "Ikhnaton, the Religious Revolutionary." *Cambridge Ancient History.* New York: Macmillan.

Bury, John B. 1932. *The Idea of Progress.* New York: Macmillan.

Childe, V. G. 1947. *History.* London: Cobbett Press.

_____.1951. *Man Makes Himself.* New York: Mentor Books.

Comte, A. 1896. *The Positive Philosophy.* Translated by H. Martineau. London: George Bell and Sons.

Cornford, F. M. 1952. *Principium Sapientiae: The Origins of Greek Philosophical Thought.* London: Cambridge University Press.

Daniel, G. 1962. *The Idea of Prehistory.* London: C. A. Watts.

_____.1976. *A Hundred and Fifty Years of Archaeology.* Cambridge, Mass.: Harvard University Press.

Donagan, A. 1962. *The Later Philosophy of R. G. Collingwood.* London: Oxford University Press.

Frankfort, H., H. A. Frankfort, J. A. Wilson, and T. Jacobsen. 1946. *Before Philosophy.* Chicago: University of Chicago Press.

Gardiner, P. 1959. *Theories of History.* New York: Free Press.

Guthrie, W. K. C. 1957. *In the Beginning: Some Greek Views on the Origins of Life and the Early State of Man.* Ithaca: Cornell University Press.

Harris, M. 1968. *The Rise of Anthropological Theory.* New York: Crowell.

Hole, F., and R. Heizer. 1973. *An Introduction to Prehistoric Archaeology.* New York: Holt.

_____. 1977. *Prehistoric Archaeology: A Brief Introduction.* New York: Holt.

Huntington, E. 1945. *Mainsprings of Civilization.* New York: Wiley.

Kroeber, A. 1944. *Configurations of Culture Growth*. Berkeley: University of California Press.

Lowie, R. 1920. *Primitive Society*. New York: Harper & Row, 1961.

Lubbock, J. 1871. "Social and Religious Conditions of the Lower Races." *Annual Report of the Smithsonian Institution for 1869*, pp. 341–362. Washington, D.C.

Marx, K. *On Society and Social Change*. With selections by F. Engels. Ed. by N. J. Smelser. Chicago: University of Chicago Press, 1973.

Morgan, L. H. 1877. *Ancient Society*. Cleveland: World, 1963.

Nisbit, R. 1969. *Social Change and History*. London: Oxford University Press.

Sorokin, P. 1937–1941. *Social Change and Cultural Dynamics*. 4 vols. New York: American Book

Spengler, O. 1926. *The Decline of the West*. New York: Knopf.

Steward, J. 1949. "Cultural Causality and Law: A Trial Formulation of the Development of Early Civilization." *American Anthropologist* 51:1–27.

_____ . 1955. *Theory of Culture Change: The Methodology of Multilinear Evolution*. Urbana: University of Illinois Press.

Teggart, F. J. 1925. *Theory of History*. New Haven: Yale University Press.

Toynbee, A. 1934–1954. *A Study of History*. London: Oxford University Press.

Vico, G. 1725. *Scienza Nuova* [The New Science.]. Translated by T. G. Bergin and M. H. Fisch from the third edition. Ithaca: Cornell University Press, 1948.

Wagner, P. L. 1960. *The Human Use of the Earth*. New York: Free Press.

White, L. A. 1949. *The Science of Culture*. New York: Farrar, Straus.

_____ . 1975, *The Concept of Cultural Systems*. New York: Columbia University Press.

Willey, G. R. 1953. *Prehistoric Settlement Patterns in the Virú Valley, Peru*. Bureau of American Ethnology, Bulletin 155.

Willey, G. R., and J. A. Sabloff. 1974. *A History of American Archaeology*. San Francisco: Freeman.

Wittfogel, K. 1957. *Oriental Despotism: A Comparative Study of Total Power*. New Haven: Yale University Press.

Chapter 2

Adams, R. McC. 1966. *The Evolution of Urban Society*. Chicago: Aldine Press.

_____ .1972. *The Uruk Countryside*. Chicago: University of Chicago.

Adams, R. McC., and H. Nissen. 1972. *The Uruk Countryside*. Chicago: University of Chicago Press.

Anati, E. 1962. *Palestine Before the Hebrews*. New York: Knopf.

Binford, L. 1968. "Post-Pleistocene Adaptations." In *New Perspectives in Archaeology*, ed. by S. R. and L. R. Binford, pp. 313– 341. Chicago: Aldine.

Braidwood, R. J. 1974. *Prehistoric Men*. 8th edition. Glenview, Ill.: Scott, Foresman and Co.

Braidwood, R. J., and B. Howe. 1960. "Prehistoric Investigations in Iraqi Kurdistan." *Studies in Ancient Oriental Civilization*, No. 31. Chicago: University of Chicago Press.

Childe, V. G. 1925. *The Dawn of European Civilization*. 6th edition: 1958. New York: Knopf.

_____ . 1928. *New Light on the Most Ancient Near East*. 4th edition. New York: Grove Press.

_____ . 1951. *Man Makes Himself*. New York: New American Library.

Cohen, M. N. 1977. *The Food Crisis in Prehistory*. New Haven: Yale University.

Davidson, T., and H. McKerrell. 1976. "Pottery Analysis and Halaf Period Trade in the Khabur Headwaters Region." *Iraq* 38(1):45–56.

El-Wailly, F. 1966. "The Excavations at Tell-es Sawaan." *Sumer* XXI(1–2).

El-Wailly, F., and B. Abu-Soof. 1965. "Excavations at Tell-es Sawaan." *Sumer* XXI(1):17–32.

Flannery, K. V. 1968. "Archaeological Systems Theory and Early Mesoamerica." In *Anthropological Archaeology in the Americas,* ed. by B. J. Meggers, pp. 67–87. Anthropological Society of Washington, D.C.

———. 1969. "Origins and Ecological Effects of Early Domestication in Iran and the Near East." In *The Domestication and Exploitation of Plants and Animals,* ed. by P. Ucko and G. W. Dimbleby, pp. 73– 102. Chicago: Aldine.

Garrod, D. A. E. 1957. "The Natufian Culture: The Life and Economy of a Mesolithic People in the Near East." *Proceedings of the British Academy* 43. London.

Gorman, C. F. 1972. "Excavations at Spirit Cave, North Thailand: Some Interim Interpretations." *Asian Perspectives* XIII:79– 110.

Harlan, J. R. 1967. "A Wild Wheat Harvest in Turkey." *Archaeology* 20:187–201.

Isaac, E. 1975. *The Geography of Domestication.* Foundations of Cultural Geography Series. Englewood Cliffs, N.J.: Prentice Hall, Inc.

Kenyon, K. 1957. *Digging Up Jericho.* London: Benn.

———. 1970. *Archaeology in the Holy Land.* 3rd ed. New York: Praeger.

Kirkbride, D. 1966. "Five Seasons at the Pre-pottery Neolithic Village of Beidha in Jordan." *Palestine Exploration Quarterly,* Jan.– June:8– 42.

———. 1973. "Umm Dabaghiyah 1973: A Third Preliminary Report." *Iraq* XXXV, pt. 1:1– 8.

———. 1974. "Umm Dabaghiyah: A Trading Outpost?" *Iraq* XXXVI, pt. 1– 2:85– 92.

Larsen, C. E. 1975. "The Mesopotamian Delta Region: A Reconsideration of Lees and Falcon." *Journal of the American Oriental Society* CXV. Philadelphia.

Legge, A. J. 1977. "The Origins of Agriculture in the Near East." In *Hunters, Gatherers and First Farmers Beyond Europe,* ed. by J. V. S. Megaw, pp. 51– 68. Leicester University Press.

Lloyd, S. 1956. *Early Anatolia.* Baltimore: Penguin Books.

Lloyd, S., and F. Safar. 1945. "Tell Hassuna." *Journal of Near Eastern Archaeology* 4:255–289.

MacNeish, R. S. 1964a. "Ancient Mesopotamian Civilization." *Science* 143 (3606):531– 537.

———. 1964b. "The Food Gathering and Incipient Agriculture Stage of Prehistoric Middle America." In *Handbook of Middle American Indians,* Vol. 1, R. Wauchope, general editor, and R. W. West, volume editor, pp. 413– 426. Austin: University of Texas Press.

———. 1969. "Speculation about How and Why Food Production and Village Life Developed in the Tehuacán Valley, Mexico." *Archaeology* 24(4):307–315.

———. 1972. "The Evolution of Community Patterns in the Tehuacán Valley of Mexico and Speculations about the Cultural Process." *Man, Settlement, and Urbanism,* ed. by P. J. Ucko, R. Tringham, and G. W. Dimbleby, pp. 67– 93. London: Gerald Duckworth.

Masry, A. H. 1974. *Prehistory in Northern Arabia: The Problem of Interregional Interaction.* Miami: Field Research Projects.

Mellaart, J. 1967. *Çatal Hüyük: A Neolithic Town in Anatolia.* London: Thames and Hudson.

———. 1975. *The Neolithic of the Near East.* London: Thames and Hudson.

Moore, A. M. T. 1973. "The Late Neolithic in Palestine." *Levant* V :36– 69.

Murray, J. 1970. *The First European Agriculture.* Edinburgh: Edinburgh Press.

Oates, J. 1966. "The Baked Clay Figurines from Tell-es Sawaan." *Iraq* XXVII:146–153.

Sauer, C. 1952. *Seeds, Spades, Hearths, and Herds.* Cambridge, Mass.: The M.I.T. Press.

Singh, P. 1974. *Neolithic Cultures of Western Asia.* New York: Seminar Press.

Smith, P. E. L. 1976. *Food Production and Its Consequences.* Menlo Park, Calif.: Cummings.

Toynbee, A. 1947. *A Study of History.* (Abridgement of Vols. I–VI.) London: Oxford University Press.

Watson, P. J., and S. Le Blanc. 1973. "A Comparative Statistical Analysis of Painted Pottery from Seven Halafian Sites." *Paleo Orient* 1:117–133.

Wheatley, P. 1971. *The Pivot of the Four Quarters.* Chicago: Aldine.

Zeuner, F. E. 1963. *A History of Domesticated Animals.* Chicago: Aldine.

Chapter 3

Adams, R. McC. 1966. *The Evolution of Urban Society.* Chicago: Aldine.

Adams, R. McC., and H. Nissen. 1972 *The Uruk Countryside.* Chicago: University of Chicago Press.

Aldred, C. 1961. *The Egyptians.* New York: Praeger.

Bibby, Geoffrey. 1969. *Looking for Dilmun.* New York: Knopf.

Braudel, F. 1972. *The Mediterranean and the Mediterranean World in the Age of Philip II.* 2 vols. New York: Harper & Row.

Butzer, K. 1976. *Early Hydraulic Civilization in Egypt.* Chicago: University of Chicago Press.

Childe, V. G. 1950. "The Urban Revolution." *Town Planning Review* (Liverpool) 21 (1):197–223.

Diakonoff, I. M. 1969. *Ancient Mesopotamia.* Moscow: Nauka Publishing House.

Emery, W. B. 1961. *Archaic Egypt.* Baltimore: Pelican Books.

Fairservis, W. A., Jr. 1975. *The Roots of Ancient India.* 2nd ed. Chicago: University of Chicago Press.

Frankfort, H. 1951. *The Birth of Civilization in the Near East.* Bloomington: Indiana University Press.

Gelb, I. J. 1952. *A Study of Writing.* Chicago: University of Chicago Press.

Hallo, W. W., and W. K. Simpson. 1971. *The Ancient Near East: A History.* New York: Harcourt Brace Jovanovich.

Hawkes, J. 1973. *The First Great Civilization.* New York: Knopf.

Helck, W. 1975. *Wirtschaftsgeschichte des Alten Ägypten im 3 und 2 Jahrtausend vor Chr.* Leiden: E. J. Brill.

Jacobsen, T. 1943. "Primitive Democracy in Ancient Mesopotamia." *Journal of Near Eastern Studies* 2(3):159–172.

Kemp, B. 1977. "The Early Development of Towns in Egypt." *Antiquity* 51(203):185–199.

Kohl, P. 1978. "The Balance of Trade in Southwest Asia in the Mid-Third Millennium." *Current Anthropology* 19(3):463–492.

Kramer, S. N. 1963. *The Sumerians: Their History, Culture and Character.* Chicago: University of Chicago Press.

Kraeling, C., and R. McC. Adams. 1960. *City Invincible.* Chicago: University of Chicago Press.

Lamberg-Karlovsky, C. C. 1974. "Urban Interaction on the Iranian Plateau: Excavations at Tepe Yahya, 1967–1973." *Proceedings of the British Academy* 59:1–43.

———. 1976. "The Economic World of Sumer." In *The Legacy of Sumer,* edited by Denise Schmandt-Besserat. Bibliotheca Mesopotamia, vol. 4. Malibu, Calif.: Undena Press.

Mallowan, M. 1949. "Excavations at Brak and Chagar Bazar." *Iraq* 9(1):48– 87.

Marshall, J. 1931. *Mohenjo-daro and the Indus Civilization.* London: Probsthian.

Masson, V. M., and V. I. Sarianidi. 1972. *Central Asia.* London: Thames and Hudson.

Matthiae, P. 1977. "Tell Mardikh: The Archives and Palace." *Archaeology* 30(4):244–253.

McAlpin, D. W. 1974. "Toward Proto-Elamo-Dravidian." *Language* 50(1):123–137.

Mendelssohn, K. 1974. *The Riddle of the Pyramids.* New York: Praeger.

Merriggi, P.(n.d.) "The Proto-Elamite Tablets from Tepe Yahya." *Bulletin of the American School of Prehistoric Research* (Cambridge). In press.

Moortgat, A. 1969. *The Art of Ancient Mesopotamia.* New York: Phaidon.

Oppenheim, A. L. 1977. *Ancient Mesopotamia.* 2nd ed. Chicago: University of Chicago Press.

Pfeiffer, J. 1977. *The Emergence of Society.* New York: McGraw-Hill.

Piggott, S. 1950. *Prehistoric India.* Baltimore: Pelican Books.

Rao, S. R. 1973. *Lothal and the Indus Civilization.* London: Asia Publishing House.

Roux, G. 1964. *Ancient Iraq.* Baltimore: Pelican Books.

Sabloff, J. A., and C. C. Lamberg-Karlovsky. 1974. *The Rise and Fall of Civilizations: Modern Archaeological Approaches to Ancient Cultures.* Menlo Park, Calif.: Cummings.

Saggs, H. W. F. 1962. *The Greatness That Was Babylon.* London: Sidgwick & Jackson.

Sahlins, M. 1976. *Culture and Practical Reason.* Chicago: University of Chicago Press.

Schmandt-Besserat, D. 1978. "The Earliest Precursor of Writing." *Scientific American* 238(6):50–59.

Wheeler, M. 1960. *The Indus Civilization.* 2nd ed. London: Cambridge University Press.

Whitehouse, R. 1977. *The First Cities.* New York: Phaidon Dutton.

Wilson, J. 1960. "Egypt through the New Kingdom: Civilization without Cities." In *City Invincible,* edited by E. Kraeling and R. McC. Adams. Chicago: University of Chicago Press.

Wittfogel, K. 1957. *Oriental Despotism.* New Haven: Yale University Press.

Woolley, L. 1954. *Excavations at Ur.* London: Benn.

Zide, A. R. K., and K. V. Zvelebil. 1976. *The Soviet Decipherment of the Indus Valley Script: Translation and Critique.* Highlands, N.J.: Mouton.

Chapter 4

Acosta, J. R. 1941. "Los últimos descubrimientos arqueológicos en Tula, Hidalgo, 1941." *Revista Mexicana de Estudios Antropológicos* 5(2–3):239–248.

———. 1956. "Resumen de las exploraciónes arqueológicas en Tula, Hidalgo, durante los VI, VII, y VIII temporadas, 1946–1950." *Anales* 8:37–116. Memorias del Instituto Nacional de Antropología y Historia, Mexico.

Adams, R. E. W. 1977. *Prehistoric Mesoamerica.* Boston: Little, Brown.

Adams, R. E. W., ed. 1977. *The Origins of Maya Civilization.* Albuquerque: University of New Mexico Press.

Adams, R. McC. 1966. *The Evolution of Urban Society.* Chicago: Aldine.

Benson, E., ed. 1968. *Dumbarton Oaks Conference on the Olmecs.* Washington: Dumbarton Oaks.

Bernal, I. 1969. *The Olmec World.* Berkeley: University of California Press.

Boserup, E. 1965. *The Conditions of Agricultural Growth: The Economics of Agrarian Change under Population Pressure.* Chicago: Aldine.

Bray, W. 1968. *The Everyday Life of the Aztecs.* New York: Putnam.

_____ .1976. "From Predation to Production: The Nature of Agricultural Evolution in Mexico and Peru."In *Problems in Economic and Social Archaeology,* edited by G. de G. Sieveking, I. H. Longworth, and K. E. Wilson. London: Duckworth.

Byers, D. S., and R. S. MacNeish, general eds. 1967–1976. *The Prehistory of the Tehuacán Valley.* 5 vols. Austin: University of Texas Press.

Calnek, E. E. 1972. "Settlement Pattern and Chinampa Agriculture at Tenochtitlán." *American Antiquity* 37(1):104–115.

Caso, A. 1958. *People of the Sun.* Norman: University of Oklahoma Press.

Coe, M. D. 1962. *Mexico.* New York: Praeger.

_____ . 1964. "The Chinampas of Mexico." *Scientific American* 211(1):90–98.

_____ . 1966. *The Maya.* New York: Praeger.

_____ . 1968. *America's First Civilization.* New York: Van Nostrand.

_____ . 1976. "Early Steps in the Evolution of Maya Writing." In *Origins of Religious Art and Iconography in Preclassic Mesoamerica,* edited by H. B. Nicholson. Los Angeles: UCLA Latin American Center.

Coe, M. D., and K. V. Flannery. 1967. *Early Cultures and Human Ecology in South Coastal Guatemala.* Smithsonian Contributions to Anthropology 3.

Coe, W. R. 1967. *Tikal: A Handbook of the Ancient Maya Ruins.* Philadelphia: University Museum, University of Pennsylvania.

Cohen, M. N. 1977. *The Food Crisis in Prehistory.* New Haven: Yale University Press.

Conrad, G. W. 1974. "Toward a Systemic View of Mesoamerican Prehistory: Inter-site Sociopolitical Organization. In *The Rise and Fall of Civilizations: Selected Readings,* edited by C. C. Lamberg-Karlovsky and J. A. Sabloff. Menlo Park, Calif.: Cummings.

Culbert, T. P. 1974. *The Lost Civilization: The Story of the Classic Maya.* New York: Harper & Row.

Culbert, T. P. ed. 1973. *The Classic Maya Collapse.* Albuquerque: University of New Mexico Press.

Davis, D. D. 1975. "Patterns of Early Formative Subsistence in Southern Mesoamerica, 1500–1100 B.C." *Man* 10:41–59.

Diaz, B. 1963. *The Conquest of New Spain.* Translated by J. M. Cohen. Baltimore: Penguin.

Diehl, R. A., ed. 1974. *Studies of Ancient Tollan: A Report of the University of Missouri Tula Archaeological Project.* University of Missouri Monographs in Anthropology, no. 1.

Diehl, R. A., and R. A. Benfer. 1975. "Tollan: The Toltec Capital." *Archaeology* 23(2):112–124.

Di Peso, C. C. 1974. *Casas Grandes: A Fallen Trading Center of the Gran Chichimeca.* 3 vols. Flagstaff, Ariz.: Amerind Foundation and Northland Press.

Drennan, R. D. 1976. "Religion and Social Evolution in Formative Mesoamerica." In *The Early Mesoamerican Village,* edited by Kent Flannery. New York: Academic Press.

Flannery, K. V. 1968a. "Archaeological Systems Theory and Early Mesoamerica." In *Anthropological Archaeology in the Americas,* edited by B. J. Meggers. Washington: Anthropological Society of Washington, D. C.

_____ . 1968b. "The Olmec and the Valley of Oaxaca: A Model for Interregional Interaction in Formative Times." In *Dumbarton Oaks Conference on the Olmecs,* edited by E. Benson. Washington: Dumbarton Oaks.

_____ . 1972. "The Cultural Evolution of Civilizations." *Annual Review of Ecology and Systematics* 3:399–426.

_____ . 1973. "The Origins of Agriculture." *Annual Review of Anthropology* 2:271–310.

Flannery, K. V., ed. 1976. *The Early Mesoamerican Village.* New York: Academic Press.

Flannery, K. V., and J. Marcus. 1976. "Evolution of the Public Building in Formative Oaxaca." In *Cultural Change and Continuity, Essays in Honor of James Bennett Griffin,* edited by Charles Cleland. New York: Academic Press.

Graham, J. A., R. F. Heizer, and E. M. Shook. 1978. "Abaj Takalik 1976: Exploratory Investigations." In *Studies in Ancient Mesoamerica, III.* Contributions of the University of California Archaeological Research Facility, no. 36.

Griffin, J. B. 1966. "Mesoamerica and the Eastern United States in Prehistoric Times." In *Handbook of Middle American Indians,* vol. 4, edited by Gordon F. Ekholm and Gordon R. Willey. Austin: University of Texas Press.

Grove, D. C. 1974. "The Highland Olmec Manifestation: A Consideration of What It Is and Isn't." In *Mesoamerican Archaeology,* edited by N. Hammond. Austin: University of Texas Press.

Hammond, N. 1974. "The Distribution of Late Classic Maya Ceremonial Centers in the Central Area." In *Mesoamerican Archaeology: New Approaches,* edited by N. Hammond. London: Duckworth.

_____. 1977. "The Earliest Maya." *Scientific American* 236(3):116–133.

Harrison, P. D., and B. L. Turner II, eds. 1978. *Prehistoric Maya Agriculture.* Albuquerque: University of New Mexico Press.

Haury, E. 1962. "The Greater American Southwest." In *Courses Toward Urban Life,* edited by R. J. Braidwood and G. R. Willey. Chicago: Aldine.

Haviland, W. A. 1975. "The Ancient Maya and the Evolution of Urban Society." *Katunob,* Miscellaneous Series, no. 7.

_____. 1977. "Dynastic Genealogies from Tikal, Guatemala: Implications for Descent and Political Organization." *American Antiquity* 42(1):61–67.

Jiménez Moreno, W. 1941. "Tula y los Toltecas según las fuentes históricas." *Revista Mexicana de Estudios Antropológicos* 5(2–3):79–83.

_____. 1966. "Mesoamerica before the Toltecs." In *Ancient Oaxaca,* edited by John Paddock. Stanford: Stanford University Press.

Katz, F. 1972. *The Ancient American Civilizations.* New York: Praeger.

Kelley, J. C. 1966. "Mesoamerica and the Southwestern United States." In *Handbook of Middle American Indians,* vol. 4, edited by Gordon F. Ekholm and Gordon R. Willey. Austin: University of Texas Press.

Lathrap, D. W., J. G. Marcos, and J. Zeidler. 1977. "Real Alto: An Ancient Ceremonial Center.' *Archaeology* 30(1):2–13.

Linne, Sigvald. 1934. *Archaeological Researches at Teotihuacán, Mexico.* Ethnographical Museum of Sweden, Publication No. 1. Stockholm.

Lowe, G. W. 1975. *The Early Preclassic Barra Phase of Altamira, Chiapas: A Review with New Data.* New World Archaeological Foundation, Paper No. 38.

MacNeish, R. S. 1964a. "Ancient Mesoamerican Civilization." *Science* 143(3606):531–537.

_____. 1964b. "The Food Gathering and Incipient Agriculture Stage of Prehistoric Middle America." In *Handbook of Middle American Indians,* vol. 1, edited by R. C. West. Austin: University of Texas Press.

_____. 1969. "Speculation about How and Why Food Production and Village Life Developed in the Tehuacán Valley, Mexico." *Archaeology* 24(4):307–315.

_____. 1972. "The Evolution of Community Patterns in the Tehuacán Valley of Mexico and Speculations about the Cultural Process." In *Man, Settlement, and Urbansim,* edited by P. J. Ucko, R. Tringham, and G. W. Dimbleby. London: Duckworth.

———. 1973. "The Scheduling Factors in the Development of Effective Food Production in the Tehuacán Valley." In *Variation in Anthropology,* edited by Donald W. Lathrap and Jody Douglas. Illinois Archaeological Survey.

———. 1974. "Reflections on My Search for the Beginnings of Agriculture in Mexico." In *Archaeological Researches in Retrospect,* edited by Gordon R. Willey. Cambridge, Mass.: Winthrop.

Mangelsdorf, P. C., R. S. MacNeish, and G. R. Willey. 1964. "Origins of Agriculture in Middle America." In *Handbook of Middle American Indians,* vol. 1, edited by R. C. West. Austin: University of Texas Press.

Marcus, J. 1973. "Territorial Organization of the Lowland Classic Maya." *Science* 180:911–916.

———. 1976a. *Emblem and State in the Classic Maya Lowlands.* Washington: Dumbarton Oaks.

———. 1976b. "The Origins of Mesoamerican Writing." *Annual Review of Anthropology* 5:35–68.

Million, R. B. Drewitt, and G. Cowgill. 1973. *The Teotihuacán Map.* (Urbanization at Teotihuacán, vol. 1) Austin: University of Texas Press.

Nicholson, H. B. 1957. "Topiltzin Quetzalcoatl of Tollan: A Problem in Mesoamerican Ethnohistory." Ph.D. thesis, Harvard University.

Parsons, J. R. 1977. "Archaeological Research 1: Teotihuacán." *Latin American Research Review* 12(1):192–202.

Pearsall, D. M. 1978. "Photolith Analysis of Archaeological Soils: Evidence for Maize Cultivation in Formative Ecuador." *Science* 199:177–178.

Puleston, D. E., and O. S. Puleston. 1971. "An Ecological Approach to the Origins of Maya Civilization." *Archaeology* 24(4):330–336.

Quirarte, J. 1977. "Early Art Styles of Mesoamerica and Early Classic Maya Art." In *The Origins of Maya Civilization,* edited by R. E. W. Adams. Albuquerque: University of New Mexico Press.

Rathje, W. L. 1971. "The Origin and Development of Lowland Classic Maya Civilization." *American Antiquity* 36:275–285.

———. 1972. "Praise the Gods and Pass the Metates: A Hypothesis of the Development of Lowland Rainforest Civilizations in Mesoamerica." In *Contemporary Archaeology,* edited by Mark P. Leone. Carbondale: Southern Illinois University Press.

Sabloff, J. A., and W. L. Rathje. 1975. "The Rise of a Maya Merchant Class." *Scientific American* 233(4):72–83.

Sanders, W. T., and B. J. Price. 1968. *Mesoamerica: The Evolution of a Civilization.* New York: Random House.

Sauer, C. O. 1952. *Agricultural Origins and Dispersals.* New York: American Geographical Society.

Soustelle, J. 1961. *Daily Life of the Aztecs on the Eve of the Spanish Conquest.* Stanford: Stanford University Press.

Spinden, H. J. 1917. "The Origin and Distribution of Agriculture in America." *Proceedings of the 19th International Congress of Americanists.* Washington, D.C.

———. 1928. *Ancient Civilizations of Mexico and Central America.* American Museum of Natural History Handbook Series, No. 3. New York.

Thompson, J. E. S. 1966. *The Rise and Fall of Maya Civilization.* Rev. ed. Norman: University of Oklahoma Press.

———. 1970. *Maya History and Religion.* Norman: University of Oklahoma Press.

Vaillant, G. C. 1962. *Aztecs of Mexico.* Revised and annotated by Suzannah B. Vaillant. New York: Doubleday.

Voorhies, B. 1976. *The Chantuto People: An Archaic Period Society of the Chiapas Littoral, Mexico.* New World Archaeological Foundation, Paper No. 41.

Wauchope, R. general ed. 1964–1976. *The Handbook of Middle American Indians.* 16 vols. Austin: University of Texas Press.

Weaver, M. P. 1972, *The Aztecs, Maya, and Their Predecessors.* New York: Seminar Press.

West, R. C. 1964. "Surface Configuration and Associated Geology of Middle America." In *Handbook of Middle American Indians,* vol. 1, edited by R. C. West. Austin: University of Texas Press.

Willey, G. R. 1962. "The Early Great Styles and the Rise of the Pre-Columbian Civilizations." *American Anthropologist* 64(1):1–14.

_____. 1966. *An Introduction to American Archaeology: Vol. 1: North and Middle America.* Englewood Cliffs, N.J.: Prentice-Hall.

_____. 1976. "Mesoamerican Civilization and the Idea of Transcendence." *Antiquity* 50(199–200):205–215.

Wolf, E. 1959. *Sons of the Shaking Earth.* Chicago: University of Chicago Press.

Wolf, E., ed. 1976. *The Valley of Mexico: Studies in Prehispanic Ecology and Society.* Albuquerque: University of New Mexico Press.

Chapter 5

Adams, R. McC. 1966. *The Evolution of Urban Society.* Chicago: Aldine.

_____. 1975. "The Emerging Place of Trade in Civilizational Studies." In *Ancient Civilization and Trade,* edited by J. A. Sabloff and C. C. Lamberg-Karlovsky. Albuquerque: University of New Mexico Press.

Culbert, T. P., ed. 1973. *The Classic Maya Collapse.* Albuquerque: University of New Mexico Press.

Flannery, K. V. 1972. "The Cultural Evolution of Civilizations." *Annual Review of Ecology and Systematics* 3:399–426.

Frankfort, H. 1951. *The Birth of Civilization in the Near East.* Bloomington: Indiana University Press.

Freid, M. H. 1967. *The Evolution of Political Society.* New York: Random House.

Lamberg-Karlovsky, C. C. 1972. "Trade Mechanisms in Indus-Mesopotamian Interrelations." *Journal of the American Oriental Society* 92(2):222–230.

Rathje, W. L. 1971. "The Origin and Development of Lowland Classic Maya Civilization." *American Antiquity* 36:275–285.

Redman, C. L. 1973. "Research and Theory in Current Archaeology: An Introduction." In *Research and Theory in Current Archaeology,* edited by C. L. Redman. New York: Wiley.

Renfrew, C. 1975. "Trade as Action at a Distance: Questions of Integration and Communication." In *Ancient Civilization and Trade,* edited by J. A. Sabloff and C. C. Lamberg-Karlovsky. Albuquerque: University of New Mexico Press.

Riley, C. L., et al., ed. 1971. *Man Across the Sea: Problems of Pre-Columbian Contacts.* Austin: University of Texas Press.

Sabloff, J. A. 1974. "Review of *Social Exchange and Interaction,* edited by E. N. Wilmsen." *American Anthropologist* 76(3):581–582.

Sanders, W. T., and B. J. Price. 1968. *Mesoamerica: The Evolution of a Civilization.* New York: Random House.

Service, E. R. 1962. *Primitive Social Organization.* New York: Random House.

———. 1975. *Origins of the State and Civilization: The Process of Cultural Evolution*. New York: Norton.

Trigger, B. G. 1976. "Inequality and Communication in Early Civilizations." *Anthropologica,* new series, 18(1):27–52.

Wheeler, M. 1959. *Early India and Pakistan*. New York: Praeger.

Whitehouse, R. 1977. *The First Cities*. New York: Phaidon.

Wilmsen, E. N., ed. 1972. *Social Exchange and Interaction*. Anthropological Papers, University of Michigan, no. 46.

Winter, M. C. 1977. "Archaeological Research 3: Mesoamerica." *Latin American Research Review* 12(1):213–215.

Index